# EARLY TEXAS NEWS

## 1831–1848

## Abstracts from
## Early Texas Newspapers

*Helen Smothers Swenson*

**Heritage Books**
**2024**

# HERITAGE BOOKS

*AN IMPRINT OF HERITAGE BOOKS, INC.*

## Books, CDs, and more—Worldwide

For our listing of thousands of titles see our website
at
www.HeritageBooks.com

Published 2024 by
HERITAGE BOOKS, INC.
Publishing Division
5810 Ruatan Street
Berwyn Heights, MD 20740

International Standard Book Number
Paperbound: 978-0-7884-7604-4

EARLY TEXAS NEWS

Early Texas News has been compiled by Mrs. Helen Smothers Swenson by abstracting from old newspapers that are housed in the 3rd floor library at the Texas State Library in Austin, Texas on microfilm.

The material in this book is strickly for the Genealogical Researcher. As I abstracted material, I kept in mind names and places.

----------------------------------------------------------------
In between this type of line you will find a new volum of newspaper
----------------------------------
In between the shorter lines you will find each abstracted article. If article is abstracted and has been shortened, I have tried to make this statement in square brackets [abstracted by HMS].
----------------------------------

When a word or words could not be read I have placed and underline with question marks.
----------------------------------

You will find many times in these old newspapers that not only a Texas newspaper is used, but that editors used material from out of state of Texas newspapers.
----------------------------------

In many of the newspapers an advertisement appeared many times and some of the court proceedings were supposed to run many times, I have printed only once and did not repeat as newspaper had printed.
----------------------------------

## CONTENTS

EARLY TEXAS NEWS

SAN FELIPE DeAUSTIN, TEXAS-MEXICAN CITIZEN


SCOTLAND    THE UNLUCKY PRESENT.
    "The Rev. Mr. L_____, minister of C_____in Lanerkshire,
    (who died within the present century,) was one of those un-
    happy persons, who to use the words of a well known Scottish
    adage." [HMS note:  Due to length of this article, it has
    been abstracted for genealogical research.]
----------------------------------
EXTRACTED ADVERTISEMENT
    "$10 Reward for Strayed or Stolen from near Villa de Austin
    in March last, a cream coloured mare mule.  Should be deliv-
    ered to Mr. James WESTALL, near Brazoria, or to the Editers
    of the Mexican Citizen"
    VILLA de AUSTIN, May 19;1831
----------------------------------
EXTRACTED ADVERTISEMENT
    "LAW--De La F. ROYSDON, of the U. States, offers his profes-
    sional services to the citizens of Austin's colony--He may
    be found at Mr. WHITESIDE'S Inn."
    VILLA de AUSTIN, May 10, 1831
----------------------------------
EXTRACTED ADVERTISEMENT
    "BRIGHAM & RICHESON, a Dry Good-Grocery store."
    BRAZORIA, May 9, 1831
----------------------------------
NOTICE--BRIGHAM & MARSH dissolving partnership.
    "A. BRIGHAM is fully authorized to liquidate the same"
    "A. BRIGHAM, S. MARSH"
    BRAZORIA, April 24, 1831
----------------------------------
STORE AT HARRISBURG--MOORE & CO.  A new store of Dry Good/Gro-
    ceries."
    HARRISBURG, May 5, 1831
----------------------------------
NOTICE--"B. M. FOLEY employed by R. J. MOSELEY to watch over
    business transactions while MOSELY is away."
    APRIL 28, 1831
----------------------------------
FOR SALE--"One Third of a League of Land, situated on LINVAL'S
    Bayou, bordering on the river San Bernardo, about 20 miles
    from the sea coast, and about half way between the towns of
    Matagorda and Brazoria.  Said land is of excellent quality,
    well timbered and contiguous to inland navigation; it is
    known as being part of league No. 36.  For terms enquire of
    Mr. JAMES NORTON, at Matagorda, or of M. M. BATTLE"
    STAFFORD'S SETTLEMENT, April 9, 1831.

----------------------------------
Dr's. PEEBLES & MILLER have just received a general assortment
    of Fresh Medicines."
    VILLA de AUSTIN, March 31 _____              No year given]
----------------------------------

San Felipe De Austin, Texas-Mexican Citizen--Continued.......

ENTERTAINMENT at Brazoria--The subscriber has opened a boarding
   house and pledges himself that his table and beds shall be as
   good as the country will afford.  He is also making arrangements for receiving horses and supplying them with corn and
   provender.  Wm. T. AUSTIN
   BRAZORIA  Feb. 25, 1831
---------------------------------

FOR SALE-A League of Land, situated on the East side of the
   Brazos river precisely at the head of tide.  For terms apply
   to R. M. WILLIAMSON.
   [HMS Note:  No name of newspaper, no date, no town given]
          [This ends the advertisements]
---------------------------------

VILLA DE AUSTIN--Thursday--May 26, 1831
   "The Reverend Doctor Muldoos, Parish Priest of Austin & Vicar
   General of all the Foreighn Colonies of Texas, already existing, or that my be hereafter established in his time."
   [abstracted by Helen]--He states that on his visits through
   the colony, he will Baptize and Marry the black race of both
   sexes, without receiving from them or their masters any
   gratification.
---------------------------------

"MESRS. EDOTORS--Riding in my official capacity, through this
   immense Parish, I was overtaken by a storm, which I giv you,
   in verse, for your amusement, and if you will, for publication.
   THE 16th OF MAY, 1831--A STORMY NIGHT
   [abstracted by Helen]-"At the residence of Mr. EDWARDS, tenant
   of our beloved Empresario Col. Austin."  [At the end of his
   long lines of poem the following was printed]--"Our last visit
   was Mr. KUYKENDALL'S, where there were upwards of one hundred
   persons Baptized, and four couple maried,--all of whom, after
   the marriage ceremony, sat down to an abundant and splendid
   feast."  "To fam'd La MANCHA'S Knight whose squire"
   "To scum the pots, sat by the fire."  "On rich COMACHO'S wed-
   ding-day"  "Here Messrs. LEAKY and KUYKENDALL the first settlers of the Colony appear as the venerable patriarchs of
   this rising generation.  Happy men to live to see their efforts crowned with so much success."
    "On my arrival at Mr. WILLIAMS'S my temporary home, I was
   greeted by an apparently mild sort of gentleman, whose first
   act was the recital of all his Ecle?iastical and Missonary
   denominations, with a long catalogue of some very respectable
   names, mostly from the Northern United States, but yet not
   qualified to confer a jurisdiction to preach in this Colony"
   [HMS note:  All of this appears to have been given by Father
   MULDOON.]
---------------------------------

ADVERTISEMENT
   "COLLINS and CO. just received more merchandise--LEWIS VEEDER
   VILLA de AUSTIN, May 26, 1831.
---------------------------------

San Felipe De Austin, Texas-Mexican Citizen--Continued......

NOTICE--Be it known that I have employed HENRY SMITH, Esq, as
    my agent to do and transmit business in my name during my
    abscence from this place.    S. MARSH
    BRAZORIA, May 26, 1831
-----------------------------------

"The concern of BENJ. B. DICKINSON _ec. was disolved on the
    1st last, by its own limitation--All persons indebted to the
    late firm will make prompt payment."
    BRAZORIA, May 1, 1831.
-----------------------------------

"Will be sold on 28th of the present month, at the house of
    WILLIAM MILICAN, a small stock of cattle, belonging to the
    estate of the late WILLIAM CUMMINS, deceased.  Terms, made
    known at the time of sale." "PLEASANT D. McNIEL, Adm'r."
    VILLA de AUSTIN, May 5, 1831.
-----------------------------------

"For Sale at the store of the subscriber a complete set of
    Saw-mill irons on the most approved plan.  GEORGE F. RICHARDSON"
    HARRISBURG, April 26th,_____          No year given.]
-----------------------------------

"Sheriff's Sale--ZENO PHILIPS Administrator of JOSEPH WHITE,
    vs. ABRAM ROBERTS.  By virtue of an execution to me directed,
    by the honorable the Alcalde of the Jurisdiction of Austin,
    I will expose to Public Sale, as the law requires, at the
    Alcable's office in the town of Austin, on the second and
    fourth Monday in May, and the second Monday in June next,
    a certain League of Land, seized in the above suit, situate,
    lying and being on the San Barnard river, known as league
    number twenty-seven.  Said League of land was granted to
    JOSEPH WHITE, and by him sold to the said ABRAM ROBERTS, and
    a special mortage retained for the payment of the purchase
    money."
    OLIVER JONES, Sheriff          AUSTIN--April 22d, 1831
-----------------------------------

ADVERTISEMENT
    "CLOTHING--Received shipment from house of BURK & WATSON,
    New York."
    EDWARD ROBERTSON--BRAZORIA--April 9, 1831.
-----------------------------------

NOTICE--My friends in Texas, will please when advising their
    correspondents to direct their letters to my care, to be very
    particular in requesting them to pay the postage, as I will
    not receive them from the office unless the postage has
    been paid."
    J. W. COLLINS, New-Orleans--3/27/1831.
-----------------------------------

"BEING under the neccesity of going to New-Orleans on business,
    I have appointed my brother J. SCANLAN, my agent during my
    abscence, who is fully authorized to transact business for
    and in my name." "P.S. For sale as above, an invaluable
    Specific for the Ague and Fever." MICHAEL SCANLAN.
    VILLA de AUSTIN, April 14, 1831.
-----------------------------------

EARLY TEXAS NEWS

San Felipe De Austin, Texas-Mexican Citizen--Continued......

"NOTICE--All persons indebted to me by note or account, are
   requested to make payment to Messrs. PERRY & HUNTER, who are
   fully authorised to give receipts in my name."
   JOSHUA FLETCHER  VILLA de AUSTIN--April 14, 1831
------------------------------------

"ENTERTAINMENT AT BRAZORIA"-[abstracted by HMS]---"A boarding
   house opened."
   WM. T. AUSTIN--BRAZORIA, Feb 26, 1831.
------------------------------------

"CHEAP GOODS"--[abstracted by HMS]-"Dry Goods store"
   McQUEEN--San FELIPE--April 7
------------------------------------

ADVERTISEMENT;  "Drs. PEEBLES & MILLER received assortment of
   fresh medicines."
   VILLA de AUSTIN, March 31,____[HMS note:  no year given]
------------------------------------

FOR SALE-"A League of Land, situated on the East side of the
   Brazos River, precisely at the head of tide.For terms apply to
   R. M. WILLIAMSON."
------------------------------------

FIRE--On Friday night the 4th ult.  the Cotton Gin of JOHN W.
   JONES, was consummed by fire.  We understand there were about
   fifty thousand pounds of seed cotton burnt.
   COLUMBIA (Ten.) MERCURY. [HMS Note: Could this be Columbia
   newspaper in Tennessee?  Was there such a newspaper in Tenn.?]
------------------------------------

[abstracted by HMS]---"The honorable PELEG SPRAGUE, at present
   an able and distinguished Senator in Congress from the State
   of Maine" N.Y., JOUR. COM.
------------------------------------

ADVERTISEMENT:  "For VERA CRUZ--The Mexican sloop General TERAN,
   GEORGE B. M'KINSTRY MASTER, having the principal part of
   her cargo engaged, will have immediate despatch, for freight
   or Passage, apply to the Captain, on board."
   BRAZORIA--April 18, 1831.
------------------------------------

FOR SALE--One third of a leagu ofland, situated on LINVAL'S
   Bayou, bordering on the river San Bernardo, about 20 miles
   from the sea coast, and about half way between the towns of
   Matagorda and Brazoria.  Said land is of excellent quality,
   well timbered and contiguous to inland navigation; it is
   known as being part of league No. 36.  For terms enquire of
   Mr. JAMES NORTON, at Matagorda, or of M. M. BATTLE.
   STAFFORD'S SETTLEMENT--April 9, 1831.
------------------------------------

[HMS Note:  The following was blurred and hard to read]
NOTICE--My suit brought against H. H. LEAGUE, for one ?uncul-
   ivated? fourth of the Matagorda Town track, has been compro-
   mised and finally settled, by a conveyance to me of one eighth

   [continued on next page...]
4.

San Felipe De Austin, Texas-Mexican Citizen--Continued.......

part of said league, as will appear by deed of sale on record;
and I further state that I ratify the sale of lots made on the
4th day of April inst.   S. RHOADS FISHER

VILLA de AUSTIN--April 15, 1831.

--------------------------------

ADVERTISEMENT                        -"The undersigned has just
    received enmerous consignments"  [Pertaining to dry goods
    merchandise]     LEWIS L. VEEDER
    VILLA de AUSTIN--April 21, 1831.

--------------------------------

"150 DOLLARS REWARD...Stop the runaways.  Runaway from the sub-
    scriber on the 15th inst.  the following servants, viz---
    SAMPSON--aged about 24 or 25 years, a bright mulatto, about
    5 feet 10 inches high, polite when spoken to by white men,
    plays the violin;  took with him a blue coat, _____rey round-
    about, three or four shirts, one of them striped gingham, the
    balance brown shirting and a black fur hat.
    JOE, aged ?22?[blurred] but believed to be ?more?[blurred]
    black complication stout five feet eleven in. high, stout
    made, humble when spoken to, had with him a cordoroy round-
    about, and five [rest is blurred.     [Advertisement then
    is in Spanish below] JEREMIAH DWYER
    SAN BARNARD--April 18, 1831.

--------------------------------

VARIETY--"One day, at the table of the late Dr. PEARME[HMS Note:
    name is blurred] Dean of Ely, just as the cloth was being re-
    moved, the subject of discourse happened to be that of an
    extraordianary mortality among the lawyers "We have lost",
    said a gentleman, "not less than sir? eminent barrister in
    as many months."--The Dean, who was quite deaf, rose as his
    friend finished his remark, and gave the company grace:--For
    this, and every other mercy, the Lord's name be praised."
    The event was irresistible"

--------------------------------

                --"FERGUSON, the self-taught astronomer,
    having met with a rigid Calvanist in a stage coach, began to
    converse"

--------------------------------

ABSTRACTED          --"ORDINANCE--By the order of the Ayuntam-
    iento, FRANCIS W. JOHNSON, Pres't.  S. M. WILLIAMS, Secretary."
    March 9 _____             no year given]

--------------------------------

NOTICE:  "An election will be held on Saturday the 16th day of
    April next, at the house of WILLIAM BARTON on the Colorado to
    be presided by R. M. WILLIAMSON sendico procurador, and at
    the house of WILLIAM ROBINSON to be presided by said WILLIAM
    ROBINSON 4th Regidor, for the purpose of electing Company offi-
    cers for the Sixth Company of Militia of the Battallion of
    Austin conformity with the Militia, Law of this State, the
    limits of the sixty company district are as follows beginning

[Continued on next page]

                        5.

San Felipe de Austin, Texas-Mexican Citizen--Continued......

at the S. W. Corner of THOMAS SLAUGHTERS League thence to the
head of Eagle Lake thence to the mouth of scull Creek, up scull
Creek, to the Atoscosito road, thence along said road, to the
Labaoon, thence following up the Lavacca and the Western boun-
dary line of this colony to the San Antonio Road, thence along
said Road Eastwardly, to the divide between the Brazos and
Colorado, thence along said divide Southwardly to the head
waters of the ?Bernard? Blurred          thence down along
the Bernard to SLAUGHTERS the place of begining.
FRANCIS W. JOHNSON, President.    SAMUEL M. WILLIAMS, Secretary.
----------------------------------

NOTICE: Mr. MIGUEL ARCINIEGA Commissioner appointed by the Governor of this State, to partition lands and issue Titles to the
   settlers of this Colony, hereby makes known to the colonists
   who are to receive titles from him for lands, on Mill Creek,
   New Years Creek, and adjacent Creek, and also on the west side
   of CUMMIN'S Creek, and all that part of the Colony known as
   Col's neighborhood, that between the 20th, and last day of the
   present month they must apply for their titles, and come prepared to pay the _?_? which will be due on the delivery of
   the _?_?
   March 12 _____[HMS Note: no year given. Above spaces that
   are blank were not legible]
----------------------------------

ADVERTISEMENT--"BRAZOS HOTEL--Now opened in house of Mr. ASA MIT-
   CHELL, at the mouth of the river Brazos."
   Wm. CHASE, G. B. COTTEN March 12 ____[  -no year given]
----------------------------------

NOTICE--PERSONS indebted to the estate of A. B. CLARK, deceased,
   are requested to pay up without delay, to avoid costs--Those
   having made purchases at the sale of the said CLARK'S effects
   are informed that their notes are past due, and that payment
   must be made without further notice.
   EDWARD ROBERTSON, ADMR. BRAZORIA-12th January 1831.
----------------------------------

## VILLA DE AUSTIN-------THURSDAY MARCH 24th 1831

" We have received intelligence from the City of Mexico, up
to the 20th of February last, by Tuesday's mail. The Official
Register, gives a detailed account of the trail, conviction
and execution of General GUERRORO, which we could not have
translated in time for the present number. He was tried by
a Military Court, and was condemned to be shot on the 14th of
February, which sentence was executed precisely at the hour
of seven, A.M. about two leagues from the cith. The subject
of this ignominious death, was a distinguished Republican
General in the revolutionary struggles for independence. He
was also distinguished for his republican principles until he
became identified with a party which, (however, justly or
unjustly, we will not take upon ourselves to say,)are"[HMS
note: Remainder of article is blurred]
----------------------------------

Villa de Austin---Continued...........

"The coffin of Col. WILLETT, who died recently in the city of
New York, was made of pieces of wood, collected by himself,
many years ago from different revolutionary battle grounds.
The corpse, in compliance with a written request of the dis-
cased, was habited in a complete suite of ancient citizen's
apparel, including an old fashioned three cornered hat, which
had been preserved for that purpose.  It is estimated that
several thousand persons passed through the house for the purpose of viewing the remains."

------------------------------------

"The ingenuity of a Frence journalist has made another remarkable discovery, namely, that the ex-king Charles X. is des-
cended from the house of STUART, being an off set _____
[HMS Note: not legible] CHARLES I.  Out learned genealogist
adduces the following memoradum in proof of his discovery.
   CHARLES I. of England married to HENRIETTA MARIA, a daughter
of HENRY IV.
HENRIETTA of England to PHILIP DUKE of Orleans, father to the
famous Regnet.
ANNE MARIA of England to VICTOR AMADEUS,II., King of Sardinia.
MARIA ADELAIDE of Savoy to the Duke of Burgundy, grandson of
LOUIS XIV.
LOUIS XV
LOUIS the Douphin
LOUIS XIV, Louis XVIII.  CHARLES X.

------------------------------------

ADVERTISEMENT--"Notice--Persons having claims against the estate
of BAKER LARKIN, deceased, will present them to the undersigned, within the delay prescribed by law, and those who are indebted to said estate, will please make immediate payment.
LAUGHLIN M'GLAUGHLIN, Administor"
March 24,_____[No year given, but probably 1831-HMS Note]

------------------------------------

"FRANCIS BINGHAM, Informs his friends and the public, that he has
opened a house of entertainment at his residence east of the
Brazos"
BRAZORIA  March 21, 1831

------------------------------------

"The death of the Pope (Pius VIII) has taken place at Rome  He
was 69 years old.  The news reached London thru Paris on Friday
Morning."

------------------------------------

ADVERTISEMENT: "A CARD--All persons indebted to the subscriber,
either by note or account, will please settle the same immediately, as no further indulgence can or will be given--Cattle
will be taken if delivered in San Felipe De Austin..
JABEZ BARNEY  March 17_____[HMS Note: no year given, probably
1831]

------------------------------------

ENTERTAINMENT-[abstracted by Helen] "A boarding house opened in
Brazoria."  Wm.T. AUSTIN
BRAZORIA, February 25, 1831.

EARLY TEXAS NEWS

Villa de Austin--Continued...........

ADVERTISEMENT--"FOR SALE--Two out Lots pleasantly situated on
    PARKER'S Creek.  March 12,_____[HMS Note: no year given,1831?]
    [No name give for advertisement]
-----------------------------------

NOTICE--ALL Persons indebted to the estate of MICAJAH BIRD, dec-
    eased, are hereby requested to make immediate payments to the
    subscriber, and those having claims against said estate, are
    requested to present them duly authenticated, within the time
    limited by law, or they will be barred.
    OLIVER JONES, ADMINISTRATOR  Jan. 22,_____[HMS Note: no year
    given, but probably 1831]
-----------------------------------

"NEW GOODS--The subscriber has just landed from New-Orleans,
    with an assortment of Goods for this market, of which the fol-
    lowing is a part"  R. J. MOSELEY  March 12,____[no year given
    but is probably 1831.  This ad pertaining to kinds of dry goods]
-----------------------------------

ADVERTISEMENT--"Dry goods for sale"
    PERRY & HUNTER--Austin, Feb. 12, 1831.[abstracted by Helen]
-----------------------------------

ADVERTISEMENT--"NOTICE--All persons indebted to me are forewarn-
    ed to settle with me direct, or with my agent L. SMITHER at
    BELL'S Landing, and not to pay any account to J. A. SCHULTE,
    because he is no longer in my service, having paid him off."
    BELL'S LANDING, March 7, 1831  H. KLONNE.
-----------------------------------

ADVERTISEMENT--"NOTICE--All persons indebted to me, are fore-
    warned to settle with me, and not to pay any amount to H. KLONNE,
    his agent of agents at BELL'S Landing as I have discharged
    said KLONNE from my service, and settled off with him and do
    not confide any longer in him.  JOHN SCHULTE
    March 17,_____[HMS Note: no year give, probably 1831]
-----------------------------------

ADVERTISEMENT--"A CARD--S. B. WALLS, M.D. [abstracted by Helen]
    states that he is doing professional services in Brazoria.
    His present residence at the hotel, occupied by WILLIAM T.
    AUSTIN."
    BRAZORIA, February 23, 1831.
-----------------------------------

ADVERTISEMENT:  "NOTICE will be sold in conformity with an order
    of the Alcalde's Court of this jurisdiction, in the town of
    Austin, on the 30th day of March next, A NEGRO, belonging to
    the estate of RICHARD GRAVES, deceased, for the benefit of the
    creditors of said estate.  Terms made known on the day of
    sale."  JAMES MOORE, Tutor & Guardian
    Feb. 28,_____[HMS Note: no year given, probably 1831]
-----------------------------------

ADVERTISEMENT:  "WOOL HATS" "sold at the store of Mr. VEEDER, in
    San Felipe de Austin."
    "made by WILLIAM H. BRIDGERS"  Jan. 22,_____[no year give, 1831?]
-----------------------------------

Villa de Austin---Continued.......

ADVERTISEMENT: "STRAYED OR STOLEN  from the premiscs of Mrs.
    MARTIN, at Post Oak Point on Turkey Creek, on sorrel horse,
    with a blaze face, and a Spanish brand, trots and paces;  Also
    one Mare Mule, dark colour, blind of the left eye, Spanish
    Brand, and some saddle spots, and gentle,  Whoever will take
    up said animals and return them to Mr. EDWARD LANG, in Aus-tin,
    shall receive ten dollors  reward."  NICHOLAS DILLAIRD.
    Jan. 29,_____[HMS Note:  no year given, probably 1831]
--------------------------------

ADVERTISEMENT:  "$5.00 reward"-[abstracted by Helen] "a lost or
    strayed horse.  from the town of Brazoria.  Return to JOHN L.
    SLEIGHT."  BRAZORIA  Feb. 23, 1831.
--------------------------------

"CONTD. ARTICLE OF POPE'S DEATH..His late Holyness, FRANCOIS
    XAVIER CASTIGLIONE, was born at Clingoll, on the 20th of Nov.
    1761, elected to the Popedom on the 31st of March,  1829.
    and crowned the 5th of April following."[HMS Note:  The remain-
    der of this article is blurred.] [HMS Note:  For more on
    the above Pope, see page 7 of this book.]
--------------------------------

ADVERTISEMENT:  "NOTICE--The undersigned having been appointed
    administrator to the estate of ISAAC FOSTER late of the juris-
    diction of Austin, deceased requests all persons who have any
    claims against said estate, to present them to Messrs.
    L_____[blurred] & WILLIAMS, his attorneys in the town of
    San Felipe de Austin, of the undersigned, residing? in Corn
    Bend, on the east side of the river Brazos."
    RANDOLPH FOSTER        Austin Feb. 12, 1831.
--------------------------------

ADVERTISEMENT:  "NOTICE  All persons indebted to the subscribers,
    by note or account, are requested during my absence to make
    payment to Mr. LEWIS L. VEEDER, who is duly aruthorized to
    give ?discharge? [HMS-not legible] for the _____in [no legible]
    my name."  WALTER C. WHITE     Feb. 12,____[probably 1831]
--------------------------------

ADVERTISEMENT--"SALE OF LOTS IN THE TOWN OF MATAGORDA--By order
    of the board of proprietors, IRA INGRAM, President."
    Austin, Feb. 12, 1831.
--------------------------------

ADVERTISEMENT:  "BLACKSMITH SHOP" [abstracted by Helen]  a new
    blacksmith shop opened by JABEZ BARNEY at DAVIS & Stand in the
    town of Austin.
    JABEZ BARNEY, Austin, Jan. 15, 1831.
--------------------------------

ADVERTISEMENT--"AGENTS FOR THE MEXICAN CITIZEN NEWSPAPER--
    Capt. MARTIN ALLEN,--Harrisburg;  GEORGE ORR--Trinity;
    Col. GREEN DeWITT, Gonzales;  ADOLPHUS STERNE--Nacogdoches;
    JAMES W. BREEDLOVE--New Orleans;  JAMES D, M'COY-Alexandris,La."
--------------------------------

"A letter written by RAMON MUSQUIZ, Bexar, Jan.38,1831 to the
Constitutional Alcalde of Austin."[HMS did not copy, not genealogical.]

Villa de Austin---Continued.............

"At the regular Session of the Ayuntamiento the following resolutions were adopted. ---- the establishment of boards of
health in different parts of the Colony, to protect as far as
may be practicable the inhabitants from the contagion of the
small pox, which the body has been officially informed, exits
at Bexar and Goliad. The here-in-after named persons were
appointed by the Ayuntamiento as members to compose boards
of health within the respective districts.
For the town of Austin, FRANCIS W. JOHNSON, Esqr. Alcable,
Doctors JAMES B. MILLER, ROBERT PEEBLES & S. S. MOSELY, R. M.
WILLIAMSON, Esqr. _indico procurador, Messrs. LUKE LESENSSIER?
& WILLIAM H. JACK.
For the town of Brazoria, A. BRIGHAM, sind., Doctors F. F. WELLS,
S. B. WALLS, Messrs. A. B. STEWART & JOHN AUSTIN.
For the town of Harrisburg, S. C. HIRAMS, COMISARIO S. BUNDICK
sindico Messrs. DAVID HARRIS, WILLIAM P. HARRIS & EPHRAIM FUQUA
For the upper settlement, Doctor WRIGHT, Messrs. THOMAS S. SAUL,
JOHN P. COLES, NESTOR CLAY, ABNER KUYKENDALL and LEVI H. BOSTIC,
Dor Bay Prairie & lower part of Colorado, LAWRENCE RAMEY Comisario,
Doctor C. G. COX, Messrs. THOMAS M. DUKE, ROBERT H. WILLIAMS,
AYLETT C. BUCKNER and JAMES CUMIDS?.
For the town of Gonzalis, J. B. PATRICK, comisario, THOMAS R.
MILLER sindico, Messrs. GREEN DeWITT, EZEKIEL WILLIAMS, and
JOSEPH CLEMENTS. [the following was abstracted by Helen] "further
ordered by the Ayuntamiento, that F. W. JOHNSON, President,
R. M. WILLIAMSON, sindico Procurado, LUKE LESASSIER, JAMES
WHITESIDE, and WILLIAM MORTON, be appointed a committee".
[abstracted by Helen] "On motion that a patrol be formed for the
town and neighborhood of San Felipe de Austin" "that as the
Ayuntamicento entertain the highest opinion of the zeal and act-
ivity of Mr. THOMAS GAY, appoint him captain of the patrol
guard." "On motion, contract be made with THOMAS H. BORDEN,
the Municipal surveyor, or some other surveyor, of the best
possible term, to extend the road leading from this place to
J. H. BELL'S, to the town of Brazoria, by the most direct and
practiable route, and that JESSE THOMPSON and THOMAS GAY be
appointed commissioners with said surveyor, to report to this
body by the first of June next, the result of said survey."
"It was unanimously resolved by the Ayuntamiento, that PLEASANT
D. M'NEEL, 3d Regidor, be fined in conformity with the provisions of the Municipal Ordinance, the sum ten dollars for
failing to attend the regular meetings of that body, and it is
further resolved that unless he attends the nest regular session,
which will be held on Saturday the 2d day of April next, that
he be reporterd by the body at said meeting to the Chief of
Department., The Ayantamiento adjourned until Sat. 2d April next."
"By Order of the Ayuntamiento,
FRANCIS W. JOHNSON, PRES'T.      S. M. WILLIAMS, SECT.
March 9,_____[HMS Note: probably 1831]
--------------------------------
VILLA de AUSTIN--Thursday March 17th 1831
  [abstracted by Helen] "Congratulations to inhabitants of
GREEN DeWITT'S Colony on appointment of Mr. ANTONIO NAVARRO, as
Commissioner."
-----------------------------------------------------------------

BRAZORIA, VARIOUS NEWSPAPERS-----

"NOTICE--A town has been laid off at the head of navigation
_____side of the Navidad, five miles _____[?ahead?] its con-
fluence with La Va--. The LOTS will be disposed of 10th. The
highest bidder, on the 20th day of September next. Terms made
known on the day of sale."
FRANCIS F. WELLS      JAMES M. ROYSTER  Aug. 24th 1832.
----------------------------------

"NOTICE--Will be sold, at public auction, on Sunday the 7th day
of October next, by JOHN AUSTIN [last name blurred,Helen], Alcalde, at his office, in the town of Brazoria The FOLLOWING
SLAVES...To Wit--SAM, a negro man--BETTY, his wife--MARYANN--
NANCY--JEFFERSON--CHARLES--JIM, and LOUISA, at a credit of six
months from and after the day of sale purchasers giving negot-
ible notes with approved personal security.
JOHN AUSTIN      Brazoria  27th August 1832
----------------------------------

"NOTICE--Persons indebted to the estate of EDWARD ROBERTSON,dec'd.
late of the jurisdiction of Austin, are requested to make immediate payment to the undersigned and those having claims against
said estate, will present them for settlement, within the delay
prescribed by law, otherwise they will be bared.  WM.T.AUSTIN,Admr.
Brazoria      August 30th 1832
----------------------------------

ADVERTISEMENT:  Drugs & medicines
LEWIS L. VEEDER, San Felipe de Austin,  June 14, 1832
----------------------------------

"FOR SALE"                    "15 yoke of oxen..apply to
M'KINSTRY & AUSTIN   Brazoria  June 9, 1832
----------------------------------

ADVERTISEMENT: [abstracted by Helen] "VICTORIA HOTEL--Opening
House of entertainment at this place, in the house formerly
occupied by Mr. EDWARD ROBERTSON"
THOMAS H. BRENAN   Brazoria  July 30, 1832
----------------------------------

"A LIKELY YOUNG NEGRO GIRL FOR SALE"
"A likely Negro Girl between 14 and 15 yrs. of age."
J. B. BAILEY      September 1,____[no year given]
----------------------------------

"BOARDING HOUSE"[abstracted by Helen ] "Mrs. JANE H. LONG opened a Boarding House in the town of Brazoria in the house lately
occupied by Mr. Wm.T. AUSTIN."   Brazoria April 11 ___[no year]
----------------------------------

"BRAZORIA, Wednesday, Sept. 5 [no year given,HMS]"
"APOLOGIES" [abstracted by Helen-] "Apologies being made for
different things done during his illness."[Apology in relation
to publication of a hand-bill] signed G. B. COTTEA
----------------------------------

"Col. MEXIA left the mouth of the Brazos with his fleet and
forces on the 26 th July for Galveston, intending to proceed immediately to Nacogdoches to attack PIEDRAS;  but finding it dif-

BRAZORIA VARIOUS NEWSPAPERS------Continued....

ficult to obtain supplies for his troops, he sailed on the 2d.ult
for Matamoros, leaving his best wishes with the people of the Colonies, who he was assured were able to work out their own salva-
tion. He requested PIEDRAS should not be permitted to escape;
which has been attended to."

--------------------------------

"IMPORTANT QUESTION" [abstracted by Helen] "There is published
in a late Arkansas paper, a letter written from Washington City
by Mr. SEVIER, the representative of Arkansas Territory"

--------------------------------

[Helen's Note: Found in large article possible full name of
Gen. PIEDRAS...JOSE de Las PIEDRAS.(Brazoria 1832 newspaper)]

--------------------------------

THE CONSTITUTIONAL ADVOCATE--BRAZORIA, WED. Sept 5, 1832, Vol.1,No1

[Helen's Note: All of the left side of this article missing so
 will abstract only the names:]
"They had organized, from _____themselves, a Volunteer
Com-_____ander the title of the Santa An-___ Volunteer Company,
of which F. W. JOHNSON, commander of the Santa Anna forces, in
the late expedition against the military post of Anahuac, had
been selected captain: F. ADAMS, 1st Liet. THOMAS GAY, 2nd liet.
and ROBERT PEEBLES, standard bearer."[Helen's note: On the name
of ROBERT PEEBLES there could possibly be a middle initial missing as the space missing in this part would be aloted a letter
and possibly a period. Possibly the same alloted space on
THOMAS GAY.] "WILLIAM H. JACK, Esqr. in the -------of the company, as follows:"

--------------------------------

"NOTICE--All persons having claims against the Estate of SYLVESTER
MURPHY, dec'd. are required to present them, duely authoricated,
to either of the _____ ____bers, within the time specified by
law, or they will be barred. All persons indebted to said Estate,
are required to make ____ inediate payment.
G. B. McKINSTRY, ____Admr. Wm.T. AUSTIN Brazoria, July 31,1832

--------------------------------

[The following in poor condition]
"DISSOLUTION OF COPORTNeeShip?" [believe this to be Corportenship]
"By mutual consent the _____heretofore existing between the
undersigned, under the style of "RUSSELL & WESTAIL", is this day
dissolved. Mr. WESTALL will continue the _____in his name."
Wm. J. RUSSELL     JAMES WESTAIL
Marion, July 12th 1832

--------------------------------

"NOTICE--[abstracted by Helen] "Strayed from this town a gray mare."
JOHN S. MOORE          Brazoria Aug 1, 1832

--------------------------------

ALONE--"The subscriber respectfally informs his friends & the
public" Black-Smith business" WILLIAM H. LEE Brazoria,May,12,1832

--------------------------------
Advertisements: Dr.J.S. COUNSEL doing business in Brazoria
Brazoria April 14, 1832.

Brazoria Various Newspapers----Continued.....

Doctor J. E. PHELPS  Orozimbo, June 2, 1832 [an advertisement]
--------------------------------

"NOTICE--R. M. WILLIAMSON & LUKE LESASSIER--Attorneys of the Law within the jurisdiction of Austin."  Brazoria April 14, 1832.
------------------------------------------------------------------

CONSTITUTIONAL ADVOCATE & TEXAS PUBLIC ADVERTISER
    Vol. I No.    September 5, 1832

[HMS Note:  This article is partly gone on the left side of
   paper.  The following name at bottom or partial of the name]
"_____ENCARN ACIAN CHIRINO"
"_____ONIO MINCHACA"
"_____ES TAYLOR"
"_____TCHKISS,"
--------------------------------

_____OF FOREIGN NEWS  "DON PEDRO's fleet with 16,000 troops, had sailed for Lisbon on the 20th of June.  Spain had united with MIGUEL.  And Great Britain had dispatched a naval force to the mouth of the Tagus, to prevent foreign interferance.  This contest is tediously slow in its progress, but we suppose the next accounts will bring us something decisive in regard to the future destiny of Lusiania, and of the for _lues of Kingly war.
--------------------------------

"There has been a new attemp at a revolution in France.  Five or six hundred were killed in Paris.  Tranquility had been restored.  Particulars in our next."
--------------------------------

DEATH OF YOUNG NAPOLEON, It is stated in the American newspapers, that the capt. of a vessel from the Mediteranean, recently arrived in the U States brought an account of the death of the young Duke of Reichstadt;  which occured about the 5th June.  The news arrived at Frankfort by express, and was generally credited.  The Paris Papers speak of his illness and of his having suffered a relapse.
--------------------------------

"COL BRADBURN--in N. Orleans....  We are not a little astonished at the tone of the following paragraph, coming from the source it does--that an American news paper should in the slightest degree countenance either Military Despotism, or admit for a moment the least apology for its meanest willing instrument!--"
    "FROM THE LOUISIANA, ADVERTISER OF AUG 9th"
    "Col. Bradburn, of the Mexican Army and late commandant at Anahuac, arrived in this city on Monday last.  We understand he is on his way to the city of Mexico, in order to procure an investigation into the recent occurrences in Texas.  He states that his conduct at Anahuac was in strict accordance with the commission deputed to him, as commander of the fort; and is preparing a statement that will place the matter in its true light.  He certainly possesses official documents and papers which give another colouring to the affair.

CONSTITUTIONAL ADVOCATE & TEXAS PUBLIC ADVERTISER..Continued...

"FROM THE PHILADELPHIA GAZETTE.  "J. M. CASTILLO, Esq. Gen.
SANTA ANNA'S Secretary, arrived in this city on Saturday last
from Vear Cruz." [extracted by Helen]-"Mr. CASTILLO is bearer
of despatches from Gen. SANTA ANNA to Gen. MANUEL GOMEZ PEDRAZA"
"Should Gen. PEDRAZA accept the invitation of Gen. SANTA ANNA,
we have strong hopes that order, tranquility and peace will be
restablished in our sister Republic." [this was a very long article]
-----------------------------------

"GEN PEDRAZA.  The Louisiana Advertiser of Aug 9th says Gen.
PEDRAZA, we are credibly informed, has refused to accept of the
invitation of Gen. SANTA ANNA.  We hope this may not be more
true than some of the wise remarks of that print, when speaking
of Mexican affairs"

-----------------------------------

"THE ELECTION--The following persons were chosen electors for
this Department by the large majority:  JUAN MARTIN de BERRI-
MENDEZ, R. JONES, FRANCIS F. WELLS, ANTONIO NAVARRO, Wm. I.
RUSSELL, JAMES KERR, LUCIANO NAVARRO, JAS. B. MILLER, S. RHOADS
FISHER, MIGUEL ARCIMAGA, FELIPE MUSQUIZ, R. M. WILLIAMSON,ELI
MITCHELL, W.D.C.HALL, JOSE MARIE de CARDENAS, Wm.PETTIS, JOSE
ANTONIO de la GARCIA,HENRY SMITH, FERNANDO de LEON, FRANCIS
BINGHAM, JUAN ANTONIO de los SANTOS."
-----------------------------------

"MARINE.  Port of Brazoria...Arrived, Schooner Comet, Calif.,
from New-Orleans."
-----------------------------------

Advertisement:  EDMUND ANDREWS, Brazoria, Aug. 30th supply of
  dry goods.
-----------------------------------

NOTICE:  Persons having claims against the estate of JOHN
RANDON, deceased, are requested to present them to the undersigned
within the time prescribed by law, or they will be bared.  Those
indebted to said estate, will save cost by making immediate
payment."
DAVID RANDON, Adm'r.    Spet 1st 1832.
-----------------------------------

Advertisement:  WILLIAM B. TRAVIS, Attorney & Counsellor at
Law, San Felipe de Austin...September 1st, 1832.
-----------------------------------

Advertisement:  "Doctor C. G. COX, tenders his professional
services to the citizens of Brazoria and the surrounding
country.  Brazoria   April 14, 1832.
-----------------------------------

NOTICE: [abstracted by Helen]"MANSFIELD & GATES, are wanting 5
Negros to work in Steam Saw-Mill in Harrisburg, for $20 per
month.    Sept. 1st [no year given]
-----------------------------------

"The second quarter of the Brazoria Seminary, will recommence
on Monday next, 10th inst.   J. W. CLOUD  Sept 5th 1832.
-----------------------------------

CONSTITUTIONAL ADVOCATE & TEXAS PUBLIC ADVERTISER..Continued..

"NOTICE: Persons indebted to the estate of ISAAC B. JAMEISON,
dec'd., are requested to make immediate payment to the undersigned; and those having claims against said estate, will present them for settlement within the time prescribed by law,
or they will be bared." JOHN S. D. BYROM,Adm'r.
MARGARET JAMEISON, Adm'x. August 30th 1832
-----------------------------------

Advertisement: [abstracted by Helen]"BRIGHAM, RITCHESON & CO.,
purchased of Messrs. SAYRE & NEXON stock and have added to
BRIGHAM & RICHESON stock. The store was formerly occupied by
Messrs. SAYRE & NEXON." Brazoria Aug 26th 1832
-----------------------------------

"EDUCATION-Advertisement:"[abstracted by Helen] "The second
session of the Brazoria Seminary will commence on Monday, next,
11th inst." J. W. CLOUD, Brazoria June 9, 1832
-----------------------------------

Advertisement [abstracted by Helen] "PUMPS--states that they can
be made for $1.00 per foot--delivered in Brazoria. Apply to
JOS. REESON Cedar Lake or to C. G. COX in Brazoria" Aug 18,1832
-----------------------------------

"AUCTIONS...NOTICE.. In conformity with a decree of the second
constitutional Alcalds of the jurisdiction of Austin, will be
sold in the town of Brazoria, at the last residence of EDWARD
ROBERTSON, deceased, on the 7th Oct. next, the whole of the
moveable property belonging to his succession, on a credit of
three months. Purchasers giving security to the satisfaction
of the Administrator. JOHN AUSTIN aug. 29, 1832
-----------------------------------

ADMINISTRATOR'S NOTICE--All persons indebted to the estates of
JOSIAH F. and FRANCES R. HAMILTON, deceased, are requested to
make immediate payment to the undersigned--and those having claims
against said estates are requested to present them duly authonticated, within the ??? prescribed by law.
Wm. J. RUSSELL, Adm'r. Brazoria, Nov. 18, 1833
-----------------------------------

EXTRA--Brazoria, Wednesday, March 27, 1834
------------------

"The present Extra closes the career of the "Advocate," until
the return of OLIVER H. ALLEN, the Editor, who is now absent in
the U.S. of the North, and expected to return in the next vessel."
-----------------------------------

[abstracted by Helen] "This EXTRA contains the proposals of Messrs.
BENJAMIN FRANKLIN CAGE and FRANKLIN C. GRAY, to publish a new paper,
to be entitled "The Emmigrant"."
-----------------------------------

"The People vs. STONE--The trail of STONE, charged with the murder of EUART, came on the 10th inst. Notwithstanding there were
some things attending the trail that I condemned, yet take it all
in all I hail it as a glorices triumph, a triumph of law and
justice over ignorannce and prejudice. Nothing can more strongly
depict our lamentable situation, than the fact that STONE was

forced into trail without his witnesses, when they had been
duly subpoenaed, and were in the jurisdiction of the court,
(however the judicial arm rescued the defendant from injustice,
and the character of our court from a indellible stain.)  What
would have been the impression on the public mind, had the defendant been condemned to death with his witnesses unheard, though
duly subpoenaed, and within the jurisidiction of the court."

-----------------------------------

"THE STEAM BOAT"--"I received a letter from Mr. STURDEVANT,(the
gentleman that we despatched to the United States, to superintend, the building of the boat, in which he informs me that Mr.
GREGORY of New-Orleans, has given him letters of credit, and that
he should proceed immediately to build the boat.") "We have a fair
prospect of haveing  a steamboat in the waters of the Brazos by
the middle of the Brazos by the middle of next summer".

-----------------------------------

NOTICE:  Pursuant to an order from the honorable the Alcalde for
the jurisdiction of Brazoria, will be sold in the town of Brazoria,
on Thursday the 24th day of April next, all the real estate belonging to the succession of  D. W. ANTHONY, deceased, consisting of land, and lots in the town of Brazoria.  Particulars made
known on the day of sale, a credit of four months will be given,
by the purchaser giving bond with approved security, and a lein
on the property until final payment.  T.F.L.PARROTT  March 25.(No yr.)

-----------------------------------

MRS. JANE H. LONG takes this method of returning her unfeigned
thanks to the citizens of Brazoria and its vicinity, for the very
liberal patronage bestowed upon her during the two years of her
keeping a public house in Brazoria, and informs them that she
has retired from business--Mr. M.W.SMITH having purchased the entire concern and being aided by Mr. and Mrs. STEPHENSON, she has
no hesitation in recommending them to the public, and feels well
assured that with ample means and strict attention to business,
they will be well prepared to accommodate and please;  and she
hopes that they may share liberal portion of public patronage.
March 22 (No year given)

-----------------------------------

Advertisement:  R. STEVENSON has purchased the stock of goods
lately owned by Messrs. HOWTH & WILLIAMS & will continue to do
business in the house formerly occupied by them.  March 27(No yr)

-----------------------------------

GODWIN BROWN COTTEN will practice law in the different courts of
Austin's Colony.  His residence is in Brazoria.

-----------------------------------

PUBLIC NOTICE--The Executors of MAURICE HENRY, deceased, have
placed in my hands all notes and accounts due his succession,
for collection.  All persons indebted to said succession are requested to come forward and make payment by the first day of January, or suits will be immediately commenced.
JOHN A. WHARTON          Brazoria Dec. 21, 1833

-----------------------------------

Advertisement:  New Goods--Staple goods.  HOWTH & WILLIAMS
Feb. 8, 1833.

-----------------------------------

PUBLIC NOTICE..A Public sale of Lots in the Town of Orozimbo,
at the head of tide navigation on the Brazos River, Texas
1st Monday of May next.
JAMES A. PHELPS. Proprietor    Orozimbo, Jan. 18, 1834
------------------------------------

NOTICE: All persons are hereby warned not to purchase a pro-
misory note, signed by myself and J.S.D. BYROM, for eight hundred
dollars, dated the 16th of December, 1333, and due about the
1st of January, 1835, payable to P. R. SPLANE. The consideration
of the above note has failed, and I am determined not to
pay (not ledgible).
SYLVESTER BOWEN         Brazoria, Feb. 6, 1834
(HMS Note: The above date of Dec. 1333 is more than likely sus-
posed to be 1833.)
------------------------------------

DEPARTMENT OF BEXAR, Jurisdiction of Brazoria.
The Creditors of A. G. REYNOLDS are notified to appear before me,
at my office, on the 2nd day of March next, for the purpose of
holding an election for ?Avadics?(not ledgible-HMS Note).
EDWIN WALLER, Alealde, and Ex-Ofico Notary Public
Brazoria, Jan. 30, 1834
------------------------------------

NOTICE. All persons having claims against the Estate of JOHN
AUSTIN, deceased, are particularly requested to present them the
undersigned, within the time prescribed by law, or they will be
barred, as we are determined to close the affairs of the estate as
soon as possible. Those indebted will save _____ by making
immediate payment.
WILLIAM T. AUSTIN, Adm'r.  ELIZABETH E. AUSTIN, Adm'r. of the
Estate of JOHN AUSTIN, deceased.  Brazoria, Nov. 30, 1833.
------------------------------------

ADVERTISEMENT:[abstracted by Helen] Salt  "The undersigned having
leased the VELASCO SALT WORKS" Applications to A. G. & R. MILLS,
Brazoria, or the undersigned in Velasco.
SILAS DINSMORE, Jr.  Velasco, Nov. 21, 1833
------------------------------------

NOTICE: The administrators of the Estate of BEVERLY A. PORTER,
deceased, have placed in my hands the notes and accounts belonging to said estate, for collection--All persons indebted to said
estate are hereby notified, if they do not come forward and settle
the same, that suits will be instituted without delay.
JOHN A. WHARTON     Brazoria, Dec. 21, 1833.
------------------------------------

NOTICE: All persons having claims against the estate of HENRY
MUNSON, deceased, are notified to present them to my agent, JOHN A.
WHARTON, esq., in the town of Brazoria, for adjustment, and these
indebted to said estate to make payment to him.
NANCY B. MUNSON, admr'x.    Brazoria, Dec. 21, 1833.
------------------------------------

NOTICE: The Executor of the estate of C. G. COX, deceased, has
placed in my hands all notes and accounts belonging to said suc-
cesion, for collection, with instructions to make them by suit or
otherwise, without delay. All persons indebted to that estate
will immediately come forward and settle the same, or they will
be coerced by law. JOHN A. WHARTON  Brazoria, Dec. 21, 1833.
------------------------------------

"DEPARTMENT OF BEXAR, Jurisdiction of Brazoria"
  "To the creditors of the firm of BRIGHAM & RICHESON:  You are
   hereby notified that ASA BRIGHAM, surviving partner of the
   firm of BRIGHAM & RICHESON, has filed a petition in my office,
   praying that a meeting of the firm be called, for the purpose
   of deliberating on the matters and things set forth in the
   showing of the petitioner, who prays the grant of a respite
   of 12 months, to be given him, for the payment of the debts
   of said firm.  The creditors are therefore notified to appear
   at my office, on the 23d Feb. to deliberate on the prayer of
   the petitioner, or otherwise it will be granted.
   EDWIN WALLER, Alcalde, and Ex-Oficio Notary Public.
   Brazoria, Jan. 22, 1834.
------------------------------------

"FROM THE NEW YORK COURIER & ENQUIRER"
  JOHN COFFIN NAZRO  <u>INSTUCTOR OF PUBLIC ELOQUENCE</u>
  "Will give instruction in his Profession, with special reference to the Philosophy of the human passions Terms, $6000 per
   annum; and will teach the perfect pronunciation of the Romaic
   or modern 'Greek language, and the reading of the best ancient
   and modern Poets, Orators, Philosophers and Historians--Terms
   $250 per quarter."
  "Mr. NAZRO deems it proper to state that he is of the family
   of Gen. WARREN, of Bunker Hill, Gov. BELCHER, of Massachusetts,
   under the crown, and Admiral Sir ISAAC COFFIN, of the Royal
   British Navy; further, that the relations of his family are,
   JOHN JAY, COLONEL RUTGERS, COMMODORE RODGERS, COM. CHAUNCEY,
   COM. BAINBRIDGE, COL. TRASK, of Springfield, Massachusetts,
   Gov. POINDEXTER, of Mississippi, the Rev. Dr. NOTT, of Union
   College, Schenociady, the Rev. Dr. ELY, of Philadelphia,
   General HARRISON of the Northwestern Army, and the KNICKER-
   BOCKERS, the BECKMANS, the RUTGERS', the CLINTONS, and the
   LIVINGSTONES, of the state of New-York."
  [abstracted by Helen] Mr. NAZRO 14 yrs. of age, and was a
   candidate for cadetship in the U. States Military Academy,
   West Point, he was honored with the highest recommendations
   from Gov. CLINTON, Gen. VAN RANSSALAER, Hon. JOHN J. MORGAN,
   Hon. ALBERT H. TRACY, Col. HAYNE, Gen. SWIFT, Gen. BROWN,
   Hon. NATHAN WILLIAMS, Rev. Dr. BLATCHFORD, Hon. Saml. L.
   SOUTHARD, Hon. C. C. CAMBRELENG, Hon. SAML. L. MITCHELL,
   HENRY REMSON, Esq., JOHN C. WARREN, Esq., Wm.H. ROBINSON,
   ?GER--DUS CLARK, Esq.[HMS Note: too dim to read] JOHN G.
   BOGART, Esq., Russian Consul, HENRY ECKFORD, Esq., GEORGE
   HOFFAMN, Esq., professor of law in the University of Mary-
   land; Hon. JOHN QUINCY ADAMS, president of the U. States of
   America; Gen. JACKSON, President of the United States of
   America, and twenty members of Congress."
------------------------------------

ADVERTISEMENT:[abstracted by Helen] "HENRY AUSTIN will draw
   and attend to the execution of deeds of transfer, in due
   form of law.  He will also translate spanish and Frnech
   documents.  Leave their notes of particulars with Mr. EDMUND
   ANDREWS, and they will be attended to promptly.
   Brazoria  Nov. 30, 1833.
------------------------------------

EARLY TEXAS NEWS

ADVERTISEMENT:[abstracted by Helen]   For sale from 4 to 500
    acres first rate Timbered Land, lying on the Bernard, and
    extending westwardly across CANEY Creek.  Can be learned by
    calling at the Law Office of Messrs. LEAGUE & AINSWORTH.
    Brazoria  Nov. 23, 1833.
    ---------------------------------

NOTICE:  All persons having claims against the succession of
    WILLIAM ARNOLD, dec'd. are requested to present them for pay-
    ment to JOHN A. WHARTON, Esq. in Brazoria, without delay, as
    it is the wish of the administratrix to liquidate the debts
    of said succession immediately; and those indebted are reques-
    ted to make payment to said attorney.
    MARTHA E. ARNOLD, Administratix  Brazoria  Dec. 21.
    ---------------------------------

ADVOCATE OF THE PEOPLES--Brazoria, Texas  Vol. I, No. 8
    February 22, 1834  & March 27, 1834
    Edited & Published by OLIVER W. ALLEN
"FROM THE NEW YORK COURIER & ENQUIRER"--"For Mr. KERNAL WEB of
    the York Currier--[a letter written to him signed Confidential.]
    ---------------------------------
A letter to THOMAS BOON, Esquire  Washington, Oct. 7, 1833.
It was signed "Your respected friend, JOHN DOWNING, Esquire."
    ---------------------------------

THE ADVOCATE  Brazoria   Saturday  Feb. 22, 1834

[abstracted by Helen] "Since the decease of the Editor of the
    Constitutional Advocate, five individuals have come forward
    and claimed that press, as proprietors, and have endeavoured
    to establish their claim by a suit at law."
    ---------------------------------
[abstracted by Helen] "Mr. Editor"--"The late JOHN AUSTIN inform-
    ed me, that the Political Chief had authorised S. M. WILLIAMS
    to pay"
    ---------------------------------

MARRIAGES  "At San Felipe, on the 31st of December last, ANDREW
    WESTALL to Miss _____HENRY."
    "In this place, on the ____ult, HENRY S. BROWN, 2nd Regidor,
    to Miss CAROLINE SCOTT."
    "In this place, on the 28th ult.  T.F.L.PARROTT, M.D. to Mrs.
    E. E. AUSTIN."
    ---------------------------------

OBITUARY
    "Departed this life, at the residence of DAVID H. MILBURN, on
    the 9th of January last, BENJAMIN FOWLER, in the 7-th year of
    his age. Mr. FOWLER was a native of Virginia, and for the last
    twelve years a resident of Texas."
    "Of a pulmonary complaint, on the 2d inst. Mrs. SARAH WESTALL,
    relict of the late THOMAS WESTALL."
    "Of the congestive fever, on the 9th inst.  Miss EMILY McNEEL,
    in the 16th year of her age."
    ---------------------------------
NOTICE: "All persons having professional business with me are
    requested (should I be absent) to call on HENRY SMITH, who is
    authorised  and empowered to act for me, and in my name."
    JOHN A. WHARTON   Feb. 22, 1834.
    ---------------------------------

19.

I HAVE FOR SALE A TRACT OF LAND....[abstracted by Helen]
   "This land is well known, it being the same originally granted
   to GEORGE HUFF, and by him sold to S. SAWYER."
   JOHN A. WHARTON        Brazoria   Feb. 22, 1834.
------------------------------------
NOTICE:     Persons indebted to subscriber, or the estate of
   JOHN AUSTIN, Deceased, are requested to come forward, with-
   out delay, and settle, or they will find their accounts, Etc.
   in the hands of an attorney for collection.
   WILLIAM T. AUSTIN        Dec. 28 [no year given]
------------------------------------
"OBSERVATIONS, HISTORICAL, GEOGRAPHICAL & DESCRIPTIVE, in a
   series of letters on Texas, By Mrs. MARY AUSTIN HOLLEY,  Just
   received and for sale by EDMUND ANDREWS."   Dec 28.[no year]
------------------------------------
NOTICE:  "The Secretary of the Velasco Association has placed in
   my hands, for collection, all notes and accounts belonging to
   said Association.  All persons indebted to said association
   are requested to make payment without delay, as no far her
   indulgence can be given. JOHN A. WHARTON  Brazoria Dec 21,1833
------------------------------------
THE REPUBLICAN  Brazoria  Nov. 1, 1834

   "INDIAN HOSTILITIES--By a gentleman arrived last night from
   Alexandria, La. we are informed that information had been received at that place from Arkansas, that a battle had taken
   place between the United States Dragoons, lately under the
   command of Gen. LEVENWORTH, and the Pawnee Indians, which resulted in the death of 80 indians and 8 of our troops.  One
   hundred and fifty Indians were taken prisoners, and were
   on their way to Fort Towson."
------------------------------------
"We received, for publication, the able and patriotic Circular
   of our Superior Judge, T. J. CHAMBERS, which shall have a
   place in our next."
------------------------------------
[abstracted by Helen]-"THE MARCH OF STEAM--Mr. MASON of Cin-
   cinnati, an ingenious mechanic has been for some months engaged in constructing a machine."
------------------------------------
"Chieftaincy of the Department of Bexar"   signed JUAN NEPOMUCENA
   SEQUIN.  To the Political Chief of the Department of Brazos.
   Bexar, October 14, 1834."[abstracted by Helen]
------------------------------------
[abstracted by Helen] "ELECTION--CHIEFTAINCY OF THE DEPARTMENT
   OF BRAZOS--"  To the citizens of the Jurisdiction of Columbia,
   Election be held Nov. 8, 1834.  "In the town of Columbia, to
   be presided by myself; in the town of Brazoria, to be presided
   by L. C. MANSON, Esq.; in the town of Velasco, to be presided
   by F. J. HASKINS, comissario; at the house of ALEXANDER HODGE,
   Esq. to bepresided by him--and the returns to be made at the
   store of A. G. & R. MILLS, in the town of Brazoria, on the
   day following, for two representives to the provisional congress, to be held in the city of Bexar, to commence their
   session on the 15th day of the same month."
   HENRY SMITH            Brazoria  October 29, 1834.
------------------------------------

[abstracted by Helen][A very long involved Political article]: The
following signed "Solemnly protesting before the S-oreme Being,
not to act in bad faith in proof of which we sign the present
in Bexar, October 7, 1834." JUAN NEPOMUNCENO SEGUIN, GASPER
FLORES, ERASMO SEGUIN, REFUGIO De la GARZA, JOSE ANTONIO NAVAR-
RO, JUAN ANOTNIO ZAMBRANO, IGNACIO CHAVES, FRANCISCO RUIZ,
JOSE ANTONIO De la GARZA, FRANCISCO XAVIER BASTELLO, DOMINGO
BUSTELLO, JOSE MARIA de JESUS CARRAJAL, IGNACIO HERRERA, JOSE
MARIA ZAMBRANO, AUGUSTIN SOTO, MIGUEL ARCEMEGA, LUCIANO NAVAR-
RO, JOSE MARIA SALMAS, JOSE MARIA CARDENAS, IGNACIO AROCHA,
JUAN McMULLIN, NICHOLAS FLE_____, JOHN W. SMITH, ____ _____,
ANTONIO D-L---, SIMON de LAON, AMBROSIA RODRIGUEZ, IGAACIO
PERES, BRUNO HUYSAR, PEDRO FLORES, NEPOMUCCNO SANCHEZ, JUAN
MANUEL RIVA, PLACIDO OLIVARRI, AUGUSTIN BARRERER, MANUEL MAR-
TINEZ, ALEXANDER VIDAL, JOSE FRANCISCO FLORES, JOSE MANUEL de
la GARZA, MANUL CARVAHAL, JOSE ANTONIO SOMBRAMA, EDWARDO RIVAS
JOSE FLORES, PEBLO SALENAS, SALVADOR FLORES, RAMON TREVINO MAN-
UEL FLORES, CLEMENTE SUSTIL--.
JUAN AN---S ZAMBRANO, Secy.        Bexar Oct.13, 1834.
------------------------------------
"PLAN FOR CALLING A PROVISIONAL CONGRESS FOR TEXAS"
Polical articles signed "In the capital of Monelova, JOSE
ANTONIO VASQUEZ, Deputy for Texas, OLIVER JONES, do. T. J.
CHAMBERS, Superior Judge of Texas, on Sept. 1st, 1834."
------------------------------------
"FOR ALCALDE, ASA BRIGHAM--FOR SHERIFF, J. S. D. BYROM, JOSEPH
CALVETT, W. B. SWENY, AUGUSTUS WILLIAMS, FRANKLIN LEWIS,
CHARLES W. STEWART.
JURISDICTION OF AUSTIN, ROBERT WILSON--FOR SHERIFF OF THE
DEPARTMENT OF BRAZOS, Col. GOWIN HARRIS is a candidate for
the above office at the ensuing election, in December next,
and will be supported by many voters. W. E. HOWTH is a candidate for the above office [HMS Note: Brazos office of
sheriff], G. M. COLLINSWORTH is a candidate for the above
office [Brazos] 1st Rigador, GREEN B. JAMERSON. The following gentleman, from their identity with Texas and its best
interests, and their well known intelligence and respectability it is believed will give general satisfaction and meet
with a general support as officers of the Ayuntannia into
of the Jurisdiction of Columbia for the insuing year, viz:
JAMES F. PERRY, 1st Regidore, WALTER C. WHITE, 2nd Regidore,
A. G. MILLS, Syndico Procurador"
------------------------------------
"DISSOLUTION. The partnership heretofore existing between the
subscribers, under the firm of MIMS & SHARP, is this day dissolved by mutual consent, and JOHN SHARP remains charged with
the concern and will continue business at the Exchange as
usual. JOHN SHARP, DAVIS R. MISS. Brazoria--Oct. 25.
------------------------------------
NOTICE Brazoria Hotel--M. W. SMITH informs his friends and the
public that the above establishment will in future be conducted by himself. M. W. SMITH  Brazoria, Oct. 27.
------------------------------------
"FOR SALE" [abstracted by Helen]-- General merchandise for sale
by: EDMUND ANDREWS        Nov. 1st.
------------------------------------

"DISSOLUTION, The copartnership heretofore existing between
M. W. SMITH & E. BAILEY under the firm of SMITH and BAYLEY
is this day dissolved by mutual consent and all the business
of the above firm will be settled by M. W. SMITH.
M. W. SMITH "    E. BAILEY
Brazoria--Oct 27

-------------------------------

LAND FOR SALE   The subscriber has 15,000 or 20,000 acres of
superior Land for sale in tracts to suit purchasers, persons
wishing to purchase, will find him at his residence a few
miles above Orozimbo.
T. F. L. PARROTT    Oakland Place,

-------------------------------

"By virtue of a decree of the Alcalde of this jurisdiction,
I will expose to public sale, on Saturday the 29th of Nov.
next, in the town of Columbia, a certain tract of land containing 163 acres;  the property of the succession of JAMES
WESTALL; formerly owned by J. H. BELL, and by him sold to
F. F. WELLS, being near the town of Columbia. Also--Three
town lots in the town of Marion, with their improvements,
and a two acre lot, not designated. Sale to take place on
the 1st Jan. next, on the premises. For further particulars
apply to J. H. BELL, Esq. Terms--Six & twelve months credit
with judicial security.   J. G. McNEEL,adm'r.   Oct. 25."

-------------------------------

"CURATOR"S SALE--By virtue of an order from EDWIN WALLER, Esq.
constitutional Alcalde for the jurisdiction of Columbia, I
will sell on Sunday the 9th of Nov. next, the entire stock
of goods belonging to the succession of the late JOHN GRAHAM,
deceased, consisting of the following articles, viz:  Cotton
Cambric Hdfks., capes, cotton check, pins, Valencias, printed
muslins, black, red, and purple silks, mosquito muslins, one
bale fancy prints, also a quantity of wearing apparel etc.
Sale to take place at 10 o'clk. a. m., terms made known on
the day of sale.   ANSON JONES, Curator    Brazoria Oct 24,1834."

-------------------------------

"NOTICE--All persons having claims against the succes'n of
LUKE LESASSIER are hereby noticed to present them to the
undersigned by the 4th, Monday in October next property authenticated, after that date suit will be brought against
every person indebted to said succession.
JAMES B. MILLER, Testamentary (HMS: this next word hard to
read, could be executor.) exe_____.

-------------------------------

Advertisement:  For Sale, New French, English and Italina goods,
Now opening in the corner room of Mr. ECKLE's new building,
Fifth and River streets. PIANO FORTE  H.B. STRATTON,
Brazoria Mar. 17

-------------------------------

NOTICE:  About the first of January last a box of Books was
landed at this port, from the sch'r. Empress, Thompson, master,
directed to "Rev. SUMNER BACON, care of JOHN OVERTON, Brazoria,
Texa." Said Box is in the possession of ASA BRIGHAM, who
desires the owner to receive the property and pa_____rges.

-------------------------------

EARLY TEXAS NEWS

## SAN FELIPE deAUSTIN
TELEGRAPH, AND TEXAS REGISTER-Vol.I,No.1-Saturday, October 10,1835
Published every Saturday, By BAKER & BORDENS, San Felipe De Austin.
------------------------

"LIFE OF ROBERT MORRIS--The important services which were rendered to the United States by Mr. Morris, during the arduous
struggle which terminated in our independence, entitle him to
the grateful recollection of every American.  For the following
particulars respecting his life we are indebted to a memoir in
the [Repository,] published in Philadelphia by Mr. DELAPLUINE.
    ROBERT MORRIS was born at Liverpool, in January 1733-4,O.S.
Of his family, little is known, except that his father was a
respectable English merchant.  When he was thirteen years of age,
he was brought to America by his parents.  After receiving a
suitable education, he was placed in the compting-house of Mr.
CHARLES WILLING, conjunction with whose son, THOMAS, he subsequently carried on the business of a merchant.  On the appearance
of a rupture with Great Britain, he was elected a member of
Congress from Pennsylvania, at the close of the year 1775, and
assisted very materially in those pecuniary arrangement which the
operations of an army and navy required.
    (Remainder has been abstracted by Helen due to length]
    "During the march of the British troops through Jersey,
in 1776, Congress removed to Baltimore, but Mr. MORRIS was left
in Philadelphia, for reasons of a commercial nature." "and Mr.
MORRIS Furnished also very large sums to general Greene, during
his difficulties in South Carolina."
    "In the year 1781 the office of Financier was created, and
this gentleman was unanimously elected to fill the station."
    "Mr.MORRIS died in Philadelphia, in May, 1806, in the sev-
enty-third year of his age."
From the Newspaper, Port Fol---.(smuge of ink)
--------------------

"A GOOD STORY--Almost thirty years since, an English gentleman
with whom we subsequently became acquainted, (Mr.BENJAMIN CRIED-
LAND, of Liecester, Eng.) detected and brought to justice a
large gang of pickpockets by unwitting adopting one of their
private signals."  From the newspaper-Troy (N.Y.) Sentinel.
----------------

"COLONIZATION LAW OF MAY 2, 1835--The Constitutional Governor
of the State of Coahuila and Texas to all its inhabitants:  KNOW YE,
that the Congress of the same State has decreed the following:
The Constitutional Congress of the free, independent and sovereign
State of Coahuila and Texas has thought proper to decree:
Article I.  All persons or families who actually reside in Texas,
and were introduced previous to the date of this law, for the
purpose of establishing themselves in the country, and who have
not received land, according to the laws of Colonization, are
declared entitled to the portions indicated in that of the 24th
of March, 1825, provided they possess the requisites therin
required.
Article 2.  Such persons as may be benefitted by the foregoing
article, who arrived previcus to the 28th of April, 1832, shall
pay as an acknowledgement, at the time of receiving their titles,
the sum fixed by the 22d article of the law of the 24th of March,
1825, and those who have arrived since, at the rate of seventy
dollars for every league of pasturage, and five dollars per labor
for arable. [temporal.]

SAN FELIPE deAUSTIN--October 10, 1835
Article 3. The Government shall appoint a commissioner for each
of the three departments of Texas, to issue the necessary titles
to the persons spoken of in this law, conformably to the instructions of commissioners of the 4th of September, 1827, without
subjection to the additional act. Said commissioners shall be
paid by the persons interested, agreeably to the decree of the
15th of May, 1828.
Article 4. The Executive shall take the necessary steps to carry
this law into effect as soon as possible.
    The Constitutional Governor of the State will have this
understood for its compliance, caustin it to be printed, published,
and circulated.                JOSE MARIA MIER, Pres't.
                               DIEGO GRANT, Sec.
                               JOSE M. J. CARVAJAL, Dep. Sec.
    Therefore, I order it to be printed, published, and circula-
ted; and that due compliance be given to it. Done in the capital
of Monclova, this 2d of May, 1835.   AUGUSTIN VIESCA.
JOSE MARIANO IRALA, Sec'ry.
--------------------
"The result of the election for delegates to the Consultation, as
far as we have learned, is as follows: S. F. Austin, Thos. BARNET,
Wyly MARTIN, Randall JONES, Jesse BURNHAM, Wm. MENIFEE, W.B.TRAVIS,
For the Jurisdiction of Harrisburg: Lorenzo deZAVALA, D.B.McCOMB,
John W. MOORE, Wm. P. HARRIS, C. C. DYER, M. W. SMITH, Geo.M.
PATRICK.
----------------
"Col.S. F. AUSTIN left this place on the 8th inst. for the head
quarters of the Army of Texas, with the expectation of returning
previous to the 15th inst. so as to take his seat as a member
of the Consultation, which is to convene on that day."
----------
[abstracted by Helen"From the best information, no doubt can
exist that General COS is now in Bejar, at the head of a large
body of troops, with which he intends shortly to invade the
colonies."
----------------
"For the information of all who may wish to obtain land under
the colonization contract of AUSTIN & WILLIAMS, we have the
satisfaction to state that the commissioner, DR. PEEBLES, is
now issuing deeds; and we would suggest to those who have made
their selections, the propriety of making as early an application
as practicable."
--------------
"MARTIN de LEON'S second colony, which was included in this
department by the third article of the decree of March 18, 1834,
was annexed to the department of Bejar, by a decree of May 17,1835."
------------------
"A translation of the law giving land to the scattered families
in Texas, will be found the second page of this paper. We will
state, for the information of the public, that FRANCIS W. JOHNSON
is appointed commissioner under this law, and that he has received
a commission from the Government to that effect, dated May 30,1835."
--------------------
[abstracted by HMS] "COLONEL UGARTECHEA is on his march from
Bejar with 500 men, to overrun our country. They come to make
us yield an unconditional and slavish submission to a military
usurpation." "Shall we surrender our country and our homes to
a military usurpation?" "This Committee are ready to answer

for their countrymen; and they answer by calling upon them to
come, and come quickly, to the assistance of their friends,
their neighbours, and their brothers, three hundred of whom are
already in the field--COLONEL AUSTIN is with them.  These have to
contend with the whole of the Mexican army; but they will contend
bravely; they will dispute every inch of ground with their
invaders until the expected aid shall arrive."
GAIL BORDEN, JR., WM. PETTIS, JNO. H. MONEY, Members of the Com. of
AUSTIN.    R. R. ROYALL, Member from Matagorda.   ISAAC BAT-
TERSON, Member from Harisburg."
-----------------------
"CIRCULAR--From the Committee of Safety of the Jurisdiction
of Austin"[abstracted by HMS]  "The substance of this information
is, that GENERAL COS was expected at Bejar, on the 16th of this
month, with more troops; that he intended to make an immediate
attack on the colonies; that there was a plan to try and foment
division and discord among the people, so as to use one part
against the other, and prevent preparation; and that the real
object is to break up the foreign settlements in Texas."
S. F. AUSTIN, Chairman
San Felipe, September 19, 1835.
-----------------------------
"Gonzales, September 25, 1825, To the Committee of Safety of
Mina, and to J. H. MOORE, Rio Colorado'[abstracted by HMS]   "A
demand, at the instance of COLONEL UGARTECHEA, has been made for
a piece of cannon, which has been in this town upwards of four
years." "The Alcalde, with the approbation of the people, has
refused to deliver up the cannon; and we are satisfied that,
as soon as COLONEL UGARTECHEA is informed of the fact, he will
immediately send a force against this colony at least, thinking
us too weak to resist him.  We therefore earnestly request you
to send what force you can collect immediately to our assistance.
You need make no delay about provisions, for we have plenty at
your service.  The time we think is most pressing and the occasion
most urgent.  In haste etc. By Order of the Committee,
signed  G. W. DAVIS, Secretary."
-----------------------------
"San Felipe De Austin, September 29, 1835--.[abstracted by HMS]
"The Committee of the Jurisdiction of Austin has received the
communication directed to the Committee of Safety of Mina by you,
in the name of the people of Gonzales, under date of the 25th inst.
stating that COLONEL UGARTECHEA had made a demand for the piece of
cannon at that place, and that the people, in a general meeting,
had refused to give it up."   "Yours respectfully,S. F. AUSTIN,
Chairman of Committee,
G.W.DAVIS, Secretary of the Committee of Gonzales."
-----------------------------
"CIRCULAR, From the Committee of Safety of the Jurisdistion of
Austin" [abstracted by HMS]  "When the circular of this Committee, under date of the 19th ult. was issued, information of
an unquestionable character had been received here, as to the
marching of soldiers from Bejar, in some short period, within
the limits of the colonies.  The object appeared to be the apprehension of certain citizens, among whom DON LORENZO de ZAVALA,
now a citizen of Texas, was particularly designated and aimed at.
This gentleman had come to Texas, as to an asylum from the per-
secution of the present administration of Mexico."

"GONZALES, September, 30, 1835--Fellow-Citizens of San Felipe
and La Baca,--A detachment of the Mexican forces from Bejar,
amounting to about one hundred and fifty men, are encamped opposite us: we expect an attack momentarily. Yesterday we were
but eighteen strong, today one hundred and fifty, and forces
continually arriving. We wish all the aid and despatch, that
is possible to give us, that we may take up soon our line of
march for Bejar, and drive from our country all the Mexican
forces. Give us all the aid and despatch that is possible.
Respectfully, yours, CAPTAIN ALBERT MARTIN, CAPTAIN R. M. COLEMAN,
CAPTAIN J. H. MOORE
------------------------------
A letter written by WM. FISHER, Chairman to Col.S.F.AUSTIN,Chair-
man of Committee of Austin.
------------------------------
"CIRCULAR-From the Committee of Safety of the Jurisadction of
Austin to the Committees of Nacogdoches and San Augustin--San
Felipe De Austin, October 4, 1835--Signed by S.F.AUSTIN,Chairman
of Committee--[abstracted by HMS] "War is declared against military despotism. Public opinion has proclaimed it with one
united voice. The campaign has opened. The military at Bejar
has advanced upon Gonzales. GENERAL COS has arrived and threatens
to overrun the country." "There are about 300 volunteers at
Gonzales at this time, and there will be upwards of 500 in a
few days." "The distinguished and virtuous patriot, DON LORENZO
de ZAVALA, formerly governor of the state of Mexico, and late
minister to France, has just arrived from his residence on San
Jacinto, and is now here, at the house of the chairman of this
Committee. He is a citizen of Texas, and enters fully and warmly into the cause of the people. He also approves very much
of the position they have taken against military despotism, and
of the circular of this Committee of the 19th ult."
------------------------------
CAUTION-All persons are cautioned from trading for a note, given
by me to W. BARRET TRAVIS, for $500 dated some time in Dec.,1834,
and payable the 1st day of January, 1836, as I am determined
not to pay said note unless compelled by law, as I have not
received value.              H. M. THOMPSON,San Felipe de Austin
October 10 2t
------------------------------
Ad--"WATCH & CLOCK MAKER. The subscriber informs his friends
and the Public that he has removed to San Felipe, where he intends
to follow the above business, and hopes, by strict attention,
to merit and receive a share of the patronage of his fellow
citizens.         WILLIAM SIMPSON
Oct 10 tf
------------------------------
Ad--"BAKER & BORDENS--Respectfully inform the citizens of Texas
that they have stablished a Printing Office in the town of
San Felipe De Austin, where they are prepared to execute every
description of Book and Job Printing, at the shortest notice,
and upon reasonable terms.
San Felipe de Austin, October 10,1835.
------------------------------
Ad--"A Card--The undersigned takes pleasure in announcing to the
Public that a Commissioner (Dr. ROBERT PEEBLES) has been appointed for the Colony of AUSTIN & WILLIAMS; that he has presented
his credentials to the political chief, JAMES B. MILLER, and

has by him been regularly installed in his office." "The office is now open in San Felipe de Austin, where the Commissioner is prepared to issue titles. All persons, therefore, who by the colonization laws are entitled to land, and who wish to acquire it in this Colony, are requested to come forward, and receive titles to whatever land they may have selected." "For the convenience of the colonists who have located themselves above the San Antonio Road, the office will, in the course of a month or six weeks, be removed for a time to Tenoxtitlan. SPENCER H. JACK, Agent for AUSTIN & WILLIAMS.
Oct 10 tf

------------------------------

Ad--"FRESH GOODS--The subscriber begs leave to inform the citizens of San Felipe de Austin and elsewhere, that he has just received, per schr.(meaning schooner,HMS note) San Felipe, a general assortment of merchandise, consinting of Groceries,Hardware,Dry Goods, Hats, Boots and Shoes, Clothing." JAMES COCHRANE.
October 10-tf
-------------------End of October 10,1835--------------------------

TELEGRAPH, AND TEXAS REGISTER-Vol.1,No.2-Saturday,October 17,1835
Published every Saturday, By BAKER & BORDENS,San Felipe De Austin
Terms of Subscription, $5.00 per annum, if paid in advance. $6.00 per annum, if paid at the expiration of six months.

------------------------------

"THE UNNATURAL MOTHER, A FRAGMENT OF ENGLISH HISTORY-The countess of MACCLESFIELD had one child, whom, regardless of shame, she voluntarily avowed to be the offspring of adultery, and gave away to a poor woman, with a small sum of money, to educate as her own. At the death of the nurse an accident disclosed to him the secret of his birth, yet his mother peremptorily d denied him the small-lest portion of her large possessions, and even prevented his father from making any provision for him, by artfully suggesting that he was dead. She afterwards endeavoured to have him kidnapped, and sent to the West Indies, and the failure of this attempt only added new stings to her resentment. Yet SAVAGE (the name of her unhappy son) flattered himself that, could he obtain one interview, he should find an advocate in natural affection that must soften her obduracy. An opportunity soon presented, and one evening, when he knew she was alone, he contrived to gain admittance into her room. On entering, he immediately threw himself at her feet, and in language poetically descriptive painted his missery, and intreated her pity. She received him with shrieks and abhorence, declared he had formed a design against her life, and had him turned from her house with ignominy. A dispute having arose in a tavern, in which one of his friends was insulted, SAVAGE, who excelled in the art of fencing, instantly drew in defence of his friend, who would otherwise have been overpowered by numbers, and killed his opponent. He was taken into custody; and, as soon as the rumor reached his mother's ears, she used all her influence to procure his condemnation; and at the moment when he stood most in need of the kindness and partiality of a fond mother, the countess appeared at the bar, and anxious to prejudice the court & jury against him, and fix his conviction, she related, with the most unheard of barbarity, the circumstances of his pretended attemp to assassinate her in her own house. Disappointed, however, in the design of driving him of life, she determined at least to

render that life a state of wretchedness; and accordingly, she
afterwards had the pleasure to resist every overture made by the
humanity of individuals for his relief, and finally suffered him,
in the prime of life, to die of want, in the gloomy mansions of
a prison, while she was in the enjoyment of every luxury of life.
It will probably be supposed, by those who are unacquainted with
the character of SAVAGE, that some intellectual or personal
defect in this unhappy youth inspired or confirmed the unnatural
prejudice. On the contrary, he was a man of the most sublime
genius and insinuating address, with all the graces of person,
and charms of conversation."
--------------------------
"VALOR AND MAGNAMITY--In the year 1781 PETER THE GREAT having made
several ineffectual attempts on Noteburg, a Swedish fortress,
now called Schlusselburgh sent Prince GALITZEN, colonel of the
guards, at the head of a select corps, to take it by storm.
That officer having by means of rafts brought his soldiers close
to the fortifications, which advanced almost to the edge of the
water, they were received with such cool intredidity by the garrison, and exposed to such a dreadful carnage, that PETER, con-
ceiving the assault to be impracticable, sent immediate orders
for the Russians to retire. PRINCE GALITZEN, however, refused
to obey. [Tell my sovereign,] said he, [that I am no longer his
subject, having thrown myself under the protection of a power
superior to him.] Then turning to his troops, he animated them
by his voice and example, scaled the walls, and took the fortress.
PETER was so struck with this exploit, that, upon his next interview with GALITZEN, he said to him, [ask what you will, except MOSCOW and CATHARINE.] The prince, with a magnanamity which
reflects the highest honor upon his character, instantly requested the pardon of his ancient rival, prince REPNIN, who had been
degraded by PETER, from the rank of marshall to that of a common
soldier. He obtained his request, and with it the confidence
of his sovereign the prince REPNIN, and the applause of the public. Few circumstances can give more pleasure to a generous
mind than the contemplation of such exalted traits of a great
and noble spirit."
-----------------------------
[abstracted by HMS]"As a large number of our subscribers are
absent from home in the service of the country, we know not where
to direct their papers."
----------------------------
[abstracted by HMS] "The papers which we have made arrangements
to receive from the United States have not yet come to hand. We
are, therefore, unable to present our readers with any foreign
news this week, and hope they will content themselves with such
as the country affords."
----------------------------
"The organization of the army took place at head quarters, on
the Guadalupe, on the 11th inst. Colonel S. F. AUSTIN was appointed commander-in-chief, and the army took up the line of march
for Bejar on the 13th. Urgent calls are made for re-inforce-
ments, and supplies of cannon, ammunition, and provisions. The
volunteers now on the way, and preparing to go, will consider-
baly augment the numbers, and form a very formidable force." "It
is not known when the attack upon Bejar will be made, but those
who are now in the field are anxious to be doing something. It

is hoped that the volunteers from the east will join them before
any important movements are made, because although there may
already be enough in the field to reduce the garrison at Bejar,
it would be accomplished at less expense, and with less hazard
by a larger number."

------------------------------

"The three officers who had the command of the garrison at Goliad were brought to this town yesterday, as prisoners.  It is not
yet known what disposition will be made of them."

------------------------------

[abstracted by HMS] "At the first meeting of the Consultation of
Texas held in the town of San Felipe de Austin, October 16, 1835.
R. R. ROYAL was called to the chair, and major SAMUEL WHITING
appointed secretary."  "On motion by DR. EVERETT, seconded by
GENERAL HOUSTON, the question was put whether the certificates
of members should not be presented to the meeting.  and carried,
Yeas 14: nays 11."  " The following members were present:  Mun-
icipality of Bevill, JOHN BEVILL, WYATT HANKS, THOMAS HOLMES,
S. H. EVERETT, J. H. BLOUNT.  Municipality of St. Angustin,A.HUSTON,
JACOB GARRETT, WM. N. SIGLER, A.E.C.JOHNSON.  Municipality of
Nacogdoches, WM. WHITTAKER, SAMUEL HOUSTON, DANIEL PARKER, JAMES
ROBERTSON, N. ROBINS.  Municipality of Liberty, No members pre-
sent.  Municipality of Harrisburg, LORENZO de ZAVALA, CLEMENT C.
DYER, W. P. HARRIS.  Municipality of Columbia, HENRY SMITH, EDWIN
WALLER, J.S.D. BYRON.  Municipality of Matagorda, I.R.LEWIS,
R. R. ROYALL, CHAS. WILSON.  Municipality of Gonzales, No mem-
bers present.  Municipality of Austin, WYLY MARTIN, THOMAS BARNETT.
Municipality of Mina, No members present.  Municipality of Vicsca,
J.G.W.PIERSON, J.L.HOOD, S. T. ALLEN, A. G. PERRY, J. W. PARKER,
ALEXANDER THOMPSON.  Municipality of Washington, No members pre-
sent."  " On motion of DANIEL PARKER, seconded by GEN. S. HOUSTON,"
"On motion of CAPT. WYLY MARTIN, seconded by DR. EVERETT, the meet-
ing was adjourned till to-morrow morning, [Oct.17,] at 6 o'clock.
Signed--R. R. ROYALL, Chairman.  SAMUEL WHITING, Secretary."

------------------------------

[abstracted by HMS] "On motion of DANIEL PARKER seconded by
JOHN A. WHARTON, Esq, the following preamble, and resolutions
were unanimously adopted."signed R. R. ROYALL, Chairman,
SAMUEL WHITING, Secretary."

------------------------------

"The following delegates to the Convention, from the municipality
of Liberty, have arrived since the first meeting: HENRY MILLARD,
CLAIBORNE WEST, A. B. HARDIN, JAS. B. WOOD, HUGH B. JOHNSON,
P. J. MENARD."

------------------------------

"By an express which arrived here on Tuesday last, from Guadalupe Victoria, we learn that a small detachment of our army,
commanded by captain COLLINSWORTH, had taken possession of the
town of Goliad (Labahia).  They entered the town about 11 o'clock,
P.M., on the 9th inst. marched into the fort, by breaking down the
door of the church which communicated with it, and after a short
skirmish, in which one soldier was killed, and three wounded,
the garrison surrendered.  On the part of the colonists, one man
was slightly wounded in the shoulder.  The officers were lieutenant-colonel SANDOVAL, CAPT. SAVARIEGO, and ensign GARZA, who
were put in charge of colonel BENJ. R. MILAM, to be conducted to
head-quarters at Gonzales.  In the fort were found stores to the
amount of 10,000 dollars and about 300 stands of arms."

------------------------------

"On account of the absence of so many of the citizens, a patrol
was formed in this town on Sunday last, of which STEPHEN MILLER
was elected captain, We hope this arrangement will secure our
horses, poultry yards, etc. from the midnight depredations of
prowling intruders."

---------------------------

COMET--On Sunday, the 11th inst. about 7 o'clock, P.M. a comet,
of considerable magnitude, in a northwestwardly direction was
spoted. "This is probably the one predicted by DR. HALLEY to
make its appearance this year, and approach very near the earth."

---------------------------

[abstracted by HMS] 13 chiefs of the Cherokees, Shawnees, and
other northern tribes, are on their way to this place as visitors
to the Convention."

---------------------------

"We are informed that the schr. Lady Madison is now in the Brazos,
having on board seven pieces of artillery, a supply of muskets,
and a considerable quantity of ammunition, destined to the use
of the colonists."  "The San Felipe has been seen off the bar,
and is expected in, with more arms for the supply of the army"

---------------------------

"FEMALE FORTITUDE--A woman by the name of McLELLAN, and her children, who had been taken by the Indians from their residence in
the upper colony, fortunately made their escape in the night,
while the Indians were sleeping, and were making the best of
their way home, when they were met by a company of men who were
going in pursuit of them.  They were very much fatigued and stated
that they had been cruelly treated by the Indians."

---------------------------

"EXPOSITION--Of the Congress of the State of Coahuila and Texas,
presented to the August Chambers of the Union, petitioning that
no reforms be made in the federal Constitution, only in the manner therin prescribed."  This is a very long article,HMS.
Signed by : JOSE' MARIA MIER, President, JOSE' MARIA CARVAJAL,
Deputy Secretary, ANDRES DE LA VIESCA Y MONTES, Sup. Dep. Secretary.  dated 22d April, 1835, the state of Coahuila and Texas,
in Monclova."

---------------------------

"LETTER FROM COL. AUSTIN., Headquarters, West Bank of Guadalupe,
October 11, 1832--Gentleman, On this day the volunteer troops
of Texas will take up the line of march for Bejar."

"I have to inform you that Goliad was taken by Capt. COLLINS-
WORTH on the 8th inst. with a force of fifty men."  "Capts.
SMITH AND ALLEY marched from here previous to my arrival, with
about 110 men, for Victoria, which, it was reported had been
attacked, and they have no doubt, formed a junction with Capt.
COLLINSWORTH." All of the above letter was extracted by Helen.

---------------------------

"ADDRESS-Of the Committee of Safety and Correspondence of the
Jurisdiction of Matagorda, in behalf of their constituents, to
the people of Texas" [Too long of an article to print all,HMS]
"We have no longer any hope but from ourselves.  Our trust is
in our arms, in the cause of enlightened liberty, and the wis-
dom of a patriotic Convention."  Signed: S. RHOADS FISHER, Chairman, Committee: CHARLES WILSON, L.H.W.JOHNSON, S. B. BRIGHAM,
JAMES HARRIS, FAIRFAX CATLETT, WM. P. CORBIN, ISAAC VANDORN,

IRA R. LEWIS, R. R. ROYALL, WM. L. CAZENEAU. Secretary, I.E. ROB-
ERTSON."

------------------------------

"DEPARTMENT ORDERS, Headquarters, Texas--Department of Nacogdoches
October 8, 1835--" [Too long of an article, HMS.] signed by
SAMUEL HOUSTON, General-in-chief of Department.

------------------------------

"OFFICIAL ACCOUNT--OF THE FALL OF THE STATE OF THE ZACATECAS--
Nine o'clock, A.M.  The arms of the government of the Union have
obtained a distinguished triumph over the troops under command
of DON FRANCISCO GARCIA, which exceeded 5000 men with a large
train of artillery."  "All, therefore, is in my power--their
cannons, their arms, their ammunitions, and about 800 prisoners--
the field of battle presenting a most horrid picture.  On our
part I estimate the number of killed and wounded at about one
hundred men."  "You will be pleased to give a full account to
his excellency the President pro. tem. for his satisfaction,
and receive the assurances of my estimation; and I communicate
it to you for your knowledge and satisfaction."  "God & Liberty.--
General Quarters of Zacatecas, May 11th, 1825."
ANTONIO LOPEZ DE SANTA ANA.  "Since writing the above, it is
ascertained that 2700 of the enemy are taken prisoners. LOPEZ DE
SANTA ANA."

------------------------------

[Article too long]--"RESOLUTIONS-Passed by the Committee of
Vigilance and Safety of the Municipality of San Augustin on the
6th inst. and concurred in by the Committee of the municipality
of Nacogdoches, on the 8th inst.--Committee-Room, San Augustine,
October 6, 1835.  Signed by PHILIP A. SUBLETT, Chairman.
A. G. KELLOGG, Secretary."

------------------------------

"COMMITTEE-ROOM, San Felipe De Austin, October 11,1835--At a
meeting of the Committee of Safety, Mr. JOSEPH BRYAN, from the
Jurisdiction of Liberty, laid before this body sundry resolutions
from the Committee of Safety, of that place, and presented the
certificate of his election to the Permanant Council."  "Resolved
that Col.WM. PETTUS be appointed a member, and that hereafter,
all business be transacted in the name of the Permanant Council
of Texas."  G. BORDEN, Jr., Chairman pro. Tem. of the Com. of
Safety."

------------------------------

"COUNCIL-HALL, San Felipe, De Austin, October,11,1835--At a m
meeting of the Permanent Council, Col.WM. PETTUS being called to
the chair, and GAIL BORDEN,Jr. appointed secretary"  "Resolved
that this body proceed to the appointment of its officers.
Whereupon R. R. ROYAL was unanimously elected president, and
C. B. STEWART appointed secretary of the Permanent Council."
"Resolved, That Mr. JOSEPH BRYAN wait upon Mr. STEWART, with
a certificate of his appointment, and request his acceptance of
the same.  WM. PETTUS, Chairman.  G. BORDEN,Jr.,Secretary."

------------------------------

"LETTER FROM GONZALES, Giving an account of the action which took
place there on the 1st of October" [Article too long,HMS] Sir,--
Agreeably to request before I left San Felipe, I proceed to give
you all the information I have been able to gather."  " I unfor-
tunately arrived after the battle on the opposite side of the
river with the Mexicans had taken place.

"Our numbers had increased to 168 men, and in an election for
field officers, the lot fell on JOHN H. MOORE, as Colonel, and
J.W.E. WALLACE as lieutenant-colonel." "The fence was then lev-
elled opposite our cannon. A parley was then sounded by the
Mexican commander, and a Mr. SMITHERS, who had been taken prisoner by the Mexicans on his way from Bejar to Gonzales arrived
and informed Col. MOORE that the Mexican commander desired a
conference, which was agreed to, but in the meantime we posted
to get possession of WILLIAMS' plantation, houses, etc. which
we occupied." "The commanders of both armies then advanced to
the centre, our accompanied by lieutenant-Col. WALLACE, and the
Mexican by one of his officers. The Mexican Commander, CASTONADO,
then demanded the cause of our troops attacking him, and the reply
by Col. WALLACE, was that he had been ordered to demand our
cannon, and had threatened, in case of a refusal, to take it
by force" DAVID B. MACOMB.
------------------ End of October 17,1835--------------------
TELEGRAPH AND TEXAS REGISTER-Vol.1, No.3-Saturday,October 26,1835
----------------------------
[abstracted by HMS due to length] "NAPOLEON'S PROJECTED INVASION
OF ENGLAND--It is still a question undecided, whether NAPOLEON
inteded seriously to invade England, or whether his great preparations in the channel were a feint, merely to give employment to his troops, and cover other designs. BOURRIENNE maintains
that he never in reality intended to attempt the descent; but
that, unknown to every one, he was organizing his expedition
into the heart of Germany, at a time when all around him imagined
that he was studying only the banks of the Thames." "Napoleon
asserts that he was quite serious in his intention of invading
England; that he was fully aware of the risks with which the attempt would have been attended, but was willing to have braved
them for so great an object; and that the defeat of the combined
squadron by SIR ROBERT CALDER frust ated the best combined plan
he had ever laid during his whole career. His plan, as detailed
in the instructions given to VILLENEUVE, printed in the appendix
to his memoirs, was to have sent the combined fleet to the West
Indies, in order to draw after it NELSON'S squadron; and to have
immediately brought it back, raised the blockade of FERROL and
CORUNNA, and proceeded with the combined fleet to join the squadrons of ROCHELLE and BREST, where 20 sail of the line were ready
for sea, and brought the combined squadron into the channel to
cover the embarkation of the army." "in the absence of Lord NELSON"
"It is a singular proof of the sagacity of Lord COLLINGWOOD,
that, at the time when this well combined plan was in progress
on Napoleon's side, he divined the enemy's intentions, and, in
a memorial addressed to the admiralty, and published in his
memoirs, pointed out the danger arising from the precise plan
which his great antagonist was adopting." "In pursuance of this
plan, his fleets were to assemble were from TOULON, ROCHEFORT,
CADIZ, BREST & FERROL, draw after them to the West Indies the
British blockading squadrons, and return rapidly on their steps,
and present themselves in the channel, before the English were
well aware that they had crossed the line." "MARSHALL NEY had
nothing to do but to follow out literally his instructions."
----------------------------
"COMMUNICATION--Messrs Editors" A letter written to editors from
Resident Citizens: BILLY BUCK, FANNY DOE. Late Emigrants: TOM
GANDER, DOLLY GOOSE.

---

"Mr. THOMAS H. BORDEN is authorized to receive subscriptions, appoint agents, and transact any other business connected with the TELEGRAPH."

---

[abstracted by HMS] "A considerable number of volunteers from Louisiana have already gone to join the Texas army, more are expected soon,--in short, we feel confident that our friends and brethren of the United States will lend us a helping hand, in contending for the principles for which our common ancestors have fought and bled."

---

[abstracted by HMS] "At the latest dates, the Texas army continued to occupy a position on the Salado creek, about 5 miles from Bejar. Volunteers are continually flocking to the ranks, from all quarters, and it is not known what number are now in the field."

---

"NEW TOWN--We are informed that a town has lately been laid out on the tide water of the river Neches, at a place known by the name of TEVIS'S BLUFF, 30 miles from the Sabine bay. Its situation is said to be one of the most delightful in Texas, and it has already commenced improving at a rapid rate. It is spoken of as a place which promises to be of considerable importance. It has received the name of BEAUMONT, which, from the description of the place, strikes our fancy as very appropriate."

---

"To secure the inhabitants residing on the frontiers, from the invasions of the hostile Indians, the General Council has made arrangements for raising 3 companies of rangers; one, consisting of 25 men, to be organized by D. B. FRIER, to scour the country between the Colorado and Brazos; one consisting of the same number, to be organized by S. M. PARKER, to range between the Brazos and Trinity: these two are to establish their head quarters at the Waco village. The other is to consist of 10 men, organized by GARRISON GREEN, and to establish their head quarters at the town of Houston, for the purpose of scouring the country east of the Trinity." [abstracted by HMS]

---

"RESOLUTIONS-Passed at a meeting of the citizens of Natchitoches-At a meeting of the citizens of Natchitoches, convened on the 7th of October 1835, at the Red River Exchange, DR. JOHN SIBLEY was called to the chair, and J. B. CARR was appointed secretary." "JOHN R. DUNN, Esq. having, in an appropriate address, declared the object of this meeting to be to express our sympathy with the inhabitants of Texas, who are about to suffer from a lawless and tyrannical attempt to trample their liberties under foot, and to deprive them of the rights and immunities to which, as men, and as freemen, they are entitled, On motion of DR. C. G. LEWIS, RESOLVED, That a Committee of 5 be appointed to prepare resolutions expressive of the sense of this meeting, on the alarming situation of affairs in the neighbouring province of Texas. Whereupon Messrs. JOHN R. DUNN, C. G. LEWIS, P. W. WIL-KINS, D. S. KAUFMAN, and J. B. CARR, were appointed on the said committee; and having retired, in a few moments reported the following preamble and resolutions, which were unanimously adopted." Signed JOHN SIBLEY, President. J. B. CARR, Secretary.

---

"CIRCULAR--From the General Council of Texas, to the inhabitants
of Texas residing east of the Guadalupe--Fellow-Citizens--The
hour has come when your country requires the services of every
man in it." " Information, received through an unquestionable
channel early yesterday, leaves not the least doubt of the movement of a very considerable force on this place from the south,
and we are informed this morning by an arrival from Bejar, of
the intention of the commander of that post, to send a large
detachment thence against this place. Four hundred men were
expected to arrive in Bejar, when our informant left there, in
2 or 3 days."         P. DIMMET, Commandant.
Fort Goliad, October 21, 1835--8 o'clock, P.M.
"Fellow-Citizens,--The above speaks its own importance, and is
dictated by the most imperious circumstances. The truth, and that
only, is here told you. It is now left for you to decide, and
for you to act.    Yours, respectfully, IRA INGRAHAM.
October 21, 1835--8 o'clock, P.M.
The foregoing requires no comments; therefore, Resolved, That 200
copies be printed and circulated. R. R. ROYALL, President,
JOSEPH BRYAN, DANIEL PARKER, A. HOUSTON, LORENZO DE ZAVALA,
WM. PETTUS."
------------------------------

"TO THE PUBLIC--We have just received by the hands of DR. HOXEY,
a letter dated 19th, from head quarters, stating that a vigorous defence may be expected from the enemy, an extract of which
we send out for your information. S. F. AUSTIN, Commander-in-chief.
------------------------------

The following article is too dim to read..HMS
"PROCEEDINGS"     "whereupon A.G.PERRY and DANIEL PARKER were a
appointed to superintend the ?meeting? of the ----?. R. R. ROYALL,
President, Fiesca-A. G. PERRY, J. T. HOOD, J.G.W. PIERSON.
ALEX. THOMPSON, S. T. ALLEN, L. W. PARKER, Natcogdoches-W. M.
WHITAKER, DANIEL PARKER. Liberty-JOSEPH BRYAN, HUGH B. JOHNSON,
PETER J. MENARD, A. B. HARDIN. J. B. WOODS. Austin-W. M. PETTUS.
Harrisburg-?ISC? BATTERSON. San Augustin-JACOB GARRETT, A. HOUSTON.
Secretary-J.G.W. PIERSON.
------------------------------

[abstracted by HMS] "And be it also resolved that R. R. ROYALL,
President of council, GAIL BORDEN,Jr. and JOHN H. MONEY, be
appointed to superintend the collection of all dues of a similar
nature, with the same powers and duties for the other juridic-
tions not above mentioned."
------------------------------

"DIED-In this town, on Saturday last, Mr. JOHN JAMES. On Sunday
morning last, Mr. PEDRO SALINAS."
--------------------End of October 26,1835-----------------------

TELEGRAPH AND TEXAS REGISTER-Vol. 1, No.4-Saturday-October 31,1835
------------------------------

"MOHOMETAN AND CHRISTIAN SLAVERY--Sir J. MALCOLM, in his interesting
Sketches of Persia, says, [Slaves, in the Mahometan countries,
are only liable, for any crimes they may commit, to half the
punishment to which the freemen would be subject.]" [abstracted by HMS]
------------------------------

"From late Lodgon papers--EXTRAORDINARY TRIAL IN PARIS-We yesterday
gave some account of a case which has excited considerable sen-
sation in Paris, relative to an individual names BANCAL, a surgeon

in the navy, who was accused of having murdered a woman with whom
he was intimately connected. It appeared from the act of accusation, that, in his capacity of medical man, he had endeavored to
procure both his own death and that of the female, but that the
latter only had fallen the sacrifice. Our readers will learn the
result of this trial with some surprize. The prisoner is a
young man, 27 years of age, of rather attractive appearance. His
demeanour was perfectly calm and resigned." "The act of accusation having been read, the prisoner was closely interrogated,
from whence it appeared that he had for some time been acquainted
with the lady, Mad.(am) PRIOLLAND, of whose murder he was now
accused; that he had kept up an intimate correspondance with her
previous to his leaving France for Senegal; that during his absence he had formed one of thos connections common in the latter
country, but that, on his return in 1834, he had renewed his
intimacy with Mad. PRIOLLAND. It appeared further, the idea of
mutual destruction originated with the lady, and that he had himself been only consenting to the act. After entering into length-
ened details relative to the mode in which their deaths were to be
effected (by administering poison and bleeding,) and which, though
employing the same means, was successful only with the female."
"The president demanded whether he persisted in stating that Mad.
PRIOLLAND was desirous of his putting an end to her life, and
received an affirmative reply." " The following witnesses were
then examined." "The first was a M. CASMECASSE, a friend of the
prisoner, who seemed to have been the witness of the last act of
the two intended victims. Mad. PRIOLLAND wrote to him in these
words: [This evening, after you are gone, we shall enter Charon's
bark. The money we leave will meet the expenses, and procure
us a wooden cross, with our names[[Zelie and Prosper]] inscribed
on it; nothing more.] He it was who received a bulletin written
by the prisoner, describing the dying moments of Mad. PRIOLLAND,
and who first ran to their assistance, and opened the door of the
chamber of death. The witness stated that he had dined with them,
on the evening of the fatal attempt. Mad. PRIOLLAND was very
gay; she sang a romance which had some reference to the wooden
cross for which she wrote. When questioned which of the two
appeared to have the ascendancy over the other, he replied, Mad.
PRIOLLAND." "Four medical men successively verified the exactness
and sincerity of the declarations of the prisoner, relative to
the various circumstances connected with the long and frightful
homicide of which Mad. PRIOLLAND became the victim. All were
of opinion that she made no resistance, and felt at a loss to
explain how the prisoner could have survived the two attempts made
by him to commit suicide." "The attorney general (MR. PLOUGOULN)
then addressed the court. He said that Providence had withheld
the suicidal hand of the prisoner, that he might be brought to
the scaffold, to offer an example to miserable--partizans of the
new doctrines. Without, however, dwelling on the acts of those
who sustained this fatal theory, he energetically declared that
no consent on the part of the victim could extenuate the crime.
This consent must have been given in a moment of frenzy, which
should have had no weight of authority with one who preserved
his reason. Moreover, suicide was an excuse which was not admissible; in such a case, the act of suicide is merely an en-
deavor to escape from human laws. He cited different judgments
of the court of cassation, in which it was laid down that homicide

was never admissible, save as a means of legitimate self defence,
and that suicide itself cannot be urged as a plea, unless the
object attempted be completed.  Mr. PLOUGOULN concluded by calling
upon the jury to condemn the prisoner in the name of morality
and civil law.  [Our justice,] he added, [may extend to indulgence; but it will be no longer justice, if it extends to impunity.]
"The prisoner's defence was conducted by Mr. HARDY, who said that
he saw only madness and fever in the acts now brought forward for
judgment, and threw the blame of these acts on the state of public
morals and liturature, which the government did nothing, he
averred, to repress.  Nothing, he urged, could be effected by
courts of justice, in attempting to reestablish the moral code.
Without, however, developing his ideas further, or admitting the
power of religion to produce that restriction of morality, Mr.
HARDY sustained that co-operation in suicide was not murder.
He admitted the extent of the evil, but declared that there was
no law which could punish it, and affirmed that BANCAL could not
be condemned."  "Mr. PLOUGOULN, after some interval, again renewed
his accusation and argument, which was eloquently answered by
Mr. HARDY, and the jury retired to deliberate.  At a late hour,
they returned into court, and the foreman, in the midst of the
most profound silence, stated the finding of the jury: [Upon my
honor and conscience, before God and before men, the verdict of
the jury, upon all questions of the case before it, is no; the
prisoner is not guilty.]  "The prisoner heard the verdict with
perfect calmness, and appeared only affected when his friends
approached to congratulate him on his escape.  Thus ended this
remarkable trial."
------------------------------
"MESSRS. BAKER AND BORDENS.--Gentlemen,--The following prudent,
but patriotic views, as regards the situation of Texas and her
relations to the republic, were given, as stated, on the 2nd of
September last.  The known character of DON ANTONIO PADILLA,
for talents, knowledge, and sound judgment, will give much might
to his opinions, in these eventful times of our adopted country.
By request of the General Council of Texas at this plan, I give
it for poblication in your paper of this week.  I am preparing
a condensed statement of all matters connected with the mission
to the supreme government, entrusted to EDWARD GRITTON, Esq.,
and myself, in last July, which must necessarily be delayed until
the return of my colleague, when it will be given you, to be
communicated, through your paper, to the people of Tezas, who
are privileged to require of all public agents a full account
of their conduct in matters intrusted to them.  D. C. BARRETT.
San Felipe, October 30, 1835."
------------------------------
"[TRANSLATION.]"-Messrs. BARRETT and GRITTEN, commisioners of the
people of Texas, having consulted me, in a private conference,
respecting the conduct to be observed by the people of Texas,
under present circumstances, my opinion was the following."  "That
by virtue of the guarantees offered to the Texians by the supreme general government, in the official comminunication of the
3d of August last, issued by the secretary of war, MARIANO, and
circulated by the commandant general of these states, on the 18th
of the same month, the Texians ought to remain tranquil up to
the present.  But as troops, both infantry and cavalry, are
collecting at Bejar by order of the same government, not for the
special purxose of exterminating the savages, or for any other

known purpose, it is prudent to advise the Texians to be prepared
to resist any invasion that military tyranny may undertake to
destroy liberty, as was done on the 12th of May last, at Zacatecas,
and was likewise done on the 4th of June, by emprisoning the person
of the constitutional governor of the state, DON AUGUSTIA VIESCA,
and suite, because, in fulfilment of an act of the legislature,
they had left the capital for Texas." "That in consequence of
the present acephalous situation of the state of Coahuila and
Texas, through the deposition of DON MIGUEL FALCON, who acted
as provisional governor, in pursuance of an act of the permanent
deputation, which deposition was effected in conformity with
an order from the commandant general, [the people of Texas are
now placed in the situation of calling, if without infringing
any law, for a legitimate government, to whom to apply in their
wants;] or to procure one for themselves, in a way best suited
to their necessities, character, and circumstances; in order that
they may not become involved in the confusion and disorder produced by an disorganized situation, nor become subjected to military laws, enforced by the bayonets. It is also my opinion that
one of the commissioners proceed to the colonies, to report on
what the mission has done in favor of the cause of Texas, and that
the other remaiu in this city, to watch over the operations of
the military force now here. Such are the sentiments of a free
republican, a friend to liberty and to Texas, and for whose pro-
sperity he is ready to sacrifice his frail existence.
Signed--J. ANTONIO PADILLA. To the Commissioners of the people
of Texas. Bejar, September 2nd, 1835."
----------------------------

"Almost every day brings with it cheering intelligence from some
quarter. The last arrival confirms the previous accounts of the
great excitement which our cause has produced in the United States.
Sixty-five volunteers, well armed and equipped, have arrived from
New Orleans on board the schr. Columbus. Seventy or eighty have
started to come by land, and many more are about to start."
"It is also said that the creoles of New Orleans have raised a
company of 150 men who are now ready to embark for Texas, to join
the army of the people. Subscriptions are opened in New Orleans,
to raise funds, to be applied to the use of Texas, to aid in carrying on the war."
----------------------------

"an action took place near Bejar, on Wednesday morning last,
between a detachment of COS'S army, 400 in number, and 90 of
the colonial troops, under the command of Capt. FANNING; in which
the former were repulsed, with the loss of about 50 men, one
piece of artillery, and a considerable number of muskets. On
our part, the only damage sustained was one man wounded. Particulars will be given hereafter."
----------------------------

"We notice in the New-Orleans Bee of September 9th, the concluding
part of an article on Texas, addressed to the citizens of Georgia,
and signed [BENJ. H. RUTHERFORD.] We have not seen the former
part of this article, but judging from what we have seen, we
pronounce the production a tissue of misrepresentations, and
its author."
----------------------------

HMS Note: An article "From the New-Orleans True American" mainly
comments about the struggle of Texas and the fighting. Another

article "From the New-Orleans Commercial Bulletin" again comments
about the struggle of Texas. This was also included in the article:
"AUSTIN, the father of the colony, and under whose prudent and
persevering efforts, Texas has reached its present growth and
strength, will, in all probability, under the new organization of
things, rendered indispensible by the hostile attitude of the country, be clothed with the chief authority. In better hands it
cannot be lodged and the same zeal, ardor, and sincere attachment which he has for 25 years devoted to the best interests
of his colony, will be even the more strongly displayed now that
his countrymen and colonists struggle for the preservation of
their dearest rights."
HMS Note: The next article has "From the same", I presume this
means from the same newspaper. "From the Same--At a numerous and
highly respectable meeting, held at Bank's arcade, last evening,
for the purpose of taking into consideration the present affairs
of Texas, WM. CHRISTY, Esq. was appointed chairman, and JAMES
RAMAGE, secretary." " The meeting was addressed by Messrs.
SCHMIDT and FISHER." HMS Note: then resolutions were adopted by
the committee. "5th Resolved, That JAMES H. CALDWELL, WM. BRYAN,
WM. BOGART, JAMES P. NEVIN, WM. L. HODGE, and THOMAS BANKS, be
appointed members of the said committee." HMS note-the following
I believe will back up my theory of this article being from the
New-Orleans Commercial Bulletin--"7th Resolved, That the officers
fo this meeting open a list forthwith for volunteers to enter
for the aid of the Texians, in defence of their rights." "In
conformity with the above resolutions, lists for money and men
were opened. On the first more than a $1000 was immediately
subscribed; and on the other we are informed, a large number of
volunteers have signed."
-------------------------------
This ended articles from New Orleans newspapers, HMS note.
-------------------------------
"EXTRACT--From the returns of the election in the juridiction of
Mina, for delegates to the general Consultation of Texas.--Members:
J. S. LESTER, D. C. BARRETT, EDWARD BURLESON, R. M. COLEMAN,
B. MANLOVE. Elected under the first resolutions, as adopted in
Columbia, in August last. BARTLETT SIMS, R. M. WILLIAMSON.
Elected under a subsequent arrangement for sending seven members
from each municipality." " I certify the above to be a true
extract from the returns made to the committee of safety for th
above jurisdiction. D. C. BARRETT, Chairman."
Mina, October 11th, 1835.
-------------------------------
"LETTER FROM NACOGDOCHES-To the Committee of Vigilance and Safety
 of San Felipe--Nacogdoches, October 20, 1835--GENTLEMEN,--We have
received your communication of the 13th inst., intimating to us
the highly gratifying intelligence of the capture of La Bahia.
The enthusiasm of the people on being made acquainted with the
fact was so great, that a general illumination immediately took
place, and every possible demonstration of joy exhibited. We will
despatch, to-morrow, to Washington, a wagon containing 1,500 lbs.
of lead, and 250 lbs. of Dupont's FFF powder. You will please
make arrangements for payment of the freight of the above, which
will probably amount to from 80 to 100 dollars. This committee
has made arrangements to forward a person to the United States,
for the purchase of 200 rifles which, we have every reason to
think, will reach us without loss of time. Yesterday, about 70 or

80 men, under the command of captain SUBLET, left to join the army of Texas, and being all well mounted, must reach head quarters without delay. We shall expect to receive as frequent intelligence as possible of the proceedings of the army, and any thing else that may be interesting.    Your most obedient servant,
                                        F. THORN, Chairman.
----------------------------

[abstracted by HMS] "GENERAL POST OFFICE, San Felipe--"The Texas mail will be established on the following routes, viz: From San Felipe de Austin, by Whitesides' in Cole's Settlement, Washington and Nacogdoches, to San Augustin, weekly.  From San Felipe, by Orozimbo, Columbia, Brazoria, and Quintana, to Velasco, weekly. From San Augustin, by Zavala, to Bevil's mill, weekly.  From San Felipe, by Harrisburg and Liberty, to Belew's ferry, on the Sabine river, weekly.  Proposals will be received until the 15th day of December.      JOHN R. JOHNS, Post Master General
Oct 31 tf"
----------------------------

"NOTICE-All persons are hereby cautioned not to accept or trade for a note drawn by me in favor of JOHN B. JOHNSON, for $50,(date not recollected, but about the 1st of October, 1835,) as I am determined not to pay the same, not having received value.
JOSEPH DAVIS.      Oct.31"

----------------------------
"NOTICE-Is hereby given to all persons owing the state on lands or otherwise, that the subscriber has been appointed collector for the department of Brazos, by the General Council of Texas, and is ready to receive, and receipt for all monies paid into his hands.      G. BORDEN, JR., San Felipe de Austin
Oct. 24"
----------------------------
Advertisements:
"WATCH AND CLOCK MAKER-WILLIAM SIMPSON
Oct. 10"
----------------------------
"BAKER & BORDENS--a Printing office in the town of San Felipe de Austin.
San Felipe de Austin, October 10, 1835"
----------------------------
"GROCERIES, CLOTHES, HARDWARE, etc.--JAMES COCHRANE
Oct. 10"
-------------------- End of October 31,1835----------------------

[HMS Note:  There are more newspapers from San Felipe de Austin in]
[          period of 1836 which I did not get to read.              ]

TEXAS REPUBLICAN--Brazoria, Texas  July 5, 1834

Brazoria---Saturday---July 5, 1834--Vol.I. No.1.
"Terms--The Republican is printed and published by GRAY & HARRIS"
-------------------------------

[abstracted by HMS]An article of polical nature written by
R. M. WILLIAMSON.

-------------------------------

"Mr. JOHN A. WHARTON, one of our delegates, despatched to Monclova, the seat of governement, to procure the recognition of
Jurisdiction of Brazoria, has returned, having proceeded, as
we understand, no farther than San Antonio.  In consequence
of his abscence from town we are unable to lay before our
readers the result of the mission."
-------------------------------

"His excellency the Governor of the State has been pleased to
direct to me the decree which follows:"[abstracted by HMS]"Sup-
reme Government of the Free--State of Coahuila and Texas."
RAFAEL De La FUENTE, President; IGNACIO CADENA FALCON, Member
and sec'y.; JOSE JESUS CRANDE, Member and Sec'y."
"Therefore I order it to be printed, published and circulated,
and that due compliadce be given to it.--Given in the city of
Monclova, on the 26th of March 1834."  FRANCISON VIDAURRI Y VIL-
LASEUNOR.
JOSE MIGUEL FALCON, Sec'y of State.
"And I communicate it to you or your intelligence, publication
and corresponding end."  RAMON MUSQUIZ.
-------------------------------

"DISASTERUS TORNADO--One of the most terrific hurricanes ever
experienced in this country occurred on Monday last in Peters-
burg Virginia, and its neighborhood.  The destruction of human
life was most shocking, and property to an immense amount was
destroyed in every direction."
-------------------------------

"From the Nantucket Inquirer."  MOST ATROCIOUS--[abstracted by HMS]
"The New York legislature has not only obeyed the dictations of
VAN BUREN through Mr. SPOIL MARCY, and pawned the property of
the state for six millions of money wherewith to enforce the
designs of the party."
-------------------------------

"From the Mobile Advertiser"  "STEAM BAOT ACCIDENT"--"The steam
boat Star of the West, on her way up the Bay, on the 19th inst.
burst one of her boilers, three of the hands badly scalded,
ROBERT HENNINGTON of Washington City, District of Columbia;
JOHN BROWN and JOHN M'HUGH, foreigners--all since dead.  The
Engineer, DUBOIS, was much scalded but we hope in no danger.
The boat had stopped to repair one of her buckets when the ac-
cident happened--there were no passengers on board."
-------------------------------

LAUNCH. "On Saturday list at Albany was launched the three masted
shooner Annesley.  This vessel, (says the Daily Advertiser of
that city) is owned by R. V. DeWITT, and is built upon the An-
nesly system, which, it it succeeds, must revolutionize the art
of ship building, make a sea voyage a matter of certainity, and

40.

be the means of saving hundreds of lives, and an immense amount
of property.  The shooner is fitting for sea under the command
of Captain GAGER."

------------------------------------

"After our paper had gone to press a friend of ours put us in
possession of the following information relative to Col. AUS-
TIN's imprisonment; which was received in a letter dated, Mexico, May 4, 1834 [HMS-could be 14, 1834]  That he is still confined in one of the prisons of the Inquisition, and until a
week previous he was emersed in the dungeon.  SANTA ANNA has
enlarged the limits of his confinement; and the writer thinks
in a week more he will be set at liberty.  We sincerely hope
this may be the case, though we are inclined to doubt.  The treatment of this gentleman as received at Mexico, taking into consideration all the circumstances, in our humble opinion, merits
the consideration of the whole people of Texas"

------------------------------------

Advertisement :[abstracted by HMS]
  "ENTERTAINMENT.--R. STEVENSON has rented the house lately occupied by Mrs. BREEDLOVE, and is opening a house of entertainment for boarders and transient visitors"
  R. STEVENSON    Brazoria  16 June 1834

------------------------------------

Advertisement: [abstracted by HMS]
  "THOMAS R. IRWI." [HMS believes that last name should have an N]
                    [Believe last name should be IRWIN        ]
  "Will parctice medicine, surgery and obsterrics."

------------------------------------

"NOTICE:  The undersigned gives this public notice that he had
been appointed Agent for the different Insurance Companies in
the city of New Orleans; and whereas in order the insurers
may be the more fully satisfied of the fairness of all losses
that may hereafter happen here or on the adjacent coast, cert-
ifies of the Agent will be required before any loss will be
paid."      EDMUND ANDREWS.

------------------------------------

Advertisement: [abstracted by HMS]
  Merchandise for sale.    EDMUND ANDREWS

------------------------------------

Advertisement:  [abstracted by HMS]
  a business.    MIMS & SHARP

------------------------------------

BRAZORIA HOTEL--MERIWETHER W. SMITH purchased the Brazoria Hotel.
  Mr. SMITH intends spending two months in the up county and will
  leave the superintendence of his business to Mr. ALEXANDER RUS-
  SELL during his absence."

------------------------------------

Advertisement:  [abstracted by HMS]
  J. WARE, Jr. or Sr. [cannot make out,HMS].  Just received per
  schooner San Felip, a large assortment of drugs & medicines.

------------------------------------

EARLY TEXAS NEWS

From: "San Felippe, de Austin, April 28th 1834--
"GLEANINGS FROM ENGLISH PAPERS BY THE VICTORIA"
"DEATH OF MRS. BURNS--It is with regret that we announce that
intelligence arrived here last night by the Defiance coach, of
the demise of the venerable relict of our national bar?[could be
a d, HMS]; the melanchelly event took place at her own house in
Dumfries, 11 o'clock on Wednesday night, and the information was
communicated in a letter to her sister in Mauchline, where we believe the eldest son of the poet is at present residing--Kilmar-
nock Journal."
"The celebrated German jurist, FUREBACH, died lately at Frank-
ford, it is supposed from poison.  He was a kind patron of the
unfortunate CASPER HAUSER, and the most zealous in his endea-
vors to discover the murderers of that mysterious youth."
--------------------------------

"A western paper announces the marriage of Mr. CALEB LAMB to Miss
EUNICE LYON.  This is a literal fulfilment of the scripture
prophecy, (The lion shall lie down with the lamb)."
--------------------------------

"Married in Matilda, Upper Canada, ISRAEL SATAN to GRACE PARLOR.
[HMS note:  the following was included with the above.  It is
not known by me if this was true marriage or just another article in the paper, as sometimes articles were of a jest nature.]
"Mankind are free, peace shall abound,  Since GRACE by SATIN has
been found,  And in full proof that peace is meant,
ISRAEL by GRACE has pitched his tent,  No more in deserts wild
he'll roam,  He's got a PARLOR for his home."
--------------------------------

Vol. I. No. 13 --Saturday--October 25, 1834--

"Messrs. Editors:--It appears that a report is in circulation on
the west side of the Brazos in this municipality that Mr. ABNER
HARRIS has declined holding a poll for the office of Sheriff.
Please contradict such report, it is undounded;  that gentleman does intend holding a poll, has never had any idea of de-
clining, and will be supported by a great number on the EAST
SIDE OF THE BRASOS."
--------------------------------

"FOR ALCALDE,--ASA BRIGHAM for Sheriff"
"J.S.D. BYROM; JOSEPH CALVIT; W. B. SWENY; AUGUSTUS WILLIAMS;
JOHN FOSTER; FRANKLIN LEWIS; CHARLES W. STEWART. Jurisdiction
of Austin. ROBERT WILSON."
"For Sheriff of the Department of Brazos--Col. GOWIN HARRIS is
a candidate for the above office at the ensuing election, in
Dec. next., and will be supported by many voters. A Citizen."
"W. E. HOWTH is a candidate for the above office."
"G. M. COLLINSWORTH is a candidate for the above office."
1st Rigador.  GREEN B. JAMERSON.
--------------------------------

Advertisement:  [abstracted by HMS] "I will expose to public sale,
on Sat. the 29th of Nov. next, in the town of Columbia, a certain tract of land containing 163 acres; the property of the
succession of JAMES WESTALL; formerly owned by J. H. BELL, and
by him sold to F. F. WELLS, being near the town of Columbia."
"Also three town lots in the town of Marion, with their improvements, and a two acre lot, not designated.  For further parti-

culars apply to J. H. BELL, Esq."    J. G. McNEEL, Adm'r.

---------------------------------

"By virtue of an order from EDWIN WALLER, Esq. constitutional
    Alcalde for the jurisdiction of Columbia, I will sell on Sunday
    the 9th of November, next, the entire stock of goods belonging
    to the succession of the late JOHN GRAHAM, deceased, consist-
    ing of the following articles, viz:  Cotton Cabric hdfks, capes,
    cotton check, pins, Valencias, printed muslins, black, red, and
    purple silks, mosquito muslins, one bale fancy prints, also a
    quantity of wearing apparel, etc."
ANSON JONES, curator.      Brazoria  Oct. 24, 1834.

---------------------------------

"For New-Orleans, The fine fast sailing schooner Dart, HOLDEN,
    master, will depart for the above port on Wed. next.  For
    freight or passage apply to the captain on board or to E. AND-
    REWS."    Brazoria  Oct. 24th 1834

---------------------------------

"Notice--By virtue of a decree of DAVID G. BURNET, primary judge
    of the municipality of Austin, I will offer for sale in the
    town of Harrisburg, on Tuesday the 18th November next, all the
    effects belonging to the succession of DANIEL VICUVE, dec'd.,
    consisting of a general assortment of dry-goods, groceries,
    hardware, and cutlery; well adapted to this market."
GEO. M. PATRICK, curator-Harrisburg, Oct 13 [no year given]

---------------------------------

"$50 reward" [abstracted by HMS] "Ranaway from the subscriber,
    some time in March last, a negro man named SPENCER, about 5 ft.
    10 inches or 6 ft. high, very black, red eyes, thick lips,
    and said negro is about 22 yrs. of age."   W. B. SWENY

---------------------------------

"CURATORS NOTICE--All persons having claims against the succes-
    sion of THOMAS A. HOWELL, deceased are requested to present
    them, and all person indebted to said succession are requested
    to make immediate payment to BYRD B. WALLER. "
WILLIAM HOWELL, Curator of T. A. HOWELL, deceased.  Oct.

---------------------------------

"NOTICE--All persons having claims against the succes'n of LUKE
    LESASSIER, are hereby noticed to present them to the under-
    signed by the 4th Monday in October next property authenticated,
    after that date suit will be brought against every person in-
    debted to said succession." JAMES B. MILLER, Testamentary executor.

---------------------------------

"PUBLIC NOTICE" [abstracted by HMS] "Proposals for the excava-
    tion of a Canal to be opened from the head of Matagorda bay to
    Caney Bayou, at the dwelling house of CALEB R. BOSTWICK, Bay
    prairie"
R. R. ROYALL; Th. J. TONE; IRA INGRAM, Canal Committee.
IRA INGRAM, Secretary of the board of commissioners,  Matagorda."

---------------------------------

"NOTICE--The undersigned wishes to close the late concern of
    BRIGHAM & RICHESON, all persons indebted to them, either by
    note or account, are requested to settle the same before the 20th
    of Nov. next, by so doing will prevent cost."
[See rest of article on page 44.,HMS]

A. BRIGHAM, surviving partner and Adm'r. Est. of E. RICHESON, dec'd.
Oct. 15th 1834  "P. S. BENJAMIN R. BRIGHAM is duly authorised
to receive and receipt in my abscence." "A.B."

---

"ADMINISTRATORS NOTICE--All persons having claims against the
Estate of HENRY S. BROWN, dec'd. are hereby requested to present them properly authenticated within the time prescribed by
law or they will be for ever barred--and those indebted, will
make payment to the undersigned ."
"S. M. HALE, adm'r."    "Caroline BROWN, Adm'r."
Columbia, Oct. 15th 1834.

---

"NOTICE--All persons indebted to the succession of WILLIAM ROBEN-
SON, dec'd., hereby requested to make immediate payment, all
persons having claims against said succession; will present
them by the 4th Monday in October next, properly authenticated
or___ey will be barred." JAS. B. MILLER, Adm'r.  July 1.

---

"PUBLIC NOTICE--A public sale of lots in the town of Orozimbo,
at the head of tide navigation on the Brazos River, Texas, will
take place on the 25th of October next.  Terms made known on
the day of sale.  Persons wishing to purchase previous to that
time, or the purpose of immediate improvement, can be accom-
modated."   JAMES E. PHELPS.

---

"NOTICE--By a decree of the honorable DAVID G. BURNET, primary
judge of the jurisdiction of Austin, made on the 31st of July
last, the letter of administration upon the estate of SAMUEL
SAWYER, deceased; granted to the undersigned, by HENRY SMITH,
acting Alcalde of Brazoria, on the 12th of October, 1833, have
been confirmed by the said judge;  and the undersigned has
been fully authorised to go on and settle said succession
agreeably to law."  "All persons having claims against said
estate are requested to present them within the time prescribed
by law, and those indebted to said succession will please make
immediate payment otherwise they may expect to be sued indis-
criminately. "  GEO. HUFF, Adm'r.
San Felipe, de Austin---August 8, 1834

---

"SILVER SMITH--J. R. WILLCOXON respectfully informs the public
that he has removed from this place to Columbia where he will
attend to all business in his ___e, with neatness and dispatch."

---

Advertisement: [abstracted by HMS] M. W. SMITH wants to employ
2 first rate carpenters for 3 or 4 months."

---

Advertisement: [abstracted by HMS]  "JOHN W. HALL offering himself as a candidate for the office of Sheriff of the Department of Brazos."
La Bahia Crossing,  Brazos River,  August 24th 1834.

---

"NOTICE--All persons indebted to the estate of JOHN W. MITCHELL,
deceased are hereby requested to make immediate payment to the
subscriber, and those having claims against said estate, are
[contd. on page 45]

notified to present them duly authenticated within the time
prescribed by law for liquidation."  JOHN W. HALL, Adm'r.
La Bahia Crossing   Brazos River   Aug. 1834.

------------------------------

"NOTICE--By order of the honorable DAVID G. BURNET judge of the
   jurisdiction of Austin, I will sell at public auction at the
   court house in the town of San Felipe on the 4th Monday in
   October next, all the lands belonging to WILLIAM COOPER, decd.
   consisting of choice selections of land made at an early time
   situated in Bay Prairie, on the San Bernardo, and Buffaloe
   Bayou, and elsewhere in Austin's Colony.  The terms, and a
   more particular description of the land will be given on the
   day of sale."   CHARLES D. SAYRE, Curator and agent for the
   absent heirs of WILLIAM COOPER, deceased.

------------------------------

"NOTICE--All persons having claims against the estate of JOHN
   AUSTIN, dec'd. will present them to the undersigned for settlement; and all those indebted to said estate, will make payment to him and no other."  T.F.L. PARROTT

------------------------------

"NOTICE--The undersigned will give to setlers with or without a
   family, 610 acres of Land out of each League for making a permanent settlement on 22 Leagues of Land in the Trinity and
   Netchez, the titles are two ?11? League grants from the federal
   Government of Mexico, and located in the names of ISAAC STONE &
   LORENZO deZAVALA."   "Plotts & titles may be seen by reference
   to the proper office at Liberty said grants are also covered
   with the Title of Script of one of the New York and Galveston
   Bay Land Company."  G. B. JAMESON, Agent for the Grantees.

------------------------------

[abstracted by HMS]-"Brazoria Hotel--MERIWETHER W. SMITH having
   returned from the up-country has formed a copartnership with
   E. BAYLEY."

------------------------------

"NOTICE--The partnership heretofore existing between JAMES WARE,Jr.
   and EDMUND ANDREWS, is this day dissolved by mutual consent."
   "EDMUND ANDREWS remains charges with the settlement of the con-
   cern."  JAS. WARE, Jr.   EDMUND ANDREWS
   [HMS Note:  Please notice on page 41-- Advertisement for EDMUND
   ANDREWS]

------------------------------

"DISSOLUTION-The Co-partnership heretofore existing between
   S. RHOADS FISHER and J.W.E. WALLACE, under the firm of FISHER
   and WALLACE, having by mutual agreement been dissolved on the
   30th day of May last"  "This is to notify the public that the
   settlement of the whole business will be adjusted by J.W.E.
   WALLACE."   S. RHODES FISHER    J.W.E.WALLACE.
   Matagorda

------------------------------

"NOTICE--Whereas Wm.P. HARRIS and ROBERT WILSON trading under the
   firm of HARRIS and WILSON and DAVID HARRIS and ROBERT WILSON as
   administrators of the estate of JOHN R. HARRIS, deceased, made
   a surrender of all their property and that os said estate for
   [contd. on page 46]

for the benefit of the creditors in one and the other case
under conditions expressed in the act of surrender.  The
undersigned appointed Syndics, for the purpose of carrying
into effect the stipulation contained in the surrender, in case
the parties failed to make payment to their creditors within the
time allowed them; and acting under the authority vested in
them by the said parties in said act of surrender;  as also
acting under the authority granted to them the said Syndics by
the decree of the honorable Judge of the first instance, citizen
ROBERT PEBLES, dated in the town of San Felipe de Austin, on
the 1st day of the present month, hereby give public notice
that they will preceed on the 1st day of January next, to sell
at public sale at the town of Harrisburg to the highest bidder
all the property real and personal belonging to the before
mentioned parties, and surrendered by them in comformity with
the schedule filed in the Alcalde's office in the town of Austin, on a credit of one and two years, the purchaser giving a
judicial bond with approved security, and the real estate remaining mortgaged until final payment.  The property will be
divided into parcels or lots wherein its nature or locality
will admit of proper division, so as to suit purchasers, and
lists of the property will be ready, on the day of sale.  Spec-
ulators and others who may be desirous of becoming possessed
of valuable lands and other real property, will find it their
interest to attend the sale as it will be remembered that there
is a very valuable steam Saw and Grist Mill to be sold, and
several valuable and well timbered tracts of Land, lying
contiguous on a navigable stream.  The sale will commence on
the day before mentioned at the hour of 10 o'clock A.M. and
continue until all the property shall be sold or enough thereof
to cover the debts due by the parties.  Titles will be made
by the Syndics and approved by the parties to the surender, at
the expense of the purchaser."
Town of Austin, Oct. 2nd 1834  W.C.WHITE, J.W.MOORE, S.M.WILLIAMS,
                                        Syndics.

------------------------------------

"A Classical and English School will be opened in the town of
  Columbia on the 15th of October next.  For character and quali-
  fications, those interested and refered to--B. T. ARCHER, Vel-
  asco; J. A. WHARTON, Brazoria; W. C. WHITE, Columbia; J. H. BELL,
  J. B. MILLER, San Felipe; W. B. TRAVIS; J. P. COLES, Coles
  Settlement."        F. T. WELLS      Columbia
------------------------------

"The subscriber informs the public that he has lately purchased
  from E. ANDREWS & R. STEVENSON, and is now opening in the house
  adjoining the Brazoria Hotel, the following articles:"
  J. A. H. CLEVELAND.
------------------------------

TEXAS REPUBLICAN--Vol. I, No.14  Sat. Nov 1, 1834

"THE ARCHBISHOP OF CANTERBURY--"  "John---, the son of a respectable butcher, in Westminister, London, was, at the age of ten
  years, employed to serve his father's customers with beef, etc.,
  at their houses.  Among the most noble and liberal of his pat-
  rons, was the lady Lord DARTMOUTH, who soon became so much pleased
  [contd. on page 47]

[contd. on page 47]

with punctuality and fidelity of the butcher's boy, that she
often condecended to treat him with such cakes and other
dainties as were considered suitable to his age and condition."
-------------------------------

[HMS Note:  There are more newspapers on this roll of film but I
  was unable to finish reading]
-------------------------------------------------------------------

TEXAS CHRONICLE---Vol. I.---Nacogdoches, Wednesday, Feb. 28, 1838
No. 39        Published weekly by ISAAC W. BURTON
-------------------------------

[abstracted by HMS]this newspaper very hard to read as print is
  disappearing.]  "JAMES TAYLOR--Attorney at Law, Will attend
  legalaly the District Courts of Nacodoches in San Augustin,
  M_____n and JASPER, Nacg. Aug. 2_, 1837. "
-------------------------------

[abstracted by HMS]Cannot read all]
  "NOTICE:  TO ALL WHOM IT MAY CONCERN:  Whereas I, _____CUNNINGHAM
  [rest, unable to read,HMS]  [At bottom of article:]  "And I do
  also inform all persons who made contracts _____my ____[looks like
  deeds] _____brother, A. P. CUNNINGHAM to clear out lands.  And I
  am his partner and legal representative, and will attend to
  the business strictly and punctually.
  DAVID A. CUNNINGHAM, San Augustine    Dec 29th 1837
-------------------------------

[HMS Note:  This is very dim and hard to read]
"NOTICE:  All persons _____b-ed _____ ____of HENRY A. JOHNSON
  [next four or five words not ledgible] to _____ ____ ---payment
  to ____ ____.  Messrs KAUFMAN & GOULD; or they will be ____
  _____ according to law.
  RICHARD SPARKS, Adm'r.  Nacodoches, Dec 23, 1837
-------------------------------

"NOTICE:  D. ROWLETT will open an Agnecy at the Seat of Justice
  for Fannin County, on the first Thursday of January, 1838, and
  will locate purchases and sell [HMS Note:  next four or five
  words not ledgible].    D. ROWLETT.
[HMS Note:  Suggest that the researcher interested in Fannin/Red
  River County, Texas early material see book by Gifford WHITE,
  "First Settlers of Red River County, Texas":  Sold by INGMIRE
  PUBLICATIONS.  Above mentioned on page 5 of this book]
-------------------------------

"LAW NOTICE--THOMAS J. RUSK & JAMES REILY.  Attornies and Coun-
  sellors at Law.  Nacogdoches, Texas.
  Will attend to all legal business put into their hands.  All
  Land business will meet with strict attention."
  Nacogdoches, Jan. 6, 1838.
-------------------------------

"HEAD QUARTERS, Nacodoches, Dec. 29, 1837.  General Order--No.3)"
  "It is ordered that DAVID S. KAUFMAN be, and he is hereby
  appointed Aid-de-Camp to the undersigned Major-General to the
  Militia of Texas, with the rank of Major, and that he be obeyed
  and respected accordingly."
  THOMAS J. RUSK        Nacogdoches, Dec. 30, 1837
-------------------------------

"DOCTOR A. HART (of New Orleans)"
  "Intends locating himself permanently in this place, and tenders
  his Professional services to the inhabitants of Nacogdoches and
  its vicinity.  He can be consulted at all hours, and on any
  subjects concerning his profession, by calling at the residence
  of Mr. A. EMANUEL."   Nacogdoches, August 26, 1837.
---------------------------------

"25 DOLLARS REWARD"  "Strayed or Stolen from the Subscriber a
  Large Brown Mare Mule, coming a years old, branded on the left
  shoulder with J. H. the letters are connected together, any information of the above mule will be thankful received and the
  above reward paid by Col. JAMES [either SMITH or SMALL,HMS note]
  if said mule is delivered to him two miles from Nacogdoches"
  JAMES HUTTON          Nacogdoches  Dec 2
---------------------------------

"BEWARE--I have observed that PETER E. BEAN, of the County of
  Nacogdoches, has issued a public notice, declaring that a contract which he made with me, has been forfeited by me, and is
  void.  He is aware that this is not the truth.  More than one
  month before the money became due, I notified said BEAN that
  the money would await his application when it became due, unless he chose to give ?fine? on the payment, and, in that
  event, I would give him ten per cent interest-payable every
  six months.  Subsequently to which time, he stated to a gentleman of the highest respectability and character, that he had
  accepted my proposition, and would not send to receive the
  money.
  He has slandered my title, the law will chastize him for it.
  The tenant who I left in possession of the premisce, I shall
  hold responsible for the rent, and delivery of the same."
  SAM HOUSTON          City of Houston,  Nov. 10, 1837
---------------------------------

" CAUTION--All persons are hereby forewarned not to cut any wood,
  nor in any other way to interfere with an improvement situated
  west of Rusk Brook, and south of the road leading to Mount
  Sterling, said place being my Labor, to which I am entitled."
  ADOLPHUS STERNE    Nacogdoches, Dec. 9, 18___
---------------------------------

"NOTICE--PUBLIC SALE OF TOWN LOTS."
  "There will be sold, to the highest bidder, without reserve,
  as many of the town lots in the Town of Crocket, Houston County,
  as will justify the sale, on Saturday, the last day of March
  next.  Terms-One half [remainder of article cut off by micro-
  filmer,HMS Note].
---------------------------------

"The Laws of the Republic of Texas--1837--An Act--To amend the
  several Laws regulating the Post Office department.  Endorsed/
  signed JOSEPH ROWE, Speaker of the house of representatives.
  S. H. EVERITT, President pro tem.  of the senate."
  Approved, Dec. 18, 1837      SAM HOUSTON
---------------------------------

"Continued Public Sale of Town Lots:"
  "Terms--one half cash, the balance in three and six months,
  with security.  By order of the Board of Commissioners."
  COLLIN ALDRICH President of the Board.
  Town of Crocket      Jan. 20, 1838
------------------------------------

VALASCO HERALD--Velasco Texas  April 21, 1837
  The original in the Museum, Alamo., San Antonio, Texas.
Friday--April 21, 1837

"GLORIOUS NEWS:"
  "On this day, the anniversary of the glorious Battle of San
  Jacinto, the United States' sloop of var Natchez, with the
  Mexican brig of war Gen. URREA in charge (as a pirate,) ac-
  chored off the Brasos Bar.  She re-captured the schr. Louisiana,
  and sent her back to New Orleans;  sunk a Mexican armed brig
  and schooner off Brasos St. Iago; landed Passed Midshipman
  RIDGELY, who communicated the above information; upon his return on board the Natchez, she got under way and sailed in
  search of the two brigs and schooner which appeared off this
  place on Monday last.
  We also learn from this source, that Tampico is in possession
  of the Insurgents.  A French fleet was off Tabsco and Tampico
  demanding indemnification for the Forced Loan and insults
  offered the French citizens at Matamoras, which, if not compiled with immediately, satisfaction would be taken at the
  cannon's mouth.  The French have sent to the West Indies for
  the remander of their fleet, with the intention of blockading
  all of the Mexican ports on the Gulf of Mexico, unless the
  above requisitions are instantly complied with.
  The schr. JAMES P. CALDWELL, Noycs, from New Orleans, has
  just came to anchor off the Brasos Bar.
  The celebration of the first anniversary of the victory of
  San Jacinto, was got up in a very interesting style by the
  officers and soldiers of this Post.  The manoeuvering of the
  soldiers was scarcely inferior to what might have been expected
  from the experienced soldiers of the United States' Army; and
  the officers ?cvinced? skill in tactics, and dignity in commanding, deserving the greatest credit and applause.
  A salute of 13 guns was fired from the Fort, and of 2 guns
  from on board the brig Sam. Houston, on the departure of the
  Natchez."
-------------------------------------------------------------------

THE NORTHERN STANDARD  Red River County, Texas  Clarksville, Texas
April 29, 1848    Vol 6 No. 1
------------------------------------

Advertisement:  "FOR ASSESSOR--JOHN M. BIVINS as a candidate for
  assessor and collector of Red River County."
------------------------------------

Advertisement:  "FOR SHERIFF--LEWIS D. BARRY as a candidate for
  sheriff of Red River County.  Col. HUGH F. YOUNG, as a candidate for Sheriff of Red River County.  ROBERT S. HAMILTON as
  a candidate for sheriff of Red River County."
------------------------------------

"CANIDIDATES FOR THE PRESIDENCY, POSITIONS DEFINED-formal an-
nunciations of Mr. CLAY and Gen. TAYLOR, by which they submit their claims to the action of a convention."
-----------------------------------

"A WEEDING INVITATION A CENTURY SINCE-The Philadelphia Ledger
says it has seen the original of the following curious paper.
It shows how they managed hymeneal preparations in the olden
time: "My sweetheart, if it may suit thy convenience and
freedom thou wilt favor us with thy company at our marriage,
which is intended to be at Burlington, the 4th of next month.
I am thy respectful friend. AARON ASHBRIDGE""
"October 19th, 1846" [HMS Note: The name AARON ASHBRIDGE was
in quoation marks and so was the date. The date was placed at
lower left of article like the newspapers placed the date of
receiving the article.]
-----------------------------------

Advertisement: "B. H. EPPERSON & G. LEWIS, Atty. at Law, Clarksville, Red River County."
-----------------------------------

"NOTICE--I have lost my certificate for six hundred and forty
acres of land, granted me by the Board of Land Commissioners
in and for the county of Red River, and the Republic of Texas,
said certificate is dated the 1st day of November, 1838, and
No. 365. If the same is not found in the time prescribed by
law, I shall apply at the proper office for a duplicate."
GEORGE FLETCHER    Clarksville    April 29th, 1848
-----------------------------------

"NOTICE--Taken up and lodged in jail in Clarksville Red River
County, on Sunday the 23d inst., a negro boy who calls his name
Reuben and says he belongs to Wm. AKINS living on Red River.
Said boy is about 25 years of age, 5 feet 2 inches high, had
on when apprehended on old seal skin cap, blu Jeans frock coat,
cotton shirt and pants. The owner of said boy is hereby notified to come forward, prove property, pay charges, and take
him away."          A. RIBBLE, Jailor
Clarksville     April 29th, 1848
-----------------------------------

"SUCCESSION OF JAMES W. GREEN-Whereas the undersigned was appointed
administrator of the estate of JAS. W. GREEN, deceased, late of
Red River County, by the Probate Court for said County, at the
March term Eighteen hundred and forty eight-this is therefore
to notify all persons indebted to said estate, to make immediate payment, and all those having claims upon it, to present
them to me, duly authenticated, within the time prescribed by
law, or they will be barred."     JAMES J. WARD, Adm'r.
Clarksville    April 22 1848
-----------------------------------

Advertisement: "FERRY AT FENTON, ON THE TRINITY--JOSEPH BARTLETT"
-----------------------------------

Advertisement: "TOWN OF CORSICANA, THE PERMANENT COUNTY SEAT OF
NAVARRO COUNTY. Advertisement for land in Navarro County for
sale to the public." THOS. I. SMITH; Wm. F. HENDERSON; E.MEL-
TON; J. M. RIGGS; JAMES JOHNSON--Commissioners. March 9, 1848
-----------------------------------

EARLY TEXAS NEWS

"ADMINISTRATOR'S NOTICE, Letters of Administration having been
  granted to undersigned by the Hon. Probate court of Henderson
  County of the estate of CHARLES R. SANDERS, Sen'r., deceased,
  notice is hereby given to all persons having claims against
  said estate to present them within 12 months from this date,
  and all persons indebted to said estate are required to make
  immediate payment."    CHAS. R. SANDERS, Jr.
  March 28, 1848        LUCY SANDERS
----------------------------------

"NOTICE TO OUR DEBTORS-Necessity compels us to call upon all indebted to us to make immediate payment.  All must be aware that
  they have received at our hands indulgences, unparalleled--
  and we now call upon you, confidently believing that you will
  respond with the CASH as our necessilties have become greater
  than yours."  H. LITTLE & CO.     Clarksville, Dec 4th 1847.
----------------------------------

"$75 REWARD-Ranaway from the subscriber, living near Daingerfield,
  in Titus County, Texas, in June  of last year, a negro man named
  BURTON, about five feet eight inches high, stout made rather
  yellow complesion, and a down look when spoken to.  He is intel-
  ligent and plausible in his conversation; has lost one or two
  of his front teeth, and is about twenty eight years of age.
  Said boy, may, very probably be in the Choctaw, or the Creek
  Nation.  Any person who will apprehend and confine said negro,
  and give me notice, so that I get him, shall receive $75 reward."
  JOHN G. CHAMBERS              April 20th 1848
----------------------------------

Advertisement:  "TO THE SPORTING WORLD--by J. C. HART, Secretary,
  "on horse races"   Clarksville      Feb 12, 1848 [abstracted]
----------------------------------

Advertisement:[abstracted by HMS]    BRACKNEY & COLLINS
  Paris,   July 3d. 1847
----------------------------------

"STATE OF TEXAS, COUNTY OF BOWIE--Prect. No.2--Shown as by H.A.RUN-
  NELS, one gray horse supposed to be over 12 years old, about
  15 and ½ hands high, no brands.  appraised at $20.
  A. L. HULME; S. H. BYRNE, Appraisors.  Sworn to before me, this
  day of March, 1848.  JOHN LOOP, J.P.  A true copy from the record J. C. McGONIGAL, Clerk C.C.B.C. by his Deputy S.M. McFARLAND"
----------------------------------

"SUCCESSION OF SAM'L. C. PRICE-the undersigned was duly appointed
  Executor with the will annexed of the estate SAM'L. C. PRICE,de-
  ceased, late of Lamar County, by the Hon. Probate court thereof,
  at that March term 1848.  This is therefore to notify all persons indebted to said estate, to make immediate payment, and all
  persons having claims against said estate to present them to
  the undersigned duly authonticated within the time prescribed
  by law for payment or they will be barred."  JAS. T. SANDERS
  Paris      April 16, 1848.
----------------------------------

  Advertisement: [abstracted by HMS]  C. LEWIS & CO.--Shreveport,
  La.  Groceries
----------------------------------

Advertisement: [Abstracted by HMS] ALDEN A. M. JACKSON-Merchant-
No. 28 ?Paudras? Street, New Orleans, La.

------------------------------------

Advertisement: [Abstracted by HMS] ALFRED & CO--Wholesale Grocers, Levee St. Shreveport La. References: C. C. ALEXANDER-
Clarksville; T. J. & W. F. CORNELIUS,Clarksville; A. M. & L. C.
ALEXANDER-Paris; RAGSDALE & WRIGHT-Paris; JOSEPH HARRISON-Bonham; PACE & Bros._Bonham; I. W. WELLS-Pine Bluff.

------------------------------------

Advertisement:[Abstracted by HMS] JENKINS & MASON-Wholesale Gro-
cers-No. 3 New Lewis & 6 _____,Pa. JOSIAH JENKINS, HENRY B.
MASON, formerly of Texas. [Under the addresses appears "New
Orleans."]

------------------------------------

Advertisement:[Abstracted by HMS]JAMES B. GILMER--Hides & Pelt-
ries. [ad also states that JAMES B. GILMER will also run the
Steamer "Belle of Illinois" to deliver].
Coshaita Bluffs     Dec 4th 1847

------------------------------------

"STATE OF TEXAS, COUNTY OF TITUS--This day shown to us by RUBEN
D. COLLINS, an estray mare which we find to be a bright sorrel.
[more description is given on horse,HMS note] Given under our
hands this the 11th day of March 1848     RUFUS MORTON; THOS.
N. WILSON
_?????_     to and subscribed before me this the 11th day of
March.A.D. 1848.  WILLIAM BURK,J.P.  J. COOK, Clerk.
Filed March the 15th 1848."

------------------------------------

Advertisement:[abstracted by HMS]  OLIVER & CHATFIELD--Bagging and
Rope        Clarksville, Feb 19th 1848

------------------------------------

"STATE OF TEXAS COUNTY OF LAMAR--This day we the undersigned
being called upon to view and appraise a certain horse to. "
By HENRY B. HEATHERLEY--this 2nd February 1848.
Given under our hands and seals the date aforesaid: R. H. DOSS;
Wm. WOOLDRIDGE.     Sworn and subscribed: 2nd February A.D. 1848
W. H. WYNNE, J.P.   A true copy Text.--JOHN R. CRADDOCK,Clerk L.C."

------------------------------------

STATE OF TEXAS COUNTY OF LAMAR--Taken up by HENDERSON BROWN-2 March
18?? [HMS Note: article at bottom of newspaper and is extremely
dim] H. R. LATIMER  Mat W. MARTIN appraisers
Brad C. or G. FOWLER, J.P.     John R. CRADDOCK, Clerk L.C.

------------------------------------

[From The Doblin Nation of March 4]
WATERFORD ELECTION "The nomination of a representative in Parlia-
ment for the city of Waterford, took place on last Saturday, in
the Courthouse.  There was a large military force under the command of Sir Charles O'DONNELL at hand in case any branch of the
peace was attempted." "At 12 o'clock, the high sheriff, Captain
William S. DOYLE, accompanied by Thomas HARRIS, Esq., his Assessor,
took his seat upon the bench; shortly after the several candidates
had made their appearance, having previously passed in procession
through the streets, with bands, banners, ke." "Mr. William

Newell BARRON appeared as counsellor Sir Henry Winston BARRON;
Mrs James K. O'DOWD, for Mr. P. COSTELLO; and Mr. DILLON on
behalf of Mr. MEAGHER." "The High Sheriff called on the friends
of Sir H. W. BARRON to address the electors (Cheers.)" "Major
SNOW then came forward, and said he had to propose Sir Henry
Winston BARRON, as a fit and proper person to reprensent the
city of Waterford." "It would be unnecessary for him (Major
SNOW) to occupy their time at any length in speaking of Sir
Henry's merits, for they were all well acquainted with him for
a period of more than 16 yrs., during which time he was their
representative." (Cheers and hisses) "He was not only their
faithful representative for that time, but he belonged to their
county, lived amongest them and was therefore entitled to a
preference before a stranger. (Cheers and an uproar)."
"Wm. AYLWARD, Esq., acconded the uomination " "The Mayor of
Waterford, Sylvester PHELAN, Esq., then came forward, and proposed Mr. COSTELLO as a fit and proper person to represent
their city. (Cheers and cries of "Go home, Paddy the Pensioner")
Honesty had placed him in the post of honor he occupied, and he
solemnly declared to the electors of Waterford that he would
not propose a candidate for their sufferages whom he did not
believe to be honest, and well calculated to carry out the principles he always upheld himself. (Cheers and cries of We Want
No Pensioners). The man who he (Mr. Phelan) had the honor of
proposing was a man that would stand up in the House of Commons."
"The Rev. Pat. CUDDIHY rose to second Mr. COSTELLO's nomination,
but his doing so was the means of creating the most dreadful
uproar and confusion." [HMS Note: Debate continues then the
following is stated:] "The Rev. Mr. CUDDIHY--(cuss word used)
the colleges; I would not give a (cuss word) for them, (Cheers
and cries of shame)" The Rev. gentleman then went on to say
he arraigned Mr. MEAGHER for indidelity, and being the cause
of O'CONNELL's death.--He said (The Nation) gang--the Robespier-
res, have come to light again (pointing to Mr. DOHENY). "DOHENY,
you were my schoolfellow, therefore I will not attack you;
I will only say, the richest soil sometimes produces the rankest
weeds.--(Cheers and uproar.)" "Who is next on my list? DAVIS
the coward, who ran away from the monster meetings; (cries of
shame) but he is dead, and I'll say no more about him." "A
voice--The devil die along with him,(cheers)." "The Rev. Mr.
CUDDIHY--There is another I must name; Richard O'GERMAN, the
hereditary enemy of O'CONNELL; yes, cut-throat felons, you are
all enemies of the man who struck the fetters off your felon
limbs."(Cheers and dreadful confusion.) "Let me forsake this
fool and filthy gang, and go back to their chief, he who is
spotted all over from head to foot with treachery and treason
(Cheers and groans)" [HMS Note: this article goes on for at
least half a page (column) or more.]

------------------------------------

"EMIGRATION--The steamboat Latona, on her last trip up, brought
201 emigrants to Shreveport, destined for this parish and Texas,
with 12 wagons and upwards of 20 horses. There were several
families left at the mouth, who preferred to wait than come in
a crowd. We (senior ed.) were on board, and took pains to as-
certain these facts, and we mention them to show the extensive
emigration to North Louisiana and Texas. We calculate that
more than three thousand emigrants have passed through Shreve-

port since the first of January. Many have come by land, but
a far greater portion by water. " CADDO GAZETTE
[HMS Note: This is more than likely a newspaper in Louisana,
 probably Caddo Parish, La.]
-----------------------------------
"The telegraph announces [says the New York Journal of Commerce,
 of Saturday,] the conviction of Dr. COOLRIDGE, tried at Augusta,
 Maine, for the murder of a young associate named Mathews.--
 COOLIDGE was a dashing fellow, of respectable connections; but
 lived beyond his means, beacme involved, borrowed money of
 MATHEWS, and to cancel the debt killed him--persuading him to
 drink brandy which had been secretly drugged with prussic acid.
 A report is current that COOLIDGE committed suicide after the
 verdict was rendered."
-----------------------------------
"CHLOROFORM AGAIN--The following paragraph appears in the New
 York Tribune; Miss MAGEL, sister-in-law of Mr. KOHLAATT, of
 Broadway, was put under the influence of this annesthetic agent
 by a dentist, for the purpose of extracting a tooth. She lay
 lifeless for several hours, and was carried home in a state of
 insensibility. She has been since its application, Friday last
 laboring under prostration and paralysis of the tongue, throat,
 the muscles of the throat, and loss of voice."
-----------------------------------
Advertisement: "Star Hotel, Clarksville--This large and commodi-
 ous establishment, recently occupied by the late Col. James H.
 JOHNSTON is now open." Henry GOODING. Feb. 25th 1847.
-----------------------------------
Advertisement: "Lamar Hotel in the Town of Paris"
 Geo. W. WRIGHT Paris, Dec. 12, 1846
-----------------------------------
Advertisement: "Town of Taos. Head of Navigation on the Trinity"
 R. H. PORTER, At the Bluff Dec. 10th 1847
-----------------------------------
Advertisement: "PINE BLUFFS, a town with the above name, has
 been laid off upon the west bank of the Trinity river, a high
 and beautiful bluff, immediately above the south line of
 Mercer's Colony, and below all rafts and obstruction to the
 navigation of the Trinity."
W. Nicks ANDERSON for Charles FENTON, MERCER & Associates.
-----------------------------------
Advertisement: "TAN YARD & SADDLER's SHOP"--Bluff Spring in
 Lamar County. N. R. HARLAND & CO. June 1847
-----------------------------------
"SUCCESSION OF AARON STARNS-Letters of Administration having been
 granted to me, at the March term 1848, of the Probate Court
 of Titus County, upon the estate of Aaron STARNS deceased, late
 of said county, notice is hereby given to all persons indebted
 to said estate, to make immediate payment, and to all persons
 having claims upon the estate, to present them to me, duly
 authenticated, within the time prescribed by law, or they will
 be forever barred." Thomas R. STARNS, Administrator
April 20th 1848
-----------------------------------
Advertisement: "LUMBER-the undersigned proprietors of the Steam-
 Circular Saw Mill near the Town of Clarksville"
 H.D.WOODSWORTH,Esq. of Paris will act as our agent for Lamar Co.
MONTGOMERY,LITTLE & CO. Circular-Saw Mill Jan.1,1847

EARLY TEXAS NEWS

Advertisement: "LANDS & TOWN PROPERTY FOR SALE-Valuable farm
  containing about 1275 acres heretofore occupied by Jas. W.
  SIMS. Red River County."
  Clarksville      April 28th 1847      Wm.M.HARRISON
--------------------------------
"THE STATE OF TEXAS-To the Sheriff of Lamar County, Greetings:
  Whereas Henry G. McDONALD a citizen of Lamar County has
  filed (his bill in equity) in the office of the clerk of the
  District Court of said county of Lamar, setting forth that on
  the 16th day of December A.D. 1839, the defendent Christopher
  BROOKS entered his file in the office of John T. HAROMN county
  surveyor upon a certain tract of land situated in said county
  and had the same surveyed by James HOURLAND Deputy surveyor
  by tirture conditional certificate No.--, issued to said defendent by the Board of Land Commissioners for Red River county and
  on the _____day of ____A.D. 18__ the complainent filed in the
  office of said Harmon county surveyor as aforesaid upon the
  land above prescribed supposing the same to be at that time
  vacant but was afterwards informed by said Harmon surveyor as
  aforesaid of the previous file made as aforesaid by the defendent BROOKS and that the defendent shortly after making the
  said file and survey as aforesaid left the limits of the then
  Republic name The State of Texas that he has not since returned
  nor has he ever taken out his unconditional certificate in
  accordance with law. Wherefore your oritor prays that the
  survey made for said defendent as aforesaid be declared null
  and void and the land so survey be declared subject to the file
  made subsequently by your oritor and that the county surveyor
  be by decree of your honor required to receive the file made
  by your oritor and cancel the one personally made by defendent
  BROOKS,--and whereas plaintiff attorney having made oath to
  the truth of the allegation of non-residence of said defendant
  BROOKS. We therefore command you that you summon said Christo-
  phen BROOKS by publication according to law in some newspaper
  published in Red River county, that he be and appear before
  the Judge of our said District court, to be holden for the
  county of Lamar, at the Court house, in the town of Paris, on
  the ninth Monday after the first Monday, in March, A.D. 1848,
  and defender said suit." "Witness Jacob LONG, Clerk of the
  District Court, for the county of Lamar, with the Seal of said
  court, at office in Paris, on the fifteenth day of January,
  Eighteen Hundred and Forty-eight, and of the Independence of
  the United States the United States the Seventy second."
  J. LONG, C.D.C., L.C.
  "To Christopher BROOKS: I, Reddin RUSSELL Sheriff of Lamar
  County, hereby summon you to appear and defend agreebly to the
  foregoing notice, this the 15th day of March, A.D. 1848
  Reddin RUSSEL, Sheriff, L.C. By his deputy, F. MILES."
--------------------------------
"The STATE OF TEXAS, County of Red RIVER-In Probate Court, March
  term A.D. 1848--The Estate of Isaac JONES, deceased. Charles
  JONES Administrator. Whereas at the above term of our said
  court, Charles JONES administrator of the estate of said decedent, filed his petition praying for a final settlement of said
  estate, at the next May term thereof--and the said petioner
  having represented that a portion of the heirs of said estate,
  to wit: Lodiada JONES, H. W. JONES, Jun., James WINTER and

55.

Continued The Estate of Isaac JONES....
Minerva WINTER, Charles JONES, Jun'r., Isaac JONES, Jun'r.,
William JONES and Wesley JONES are non residents of the State
of Texas and not represented in this State--wherefore it was
ordered by the court that publication by advertisement be
given of said petition in the "Northern Standard" a newspaper
published in the town of Clarksville, and county of Red River;
now therefore the heirs aforesaid and the creditors of said
estate are hereby cited to appear at the next May term of our
Probate for said county, at a court to be holden at the court
house in the town of Clarksville on the twenty-ninty day of
May next A.D. 1848, then and there to show cause, if any you
can why the final account of said administrator should not
be allowed, and a decree made therefor accordingly, and further
to do and suffer such things as shall be considered and ordered
by the court aforesaid in the premises.
By order of J.M.MONTGOMERY, Probate Judge of Red River County.
Witness George F. LAWTON, Clerk, with the impress of the Seal
of our said Court, at office in Clarksville, this 7th day of
April, A.D. 1848, and of the Independence of the United States
of America the 72nd year.          George F. LAWTON, Clerk.
------------------------------
Advertisement: "Attorneys and Counsellors at Law--Geo.W.PASCHAL
and J.A.PASCHAL"  George W. PASCHAL will reside premently at
Galveston, and J.A. PASCHAL at San Antonio.  One of them will
regularly attend the Supreme Court, at Austin, and the U. States
District Court at Galveston.
Galveston, Feb. 17th 1848
------------------------------
Advertisement: JOHNSON & GRAY, Attorneys and Counsellors at Law.
Will practise in the courts of 8th Judical District. Ala. in
Cass & Upshur in the 5th District and in the Supreme Court.
W. H. JOHNSON      and B. W. GRAY    Dec. 25th 1847
------------------------------
Advertisement: MARTIN, EPPERSON & LEWIS, Attorneys & Counsellors
at Law, Clarksville, Texas.  Will Practise in all the Courts of
the Eighth Judical District, and in Cass County.
B. H. MARTIN, E. H. EPPERSON, G. LEWIS      Jan. 4, 1848
------------------------------
Advertisement: S. H. PIRKEY, Attorney and Counsellor at Law,
Will practice in the several counties of the 8th Judicial
District, and in Cass of the 5th.  Address Houston,Bowie County.
Dec. 7th 1847
------------------------------
Advertisement: T. J. RUSK & A. S. THRUSTON  Having formed a law
partnership, will attend the courts of Harrison and of the
Sixty Judicial District.   Thos. J. RUSK, Nacogdoches--A.S.
THRUSTON, Marshal        May 16, 1846
------------------------------
Advertisement: LAW ASSOCIATION--Will regularly attend the courts
in Bowie, Titus, Hopkins, Grayson, Fannin, Lamar and Red River
in the 8th Judicial district and the county of Cass in the
3rd district.    Wm. S. TODD, Boston--Burrell P. SMITH,Clarksville
------------------------------
Advertisement: James M. MORPHIS, Attorney & Counsellor at Law.
Will practice in all counties of the 8th Judicial district.
Address, Lamar County.
------------------------------

EARLY TEXAS NEWS

Advertisement:  S. K. McGOWEN, Attorney at Law, Bonham & Fan-
    nin County.
    '46 [HMS Note:  believe this means 1846]
------------------------------------
Advertisement:  P. J. PILLANS, Attorney & Counsellor at Law and
    Notary Public  Will attend the courts of the 8th district.
    Offices Bonham, Fannin County.
    March 13th 184_  [HMS Note: this could be 1845]
------------------------------------
Advertisement:  Dr. R. R. ROGERS,  having located permanently
    in Clarksville, Texas    Office East side of the public square.
    March 4th 1848
------------------------------------
Advertisement:  Drs. MARTIN & GILLIAM, Paris, Texas.
    [HMS Note:  a piece of tape covers the majority of this ad]
---------------------------------------------------------------

NORTHERN STANDARD, CLARKSVILLE, TEXAS RED RIVER COUNTY,
    Saturday, May 6, 1848  Vol. 6 No.2
------------

"FOR ASSESSOR--John M. BIVINS as a candidate for Assessor &
    Collector for Red River County."
"FOR SHERIFF--Lewis D. BARRY, as a candidate for Sheriff of Red
    River.  Col. Hugh F. YOUNG as a candidate for Sheriff of Red
    River Co., John H. DUKE, as a candidate for sheriff of Red River
    Co.  Col. Robert S. HAMILTON as a candidate for sheriff of Red
    River County."
------------------------------------
"SODA LAKE HOTEL-Passing through Jefferson, in Cass Co., two or
    three weeks since, we stopped for two days at this house, former-
    ly kept by Mr. PERRY, and now by Messrs. NESMITH & BROWNELL."
------------------------------------
"KENTUCKY CANDIDATES FOR GOVERNOR--A. Mr. Lazarus POWELL, has
    been nominated by the Democratic Central Committee, as the regu-
    lar candidate for Governor, Lynn BOYD having declined the
    acceptance of the nomination tendered him by the late Democratic
    Convention.  In the meantime however, Col. R. M. JOHNSON has
    declared himself an independent Candidate for the office.  The
    Hon. John J. CRITTENDEN is the Whig Candidate, and whoever
    beats him, will certainly prove himself extensively popular."
------------------------------------
"IRISH POTATOES--We are endebted to our neighbor Mrs. Wm. P.
    DICKSON, for a fine mess of Ireish potatoes, the first we have
    seen of the growth of this year."
------------------------------------
"MR. ADAMS'S REMAINS IN NEW YORK--The funeral ceremonies of the
    venerated ADAMS, at New York, on Tuesday, the 7th, are thus
    alluded to in a letter from that city to the Philadelphia
    Ledger:  The scene has changed.  The Clay pageant of yester-
    day is passed and is followed by a demonstration of public
    Mourning, anything approaching a description of which would fill
    several sheets such as this."  "All that was unspiritual of
    the lamented ADAMS, arrived here about two o'clock, and is now
    progressing thro' Broadway, attended by a cortege never sur-
    passed in the city, including all the civil, judicial military,
    fire and other public departments of the city, amidst the
    booming of minutes guns from several locations."
------------------------------

"INDIAN FIGHT ABOVE AUSTIN, San Antonio, March 30,1848"  "I received instruction from Lieut. Col. BELL, commanding the frontier, dated the 5th March, directing me to take charge in person of a strong detachment from my company, for observation of any Indian movements in the country adjacent to the German settlement on the Llano; and also to extend my scot to, and some distance up the San Saba Valley.  The movement to the latter point was made with special reference to a party of Ten-A-Wish Comanches, who had threatened to destroy the advance settlements, and who, there were many reasons to believe, were lying in wait for a favorable moment to strike.  In compliance with my orders I fitted out a scout consisting of Liets. WILLIAMS and CONWAY--43 privates, John CONNER, my interpreter, and accompanied by Mr. MELLER and Dr. McGINNIS." Signed:  S. HIGHSMITH, Comm'd'g Enchanted Rock Station. [from Austin Democrat, a newspaper]

-----------------------------------

Advertisement:  "Dress Goods and articles--C. C. ALEXANDER" Clarksville,      May 5th 1848

-----------------------------------

Advertisement:  "A. K. ELLETT, M.D., Clarksville.  Attended several years, Alma House & Hospital practice in Philadelphia and the Alma House and Penitentary practise in Richmond Virginia, together with an experience of 16 yrs. of practice in the South."    Office: on the East side of the Public Square.  Residence: the late dwelling of R. H. GRAHAM."

-----------------------------------

Advertisement:  Drs. GORDON & WALKER, Clarksville and vicinity. Feb. 1, 1846

-----------------------------------

Advertisement:  "Tan Yard and Saddler's Shop--The undersigned having bought the well known Bluff Spring in Lamar County, 12 miles east of Paris, and one and a half mile north of Mr. GRESHAMS, in the north end of Blossom Prairie, have now got their shop up, and the building for, and sinking of the yard in in rapid progress."    N. R. HARLAND & Co. June 1847

-----------------------------------

Advertisement:  "DALLAM's Digest--5 copies of this valuable work still on hand.  Apple immediately to OLIVER & CRATFIELD." Clarksville      May 5th 1848

-----------------------------------

Advertisement:  "Furniture--BRACKNEY & COLLINS"(Cabinet Shop in Paris)   Paris    July 3rd 1847

-----------------------------------

Advertisement:  "Town of Corsicana, The Permanent County Seat of Navarro County"  Selling land. Thoas. I. SMITH; Wm. F. HENDERSON; E. MELTON; J. M. RIGGS; James JOHNSON--Commissioners        March 9, 1848

-----------------------------------

"STATE OF TEXAS, COUNTY OF LAMAR--This day we the undersigned being called upon to view and appraise a certain horse to us shown as a stray, by Henry B. HEATHERLEY, do find the same to be as follows to wit, a black poney 14½ hands high with a blaze in the face, seven years old last spring, some saddle marks on the back, no other brands perceivable, appraise the same at thirty dollars, this 2nd Feb. 1848.  Given under our

Continued.."State of Texas, County of Lamar---

hands and seals the date aforesaid.    B. H. DOSS; W. H. WYNNE,J.P
A true copy Test.  JOHN R. CRADDOCK, Clerk L.C."
--------------------------------

"THE STATE OF TEXAS COUNTY OF LAMAR--Taken up by Pedanrum BROWN
and posted before the undersigned Justice of the Peace in and
for Precinct No. 10 State and County aforesaid on this the
22nd day of March A.D. 1848 one flea bitten gray gelding
about 8 yrs. old, about 14 hands high.  Collar marks upon his
shoulders; badly crease fallen, with no other marks or brands
perceivable appraised to fifteen dollars.   H. R. LATIMER
Mat. W. MARTIN, Appraisers.  Sworn and subscribed to before me
this the 22nd day of March A.D. 1848.  Brad C. FOWLER,J.P.
A true copy Test.    John R. CRADDOCK, Clerk, L.C."
--------------------------------

"STATE OF TEXAS COUNTY OF BOWIE, Precinct No. 2--Shown us by
H. A. RUNNELS, one gray horse supposed to be over twelve years
old, about fifteen and a half hands high, no brands perceptible,
appraised at twenty dollars.  Also one sorrell Mare Male, sup-
possed to be over 15 yrs. old, branded with R. H. on the left
shoulder, with one shoe on the right hind foot; appraised at
$15, this March 18th 1848.  A. L. HULME  S. H. BYRNE, Appraisers
Sworn to before me, this day of March 1848--John LOOP, J.P.
A true copy from the record.  J. C. McGONIGAL, Clerk, C.C.B.C.
By his Deputy S. H. McFARLAND."
--------------------------------

"ADMINISTRATOR'S NOTICE--Letters of Administration having been
granted to the undersigned by the Hon. Probate Court of Henderson
county on the estate of Charles R. SANDERS, Sen'r. deceased,
notice is hereby given to all persons having claims against
said estate to present them within 12 months from this date.
and all persons indebted to said estate are required to make
immediate payment. "  Chas. R. SANDERS, Jun.   Lucy SANDERS
March 28th 1848
--------------------------------

"SUCCESSION OF JAMES W. GREEN--Whereas the undersigned was
appointed Administrator of the estate of Jas. W. GREEN, deceased,
late of Red River County, by the Probate Court for said county,
at the March term, 1848--this is therefore to notify all
persons indebted to said estate, to make immediate payment,
and all those having claims upon it, to present them to me,
duly authenticated within the time prescribed by law, or they
will be barred."   James J. WARD, Administrator
Clarksville, April 22, 1848
--------------------------------

"STATE OF TEXAS COUNTY OF RED RIVER  THE STATE OF TEXAS, TO THE
SHERIFF OF SAID COUNTY--GREETING:  You are hereby commanded to
summon William K. REVERE, personally to be and appear before the
Hon. the District court of said county, on the 1st day of the
next term therein to be holden at the court house in the town
of Clarksville, on the fourth Monday in May next to answer the
petition of Willis DEAN, now filed, of which the following is
a brief statement viz, (said petioner sets forth that on the 21th
day of May, 1845, William K. REVERE by the name and description
of W. K. REVERE, then a citizen of Lamar County,) since removed
to, and now a citizen of Colorado county, and State aforesaid,

Contd. "State of Texas County of Red River"...

executed, and delivered unto Willis DEAN his certain promisery
note in the words and figures following, to wit--(On ___close
the first day of January next, I promise to pay Willis DEAN
or bearer the sum of $300, with 10% interest per annum from
date until paid, value received of sum this the twenty-fourth
day of May 1845.)  (signed W. K. REVER)
which note is annexed to said petition and made a part thereof--
and alledges, that on the same day--24th May, 1845--said REVERE,
to secure the payment of said sum in said not specified, executed
and delivered to said DEAN his certain mortgage on a negro
woman named DIAK, aged twenty-two years old-- said mortgage
conditioned to be void if said REVERE should pay said sum to
said note specified according to the tenor and effect thereof
wherewise to remain in full force, and the property therein
mortgaged to become absolutely the property of said DEAN--
which mortgage in annexed to said petition as a part thereof--
said petition ____ that said note has not been paid in accord___
with the debtor and effect thereof, and that the same is still
due and payable--also ___that said mortgage has been recorded
as the law requires--and praying that said mortgage be fore-
closed and for judgment in favor of said DEAN against said
REVERE for debt, interest and costs of suit and general relief
etc.--which said petition was filed on the 25th day of May 1847.
And whereas the said platintiff has this day made oath that
said defendant is now beyond the limits of the State of Texas,
and that he is now a transient person."
"Witness Wade H. VINING, Clerk of our said District Court, with
the seal thereof hereon impressed, at office in Clarksville,
this 23d day of March, A.D. 1848; and of the independence of
the U.S. the 72d year.  Test: W.H.VINING, Clk.D.C.R.R.C. By
John W. CHENOWETH, Dep'y. Cl'k.  I hereby certify that the
above is a true copy of the original writ in my hands--Given
under my hand this 23d day of March, A.D. 1848: Edward WEST,
Sheriff R. R. Cty.
------------------------------

"AGENTS FOR THE STANDARD--Gen. E. H. TARRANT, Navarro County;
Dr. R. GRAHAM, Buffalo, Henderson County;  M. M. KNIGHT, P.M.-
Greenville, Hunt County;  S. K. McGOWES, Esq., Bonham, Fannie
County;  John R. CRADDOCK, Esq., Paris, Lamar County;  Jacob
LONG, Esq., Lamar County;  Eldridge HOPKINS P.M., Tarrant,
Hopkins County;  B. W. GRAY, Esq., Mount Pleasant, Titus County;
Thos. R. WATSON, Esq., Cass County;  R. P. CRUMP, Esq., Jef-
ferson County
------------------------------

NORTHERN STANDARD--Vol. 6, No. 3, Saturday May 13, 1848, Clarksville
Red River County.
------------------

"ACTS AND RESOLUTIONS PASSED AT THE FIRST SESSION OF THE THIRTIETH
CONGRESS" [HMS Note: then the acts are listed]
Signed By:  Robert ___. WINTHROP, Speaker of the House of
Representatives.  G. M. DALLAS, President of the Senate.
Approved February 15, 1848--James K. POLK.
------------------------------

"EXTRAORDINARY TRIAL AT PARIS--A suit between M. de PONTALBA and
his wife, lately pending in one of the Frency Courts, is thus
sketched in the (Montirur). M. de PONTALBA is one of the
greatest proprietors of France. His son had been a page of
Napoleon's and afterwards a distinguished officer, aid de camp
to Marshal NEY, and a protege of the Duke of ELOCHIUGEN. He
married the daughter of Madame d'ALMONASTER, and for some
time they lived happily: but on the death of her mother,
Madame de PONTALBA began to indulge in such extravagances
that even the enormous fortune of the Pontalbas__ was unequal
to it. This led to some remembrances on the part of the husband:
on the morning after which she disappeared from the hotel, and
neither he nor her children had any clue to her retreat. At
last, after an interval of some months, arrives a letter from
New Orleans, in which she announces that she means to apply for
a divorce; but for eighteen months nothing more was heard of
her except by her drafts for money. At last she returned,
but only to afflict her family. Her son was at the military
academy of St. Cyr____she induced him to elope, and the boy was
plunged in every species of dubanchery and expense. This af-
flicted in the deepest manner his grandfather, who revoked a
bequest which he had made him of about £4000 a year, and seemed
to apprehend for him nothing but future ruin and disgrace. The
old man, eighty-two years of age, resided in his chateau at
Mont Leveque, whither in October, 1834, Madame de PONTALBA went
to attemp a reconciliation with the wealthy senior. Then and
there occured the most estraordinary and unaccountable scene
that though we have read one hundred French novels, we have ever
met with. On the 19th of October, the day after Madame de
PONTALBA's arrival, she found she could make no impression on
the father-in-law and was about to return to Paris, when old
M. de PALTALBA, at the age of eight-two, observing a moment
when she was alone in her apartment, entered it with a brace of
double barrelled pistols, locks the door, and approaching his
astonished daughter-in-law, desires her "to recommend herself
to God for that she has but a few minutes to live" ; but he
does not even allow her one minute--he fires immediately, and
two balls enter her left breast. She starts up and flies, her
blood streaming about, to a closet, exclaiming that she will
submit to any terms, if he will spare her. "No! No! You must
die!" and he fires his second pistol. She had instinctively
covered her heart with her hand, that hand is miserably frac-
tured by the balls; but saved her heart. She then escapes to
another closet, where a third shot is fired at her without
effect--and at last she rushes in despair at the door--and while
M. de PONTALBA is discharging his last barrel at her, she succeeds in opening it. The family, alarmed by the firing, arrives,
and she is saved. The old man, on seeing that she is beyond
his reach, returns to his apartments; and blows out his brains.
It seems clear that he had resolved to make a sacrifice of the
short remsant of his son and his grandson from their unfortunate
connection with Madame de PONTALBA. But he failed--none of
her, wounds were mortal; and within a month after, Madame de
PONTALBA, (perfectly recovered, in high health and spirits,
radiant and crowned with flowers, was to be seen at all the
fetes and concerts of the capital.)"
In the mean time a suit for restitution for conjugal rights was

Continued "Extraordinary Trial at Paris"...

pending between her and her husband; and towards the end of last
  October a final decree of the court enjoined that Madame de
  PONTALBA should return under marital authority, and should
  resides in such of her husband's houses as he should appoint--
  excepting only with admiraboe delicacy--the Chateau de Mont
  Leweque, whereon the bloody scene had been acted."

-------------------------------------

"MURDER WILLOCT--The following letter in relation to examination
  on a charge of murder fourteen years ago, by a man of his wife
  appears in the Worcester (Mass.) Telegraph:  Fitchburg, March
  17, 1848,  The last two days have witnessed an exciting invest-
  igation before Ives PHILIPS, Esq., Chief Justice, assisted by
  Ebenezer TORREY, Esq., as Associate Justice.  It is a case of
  the Commonwealty vs. John COOK, Jr., of Winchedon, formerly of
  Ashburnham:  in which the prisoner is charged with poisoning
  his wife in Ashburnham, fourteen years ago the last February,
  or February 1848.
The facts in brief are, that the wife on a certain Sabbath
  afternoon, about tea time, was asked by the defendent to try
  some of his cider, which he had kept remarkably well or sweet.
  She did drink.  About an hour afterwards, the husband called
  in witness, (Mrs. Malinda WAND, a sister of his wife wupposed
  to have been murdered), from the other part of the house.  The
  witness found the wife on the bed in great distress, and trying
  to vomit.  She gave her some peppermint, but without creating
  relief.  The wife continued to grow worse.
During the night the defendent told the witness to go and lie
  down with a child which slept in an adjoining room.  While there,
  the witness heard the defendant mix something in a tubler,
  and which he gave the wife to drink, who then began to grow
  worse, so fast, that the witness insisted on knowing what he
  had given her.  He said it was hot sling.  A physician was
  also called in the night, but he could do nothing _____
  _____[HMS NOte: rest of line not legible]
died about ten o'clock next morning.  The witness insisted on
  a post mortem examination, but was refused.
After death, the body became very much swollen, a circumstance
  which caused great anxiety in the mind of the saxton, (Mr.
  John HASTINGS, of Ashburnham) who says he has kept an eye on
  it ever since it was placed in the tomb, which was on the
  Wednesday after the death.  The sexton testifies that the body
  did not change as is usually the case.  The chest continued in
  in a remarkable state of preservation till the last of Jan.1848,
  when he accompainied two gentlemen to the tomb, and the contents
  of the stomach were taken out and carried to Prof. WEBSTER, who,
  after a thorough annalynis, reports that he found about five
  grains of arsonic in what was sent to him.
The editor of the TELEGRAPH remarks:  We knew the defendent
  many years ago, as a farmer of reported respectability.  At the
  time of his arrest for this crime, he was living with his fourth
  wife.  COOK was brought to this town, and is committed till the
  next criminal term of the Common Pleas, when the case will
  go before the Grand Jury."
-------------------------------------

EARLY TEXAS NEWS

An article from New York Express----
"LOUIS PHILLIPPE--The Ex-King of the French was born in Paris
October 6th, 1773; and consequently is now in his 75th year.
He succeeded to the title of Duke of Orleans in 1793, after
the death of his father, Phillippe EGALITE, who it is well
known, suffered by the guillotine, in the sanguinary days of
the Revolution.  The Orleans branch of the Bourbon family of
which Louis PHILLIPPE is now the head, originated in Phillippe,
a younger son of LOUIS XIII, created Duke D'ORLEANS by his
brother, LOUIS XIV.  The first Duke of Orleans was twice married,
his second wife being Elizabeth Charlotte of BOHEMIA; grand-
daughter of JAMES I, of England; thus connecting the houses
of ORLEANS and STUART, from the latter of whom the Queen of
England, VICTORIA, is descended.
For many years Louis PHILLIPPE was exiled from France, travelling in various countries of Europe, and visiting the United
States in his exile.  While in Switzerland he engaged as a
teacher in an academy for eight months, being then twenty
years of age.  It is a mistake however, that he ever taught
school in the United States as is generally supposed.
He arrived in this country in November 1796, and was joined by
his brothers; the three spending some time with Gen. WASHINGTON
at Mount Vernon, by invitation, previous to making a journey
through the Western country.  After a tour to the Lakes and
the Falls of Niagara, the Princes returned to Philadelphia,
where they resided a few months.  Having determined to join
their mother in Spain, the Princes concluded to go there by
way of New Orleans and Havana.  For that purpose they again
crossed the mountains to Pittsburgh, and descending the Ohio
and Mississippi rivers in a boat, arrived at New Orleans in
February, 1768.  Being refused a passage to Spain from Havana,
whither they went from New Orleans, they sailed to New York,
whence an English Packet carried them to Falmouth, at which
place they arrived in February 1800.  The Princes then took
up their residence on the banks of the Thames, at Twickenham.
They received much attention from the English nobility.  They
made a voyage to the Island of Minorea, a passage being given
them in a frigate by the British government; but finding no
opportunity of passage thence to Spain, which was then in a
convulsed state, they returned to England, and resided for
some years at Twickenham.  The Duke of Orleans had the misfortune to lose both of his brothers while in exile.  The
Duke of MONTPENSIER died in England, in Westminister Abbey.--
The Count BEAUJOLIAS died at Malta, whither his brother
accompanied him in 1808.
From Malta Louis PHILLIPPE went to Sicily, and accepted an
invitation from FERDINAND, the King of Sicily, to visit the
Royal family, at Palermo.  During his residence there, he
gained the affections of the Princess AMELIA, the second daughter of the Kin g, and with the consent of FERDINAND and the
Duchess of ORLEANS, who had joined her son in Sicily, their
marriage took place in November, 1800.  By this lady, late
Queen of the French, Louis PHILLIPPE ..has had eight children,
of whom six still survive--viz:  1.  Louisa, Queen of Belgium.
(wife of LEOPOID) born 1812.  2.  LOUIS, Duke of NEMOURS, born
1814, married Victoria AUGUSAT, of Coburg, cousin of Prince
ALBERT.  3.  Maria CLEMENTINA, born 1817--unmarried.  Contd.....

63.

Continued "LOUIS PHILLIPPE---"

4. FRANCIS, Prince de JOINVILLE, born 1818, Admiral of the French Navy, married FRANCISCA, a sister of the Emperor of Brazil, and of the Queen of Portugal. 5. HENRY, Duke D'AUMALE, born 1822, married to CAROLINA, cousin to the King of the Two Sicillies. 6. ANTHONY, Duke of MONTPENSIER, born 1821, married a sister of the Queen of Spain.

The oldest son of Louis PHILLIPPE was FERDINAND, Duke of ORLEANS, born 1810; killed by jumping from his carriage July, 1842. He married in 1837, HELENA, daughter of the Grand Duke of Mecklenburg, SCHWERIN, by whom he had two children, viz: Louis PHILLIPPE, (Count of Paris) born 1838, and now 10 years of age, and Robert PHILLIPPE, Duke of CHARTRES born 1840.

At Palermo, Louis PHILLIPPEE remained after his marriage until 1844, when in the restoration of the BOURBONS he repaired to Paris, and was restored to his rank and honors.--The return of NAPOLEON from Elba in 1845 broke up his arrangements and he sent his family to England, where he joined them, and again took up his residence at Twickenham.

On the restoration of LOUIS XVII, the Duke returned to France, in September, 1845, and took his seat in the Chamber of PEERS. The large estate to which he was entitled by inheritance being restored to him, he devoted his attention principally to the education of his family.

His opulence enabled him to become the protector of the Fine Arts and the Patros of Letters, and few men in France were more popular during the career of the BOURBONS. He was unexpectedly called from private life by the Revolution of the three days in July, 1830, when on the addication of CHARLES X., the Chamber of Duputies offered him to Crown, which he accepted on the 9th of August 1833, adopted the style and title of Louis PHILLIPPE, King of the French.

The Ex-King was handsome man when young; his frame is now bulky, but there is much ease in his manners. He is ready in conversation, and was remarkably affable to all.--NEW YORK EXPRESS."

------------------------------------

"COMMERCIAL--The STATE OF TEXAS, COUNTY OF HOPKINS--Taken up by John HANKINS, and posted before Peter VISOR, a Justice of the Peace of the county & state aforesaid, one brown stud horse five years old, thirteen and a half hands high, with four white feet; knock need and pigeon toed, star and snip on the nose-- appraised to sixteen dollars, by us this 9th Feb. 1848. John TERREL, A. HERRIN. Sworn to and subscribed before me this 9th day of Feb. 1848. Peter VISOR, J.P. Filed and recorded March the 1st, 1848. E. HOPKINS, Clerk. A true copy of the original recorded in my office, May the 6th A. D. 1848. E. HOPKINS, Clerk, C.C.H.C."

-------------------------------------------------------------------

THE NORTHERN STANDARD-SATURDAY, MAY 20,1848- CLARKSVILLE, RED RIVER COUNTY Vol. 6, No. 4

"DEATH OF SENATOR ASHLEY,--To our friend Wm. STEWART, of Sevier Co., Ark. we are indebted, by private conveyance, for an Arkansas Democrat of the 12th inst., which given us information of the death of this distinguished gentleman. The account from the Union, and the action in Congress usual upon such events, Contd....

Continued.."Death of Senator Ashley"-----
will be found in another column.  The disease causing the
death of Senator ASHLEY, was inflamation of the bowels and
liver.  His new collegue, Maj. BORLAND, had the benefit of
his introduction to the Senate, and was then called upon to
attend his bed of death, and his burial.
Senator ASHLEY was a gentleman of a high order of capacity,
and took rank in the Senate, immediately upon his introduction;
a rank which he had maintained ever since.  At the time of
his death he was Chairman of the Judiciary committee; a very
elevated position, in that body, showing of itself, how highly
his acquirements and judgment were appreciated by the Senate.
Arkansas has lost her ablest citizen."

-----------------------------------

"ANOTHER STAR EXTINCT--DEATH OF GEN. ASHLEY--It is with profound
regret that we have to state the death of Chester ASHLEY, Esq.,
one of the U. S. Senators from the State of Arkansas.  He
was walking about in perfect apparent health on Monday, was
attacked on Tuesday, and is now no more.  This rapid and
emlancholy event has filled both houses of Congress and this
whole community with the deepest commiscration.  Yesterday the
Senate remained but a short time in session, and adjourned out
of respect to their dying colleague.  In an hour afterwards he
breathed his last.  Very soon after the melancholy tidings
reached the House, they too adjourned.
General ASHLEY was an influential and respected member of the
dignified body to which he was belonged for several years.--He
was Chairman of the Judiciary Committee; and his voice, though
not often heard in the chamber, was always heard with respect.
He was beloved in his domestic circle, and amiable in his
private relations.  We cannot adequately express the sympathy
which the whole community feel for his emibable wife and
daughter, who administered the last offices of love to the
expiring Senator."                          UNION.

-----------------------------------

"DEATH OF SENATOR ASHLEY, Washington, April 29, 1848:  To the
Editor of the Louisville Journal:"[Helen has abstracted portions that have not appeared in the above articles]
"Senator ASHLEY, who died in the afternoon."  "Washington, May
1.--Major BORLAND announced the death of Mr. ASHLEY--highly
eulogizing his private character."
"Mr. BREESE followed, after which the usual resolutions of
condolence and mourning were adopted, and a committee of arrangements appointed to make the necessary preparations for
the funeral, which will take place tomorrow."  "Mr. JOHNSON,
of Arkansas, pronounced a brief but eloquent eulogy on the
deceased, and offered the usual resolution of mourning."
"Mr. WHITE seconded the resolution and spoke briefly but
feelingly relative to the public and private character of Mr.
ASHLEY."  "Washington, May 2, 10 p.m.--The two houses of
Congress today were engaged in attending the funeral of Senator ASHLEY."  "The President and cabinet, the officers of the
army and navy, and a few of the foreign ministers were present."
"An appropriate prayer was delivered by the Rev. Mr. GURLEY,
and the funeral sermon delivered by the Rev. Mr.[HMS Note: looks
like SLICER]."  "The ceremonies were of an imposing and solemn
character."

-----------------------------------

EARLY TEXAS NEWS

"FROM THE GALVESTON NEWS OF THE 25th ult.--The steamer Tom M'KIN-
NEY returned this morning from her trip.  She ascended the
Trinity as far as Smithfield.  She has brought the following
freight and passengers:  65 bales cotton, belonging to V.P.LEE,
taken at DAVIS' Landing; 41 do., belonging to B.F. ELLIS,
taken at CHERRY's Landing; 2do., consigned to V. P. LEE, taken
at HOLLOMAN's Landing; 10 do. consigned to S. SOUTHWICK, taken
at Liberty; 97 do.; consigned to RICE, ADAMS & Co., taken at
mouth of Trinity; 88 do., consigned to H. H. HOLLOMAN, taken at
the mouth; 154, do.; consigned to A. PAUL, taken at the mouth.
In addition to the above the M'KINNEY has a considerable
quanity of sundries, as corn, corn meal, hides, buffalo skins
peltries, beeswax, furs, leather, etc., making a freight equal
to about 600 bales of cotton.  The M'KINNEY reports one other
flat boat, which has probably reached the mouth of the Trinity
by this time.  We understand that there is now on the Trinity
between three and four thousand bales ready for shipment, besides
a large quanity of corn and other produce.  A gentleman who went
and returned by the M'KINNEY as a passenger, states that this
new boat has performed very well on this her first trip."
---------------------------------
"Telegraphic Report of the Louisville Democrat, May 1--LATER
 FROM EUROPE--ARRIVAL OF THE STEAMER AMERICA..New York, April 29,
 11,P.M.--The royal mail steamer America, Captain JUDKINS, which
 sailed from Liverpool on the 15th inst., arrived here today."
 "The Arch-duke STEPHEN has been declared King of Hungary."
 "It has been reported that Louis PHILLIPPE has arrived in
 America." [HMS Note: see more about PHILLIPPE on Pgs. 63-64]
"From the N.O.Mercury, May 17...LATEST FROM MEXICO--Arrival of
 Mr. SEVIER in Mexico.."  "The schooner Heroiue, arrived last
 night from Vera Cruz, bringing news from that city to the
 26th ult. and from the city of Mexico to the 29th."  "Mr. SEVIER
 arrived at the capital on the 18th ultimo."  "Messrs. SEVIER &
 CLIFFORD were invited to Queretaro, where, the Mexicans suppose,
 our Commissioners will modity the treaty."
---------------------------------
"MARRIED--On the 18th of April, at Carlisle, Pa., by the Rev.
 Mr. NADAL, Hon. T. PHILSBURY, formerly of the State of Maine,
 and now Representative in Congress from Texas, to Rebecca S.,
 second daughter of Col. J. CARPENTER, of Penobscot County, Maine."
---------------------------------
"CORPORATION ORDINANCE--At a called meeting of the Board of Alder-
 men, on the 15th day of May, A.D. 1848, it was--[HMS Note: will
 not copy all of article due to length.]  John A. BAGBY, Mayor
 Clarksville, May 20th 1848."
---------------------------------
"CATCH THE THEIF:  $150 Reward--I camped last night, at the house
 of G. W. MORGAN, near the Falls of the Brazos river, with a
 small lot of Negroes.  Among the lot I had a Mulatto Girl, about
 15 years of age.  The Girl will weigh about one hundred and
 twenty pounds, has broad face, and very good looking.
 Her name is Mary, but from a child she has generally went by
 the name of _____[Possibly Bett.,HMS Note] I believe she was
 taken by some White Person.  I will give Fifty Dollars reward,
 for the apprehension and delivery of the Girl, either to me, or
 in some Jail so I can get her, and One Hundred for the thief.  I
 live at Porter's Bluff, on Trinity river, Navarro County, Texas."
R. H. PORTER  May 6,1848

"MELANCHOLY SUICIDE--A suicide of a distressing nature, took place in the neighboring parish of Rattray a few days ago. About three months ago, the hands of marriage were published between a girl belonging to ATHOL and a young man residing in Edinburg. The [HMS-not legible]adage, (the course of tru love never did run smooth), was verified in their case to the bitter letter. The friends of the bride thought to be exceedingly indignant to the match, and to mark their disapprobation, by refusing to give her that important something which is an object of great solicitude and of honest pride to every respectable Scottish maiden on the eve of her marriage--(her providing.). Her treatment had been such as to induce her to leave her mother's house and seek a shelter in the house of a widow sister, who occupies a farm in the neighborhood of Rattray, where she hoped to meet with some sympathy; but in this, too, she had been disappointed, as the marriage was never allowed to go forward. A few days ago, however, the betrothed resolved to have the matter brought to a conclusion, and for this purpose had appointed to meet in Perth, with the view of having the nupial knot tied. The girl being crossed and thwarted in so important a matter, in which her feelings and future prospects were so intimately concerned, had, in the meantime, become the victim of a settled melancholy; and in that state of mind disappeared from home on the evening of the intended marriage; and her body was found a few days after in the Erichi, between two and three miles below her sister's house. There was circumstance connected with this tragical affair which invests it with a horrid and melancholy interest. The girl left the house between five and six o'clock in the evening and returned about eleven o'clock in a state of convulsive agitation, her eye [HMS-not legible] her hair disheveled and her dress disordered and torn and dripping with wet; and she bore evidence of having been engaged in an agitating and violent struggle. She spoke not, but, opening the door, thrust in the housedog, by which she had, been accompained, and shutting the door immediately disappeared. It is conjectured and that with a great degree of probability, that this sagacious animal, with that almost reasoning instinct, for which the Newfoundland dog is so much noted, had by force prevented her from committing the rash act, which she had attempted, but which she could not accomplish, until she returned with him, a distance of between two and three miles." DUNDEE ADV.
[HMS Note: This article actually appeared below article on Page 66 "Telegraphic Report of the Louisville Democrat". But due to space I have placed here in order not to continue onto another page._

-----------------------------------------------

"THE HON. D. S. KAUFMAN" [abstracted by Helen ]
"Among other articles which have been postponed for this cause, is the following sketch of an address delivered at Norwich, Connecticut, by the gentleman named above, which we had cut from the Aurora, and promised ourselves the pleasure of its publication as soon as the pressure of our columns would permit. It will be remembered that Col. KAUFMAN accompanied his frined and collegue Gen. Sam HOUSTON on his late visit to New England---UNION."
"Hon. Davis S. KAUFMAN was a young noble-looking man, a native of Pennsylvania, from which State he removed to Texas about
Contd......

Continued--"THE HON. D. S. KAUFMAN"---
 eleven years ago. He distinguished himself in the military
 service of that republic, was a member of the lower house of
 the Texas Congress, and for two years Speaker of that body.
 He now enjoys a high reputation as a member of Congress from
 the State of Texas. We regret that we have room for but an
 imperfect sketch of Col. K.'s remarks."
--------------------------------------------------------------
THE NORTHERN STANDARD-SATURDAY, MAY 27, 1848, Vol. 6, No.5
--------------------------------

"HORRIBLE SCENE--Some mills and workshops were recently burnt
 in Watertown, N.Y. We make an extract from an appalling account:
 The loss of property is very heavy--much greater than ever
 before experienced by Watertown, excepting that which destroyed
 BEBEE's Factory, in 1833; and would that we could stop here, but,
 alas; the most horid portion of our tale yet remains to be told.--
 Two men who were actively engaged in securing the property of
 Mr. CONKEY in the factory building were burned to death.--They
 were in the third story, with two or three others, when the
 wind forced the flames through the windows, and in an instant
 the whole room was in a perfect blaze.
 One of the men named DeLONG, rushed to the outside door, hesi-
 tated a moment, and finally threw himself down, and escaped with
 slight injury. Another one named Leonard WRIGHT, attempted to
 reach the door, but was too much burned to do so, and when
 within a few feet of it, reeled and fell. We saw him distinctly
 writhing and twisting to avoid the intense heat, and finally
 saw him fall upon the floor, still convulsed and wrathing his
 body in the torture of his fiery death--a sight too horrid to
 behold, yet too painfully interesting to turn from. He was a
 very worth man, a workman in the factory, aged about fifty
 years, and leaves a family to mourn his awful death.
 The remains of another man Levi PALMER, a wagon-maker in the
 employ of Mr. COLWELL, were found near the southeast corner of
 the same building. He was in the building a few minutes before
 the flames burst in, but it was hoped that he had left as
 Mr. CONKEY implored all to do so, and not to peril their lives
 to save his property. He was a reputable young man, and leaves
 a wife and four children, who were dependent upon him for support."
------------------------------------
"Miss Susan CUSHMAN, the actress, was married on the 22d ult.,
 at Sefton Church near Liverpool, to Dr. Sheridan MUSPRATT, a
 wealthy gentleman residing at Seaforth Hall, near Liverpool."
------------------------------------
"JOHN JACOB ASTOR-- wife died recently at the age of eighty-five
 years, it is said by those who had the means of knowing, possessed an estate worth at least forty millions of dollars. All
 this was the product of his own industry and good management.
 He has bequeathed the sum of $320,000 for the establishment
 of a free library, to be called the ASTOR Library, of which
 Dr. COGSWELL, who has resided with him for some years, is to
 be librarian. The cost of the building is limited to $60,000.
 Mr. ASTOR was born in the village of Waldrop, near Heidelburg,
 in the Duchy of Badon, Germany, July 18, 1793. His parents,
 although poor, gave their children sufficient education to
 enable them to read and write and understand arithmetic.
 Deceased wrote a neat running hand, and was passionately fond of
 Contd......

Continued "JOHN JACOB ASTOR--"
  the study of geography, in which he educated himself.
  At the age of eighteen he left home, and spent three years with
  his oldest brother, a music solier, in London.--He then came
  to America at the request of his brother Henry who was in the
  employment of a butcher in this city.  He soon obtained work
  with a furrier, and ____[HMS Note: possibly saring or sparing]
  his earnings started out with the Indians on account, exchang-
  ing trinkets for furs, and by this means, with the aid of his
  brother Henry, who had established himself as a butcher, he
  was enabled to open a store; as per following advertisement
  from the N.Y.Daily advertiser, of January 2, 1789:  "JOHN
  JACOB ASTOR, at No. 81 Queen Street, next door but one to
  (The Friends' Meeting House) has for sale an assortment of
  Piano Fortes of the newest construction, made by the best
  makers in London, which he will sell on the most reasonable
  terms.  He gives each for all kind of Furs, and has for sale
  a lot of Canada Beaver and Beaver Coating, Raccoon Skins etx."
  ASTOR's enterprise in Oregon, owing to the treachery of some
  of his agents, was not successful.  The post was sold to a
  British Company by MACDOUGAL, his agent: and the members of
  the expeditian who remained faithful to Mr. ASTOR and the
  United States, returned overland, suffering the greatest
  [HMS Note: not legible] at the Rocky Mountians.  Among those
  who thus returned was Ramsey CROOKS, Esq., President, and now
  the principal proprietor of the American Fur Company on Ann
  Street.  In 1830 Mr. ASTOR sold the Fur Company to Mr. CROOKS
  and others, the former agents and clerks of the Company, and
  retired from commercial life; and to his credit we record the
  fact that he was liberal to his employes and cheerfully aided
  them in establishing themselves in business.--Much of his
  immense estate had been amassed by speculations in land in the
  new States-he bought large tracts before the country was settled and sold them at high prices to settlers.  He leaves his
  executors $5,000 each per annum, and we understand that to
  prevent any breach of his will, he executed deeds a few days
  ago for nearly all his real property.  His bonevolence did
  not extend far, and in proportion to his means, we never had
  a wealthy citizen who did less, in his lifetime, to promote
  charitable, religious or benevolent object.  He has nobly
  atoned for the omission by liberal donations and bequests in
  his will.  Mrs. ASTOR died about eighteen years ago, leaving
  two sons and four daughters.  Two of the daughters have since
  died.  The second son has been imbecile from birth."
-------------------------------------
"In the Louisville Journal of the 4th inst., we find the following
  letter in relation to the statement made a short time since to
  that paper, on the authority of Major BORLAND, that Cassius M.
  CLAY, when a prisoner among the Mexicans begged them to spare
  his life, telling them he was a son or relation of Henry CLAY,
  who was opposed to the war, and who if he was slain, would
  take vengeance on Mexico. (Major BORLAND is Solon BORLAND)."
-------------------------------
"FROM THE JALAPA WATCH TOWER:  ARRIVAL AND RECEPTION OF GEN.
  SANTA ANNA AT JALAPA--Fro some time past, our town has been
  filled with rumors that a correspondence has been going on
  between the ex-President of the Mexican Republic, Gen.Santa
  Contd......

Continued--"FROM THE JALAPA WATCH TOWER"----

Anna, and Col. Geo. W. HUGHES, our Governor; and that the
former had agreed to accept a safe-guard from Governor HUGHES
and to place himself under his protection until he could leave
the country.  On Tuesday last, the 28th inst., it was generally
understood that the General would arrive, and at 8 o'clock in
the morning, three companies of cavalry, of the D.C. and Md. Regiment, were formed in the Plaza.  The companies consisted of
Capt. TAYLORs Mrd. Riflemen, Capt. TILGHMAN's Artillerists,
and Lt. McDONALD's Dragoons, the whole forming an escort of
honor under the command of Major KENLEY, of the Md. Vols.  At
9 o'clock, Gov. HUGHES and staff, accompanied by the escort,
left the town and proceeded to the village of Banderilla,
some six miles from Jalapa.  Here a halt was ordered, and the
Governor was hospitably entertained by Gen. DURRAND, at whose
beautiful residence the escort remained until the approach of
Santa ANNA was reported.--At 2 o'clock, p. m., the cavalcade was
seen approaching, preceded by Lieut. McDONALD's Dragoons,
which had been despatched for the purpose.  In front of the
General's carriage, (which was a handsome travelling vehicle,
drawn by eight mules), road five well appointed and equipped
Lancers; in the rea, was a number of Mexican officers and a
small detachment of cavalry, with a company of mounted volunteers from Perote.  As the Gen. approached our escort, which
was in line to receive him, sabres were presented and the
customary salutes made, which the General returned by rising
from his seat, taking off his hat, and bowing deeply.  As soon
as the carriage halted, Gov. HUGHES approached and assisted
the General and his lovely young wife and daughter to alight;
the General then embraced the Governor and entered the house
where the officers, and all others that desired it, were duly
presented to him.  He appeared to be in good spirits, and re-
minded the Governor that he had had the pleasure of seeing him
in Washington, and that he well recollected many others whom
he had met with the United States.

After a sumptuous repast prepared by Gen. DURAND, Santa ANNA
and his family entered the carriage, which moved off rapidly
towards Jalapa.  In the advance rode Lieut. McDONALD's company
on the right side of the carriage, Capt. TAYLOR's, on the left,
Capt. TILGHMAN's and in the rear, the Mexican Guard.  The effect
produced by the whole cortege was very impressing, and which
was much hightened by the (Stars and the Stripes), which were
borne on each side of the carriage by Sergta STEWART and MURRAY.
As the column approached the Texas camp, some apprehension was
felt that the Texas might show some ill-felling towards their
old enemy; but the gallant Rangers behaved as soldiers should
to one who was now harmless and in misfortune; they received
him in decent silence, and manifested no other feeling than
that of a lively curiosity to see the memorable Santa ANNA.  At
the outer garita of Jalapa, the escort halted, with the excep-
tion of Capt. TILGHAMN's company, which was ordered to ac-
company the general to Encero, where he proposed to halt until
he could complete his arrangements to leave Mexico.  Before the
general left the garita he bade farewell to Gov. HUGHES, thanked
him most warmly for his kindness and attention to him and his
family.

On Thursday last the governor, accompanied by nearly every
officer of his garrison, visited the general by invitation,
Contd.....

Continued "FROM THE JALAPA WATCH TOWER"---
at his hacienda of Encero, where, owing to the scarcity of
household furniture, but a few of the officers had an opportunity of partaking, with his family, of an elegant breakfast,
which had been prepared for them.  Here again, we understand
that the general appeared most grateful to Col. HUGHES and the
officers, for their kindness to him, and begged him to accept
his grateful acknowledgement of their courtesy.
Whilst at Encero, the general has been guarded by two companies
of infantry under the command of Capt. ?DEGGES, D. C. and Md.
Regt.  We learn that Santa ANNA will leave immediately for
Jamaica, embarking from the port of Antigus, to which place
the governor has tendered him the escort of Capt. TILGHMAN's
company.
Santa ANNA is accompanied by his lady, a woman of exceeding
beauty and fascinating manners.  Her presence will do much
towards smothering the cares of the (self-exiled soldier).
The general left on Friday morning for Autigua, escorted by
Capt. TILGHMAN's company where a brigantine is waiting to carry
him to Jamaica.  We believe he intends visiting England."
--------------------------------------------------------------
THE NORTHERN STANDARD-SATURDAY-JUNE 3, 1848.
CLARKSVILLE, RED RIVER COUNTY, TEXAS--Vol. 6, No. 6
---------------------------------
" A friend writing to us on the 20th ult., from Buffalo, Hender-
son County says "Our District Court is in session, Hon. B. H.
MARTIN, presiding--a good Judge, and will be very popular.""
---------------------------------
"CONVICTED--The re-trial of the Slave NELSON, for the murder of
LUCKEY, took place at the court house on Thursday, a special
term being held for the purpose.--He was found guilty as before,
and on Friday morning, was sentenced to be hanged on Friday next.
This negro was first tried at the Fall term 1846.  An appeal
was taken by his counsel to the Supreme Court, and upon examination of the record it was found to be imprefect, there being
no statement that the Jury had been sworn, though they really
were sworn.  The case was sent back for a new trail which has
resulted as we have stated.  There is no doubt the accused
was guilty of astrocious, premediated murder.
As proof of the law aluding character of our population, is
the case of this negro.  Upon a mere quibble, he has been
kept for a year and a half at a serious expense to the county,
and has had the benefit of all the legal courtesy and formal-
ity which would have been extended to any one, and this too,
by a county seriously embarrassed in its county finances, and
not a doubt upon any one's mind of his guilt.  It is to be
presumed that at the appointed time he will expiate--his guilt
upon the seatfold, a warning to all offenders, of the correctness and certainty of the administration of the laws in this
community."
---------------------------------
"DEATH FROM THE BITE OF A CAT--The New York Morning Star says--
"A boy named KEELER, whose parents reside in L___rens at,
died wednesday morning, after paroxysms of raving madness.  The
boy was bitten some months ago by a cat, supposed at the time
to be rabid, but no evil effects were observed at the time, or
since, until a few hours before his death, when the symptoms of
hydrophohia became apparent, and [HMS Note: no legible] a most
violent and distressing form.""

EARLY TEXAS NEWS

"TO THE DEMOCRATIC REPUBLICAN, PRECINCT COMMITTEES, FOR THE
   COUNTY OF RED RIVER--Prec. No. 1--A. J. TITUS, A. W. KING,
   Thos. L. COWAN.  Prec. 2--John STILES, Jas. McGOWEN, John
   CAMERON.  Prec. 3--W. P. CRITTENDEN, Nelson DOAK, A.J.RUSSELL.
   Prec. No. 4--Wm. EDMONSON, Gid. MIMS, Wm. A. PARK.
   Prec. No. 5--Martia GUEST, F. or T. C FORBES, Lovell COFFMAN
   Prec. No. 6--Wm. HUMPHREYS, B. CROWOVER, D. FULBRIGHT."
-------------------------------
"RECEPTION OF THE IRISH DEPUTATION--The 3d inst. being the day
   fixed by the provisional government for the reception of the
   Irish deputation, Mr. Smith O'BRIEN and the other members of
   the Irish Confederation went to the hotel at half-past three
   o'clock, to present their address.  They were received by
   M. de LAMARTINE alone.--Besides the address of the Irish Confederation, addresses were presented by R. O.'GORMAN,Jr. from
   the citizens of Dublin; by Mr. MEAGBER, from the repealers of
   Manchester; and by Mr. McDERMOT, from the members of the
   Irish Confederation resident in Liverpool."
-------------------------------
"STATE OF TEXAS, COUNTY OF LAMAR, PRECINCT No. 6--This day shown
   to us by E. F. ANDERSON one certain stray, and we find the
   name to be a sorrel mare colt, one year old this spring; no
   marks or brands perceivable; appraised to fifteen dollars."
   R. Q. HUDSON, (seal)  J.O.LOGAN,(seal) Appraisers
   Sworn to and subscribed before me, April 26, 1848, John A.
   DILLINGHAM, J.P.  A tru_ copy as on file in my office. J. R.
   CRADDOCK, Clerk, L.C.
-------------------------------
"STATE OF TEXAS, COUNTY OF LAMAR, PRECINCT No.6--This day shown
   us by Stephen BREWER, a certain yellow bay horse, and we find
   him to be as follows the horse is about 15 hands high, with a
   star and a snip, and some saddle spots on his back, with three
   white feet, and we suppose him to be six years old, and we
   appraise the same to thirty dollars, this the 23d day of May
   A.D. 1848    J. L. DILLINGHAM(seal)  M. S. BOYD (seal)Appraisers
   Sworn to and subscribed before me this the 23d day of May A.D.
   1848.   John A. DILLINGHAM, J.P.   A true copy as on file in
   my office.  J. R. CRADDOCK, Clerk, L.C.   Paris, 26 May 1848"
-------------------------------
"THE STATE OF TEXAS, COUNTY OF HENDERSON-Taken up by Walter FAR-
   REL, and estrayed before me, J. L. AUSTIN, an acting Justice
   of the Peace for said county, and duly appraised by F. W. BRID-
   GEW and Peter HIGH, according to law, two stray nags--described
   as follows: one roan horse, with a bald face--shod all round--
   right and left fore feet white up to the pastern joint--sup-
   posed to be fourteen of fifteen years old.  The other a sorrel horse eight or ten years old--with a white snip on the nose-
   both hind feet white--hip shot in the right hip--appraised to
   $25 each, this 13th April, 1848.  The above I do hereby certify
   to be the substance of the original certificate filed in my
   office, this May 16th, 1848.  Jas. BOGGS, Clerk Co. Court,Hern.Co."
-------------------------------
"THE STATE OF TEXAS, COUNTY OF HENDERSON--We the undersigned
   being called upon by A. J. HUNTER, an acting Justice of the Peac
   Peace for said county, to appraise a stray horse taken up by
   P. M. HARRISON--we find the same to be a dark grey horse, 14½
   hands high--about eight years old this spring; some white spots
   Contd.......

Continued: "THE STATE OF TEXAS, COUNTY OF HENDERSON"
 on the back, supposed to be saddle marks; the right hand leg
 black to the hock; no other marks or brands perecivable. We
 value the horse at $45, this April 1st, 1848.
 N. G. HALLARD; G. B. MASON, Appraisers. The substance of the
 original certificate filed in my office, May 10th, 1848.
 Jas. BOGGS, Clerk, Co. Court Henderson County."
----------------------------------
"TOWN OF BUFFALO, March 29th, 1848--Shown to us this day by
 Ephraim GUTHRIE one bay horse six years old this spring,
 15½ hands high; saddle spots on each side--two hand feet white--
 no brands perecivable; with a small star in the forehead,
 appraised to sixty-five dollars. Given under our hands and
 private seals, day and date above written.
 J. P. MOORE, (seal)  J. L. GOSSETT( seal,) Appraisers.
 I, James STEPHENSON do certify that the above was sworn to
 before me, an acting Justice of the Peace in and for the above
 county and State aforesaid. Given under my hand and private
 seal day and date above written. James STEPHENSON, J.P.
 The above is a true copy of the original certificate filed in
 my office, this May 10th 1848. Jas. BOGGS, Clerk, Co.Crt.Hen.Co."
----------------------------------
"HEAD QUARTERS 2d BRIGADE, 1st DIVISION TEXAS MILITIA, Dainger-
 field, May 26th 1848--Col H. F. YOUNG, Col. Com. 1st Reg. said
 Brig.--Giving orders to hold Huttalion and Regimential Drills
 and Musters on the following days. James H. ROGERS, Brig.
 Gen. Commanding."  [above abstracted by Helen]
----------------------------------
"The Davidson County Criminal Court has been engaged for several
 days in the trial of James MARTIN, who, it will be recolicted,
 shot and killed F. H. STUMP a few months since. The trial
 closed yesterday. Mr. MARTIN was sentenced to confinement
 and labor in the State prison for twenty years. The trial
 elicited much interest. Messrs. HOUSTON, MILLER, and McEWEN,
 were MARTIN's counsel, and Messers. Attorney General FOSTER,
 BAXTER and HOLLINSWORTH, for the State. No motion has yet
 been made for a new trial.   NASH. UNION."
----------------------------------
"We learn by telegraph from Philadelphia, that a dreadful accident occured in that city at an early hour this morning. It
 appears that Mr. Joseph L. RITCHIE, the proprietor of an
 extensive sugar refinery in that city, whilst passing through
 his establishment, heard groans proceeding from one of his
 vats; and on making a examination, discovered that a negro
 man had fallen in. He immediately reached his hand down to
 help him out; but the vat being filled with boxious gases, he
 also fell in, and when taken out both were perfectly dead.
  UNION."
----------------------------------
"SYMPATHY FOR LOUIS PHILLIPEE--When the news of Luuis PHILLIPPE's
 flight from France arrived in Boston, a brilliant party was
 coming off in a fashionable quarter. The King's fall from
 greatness became the subject of conversation and one super-
 lative specimen of tall society--a real topsawyer among them--
 remarked: I'm really sorry for Lewce FILEEPE, I think he is
 to be pitied. He is an accomplished gentleman, and there
 ought to be a meeting of the gentleman, of Boston, qualified
 by their wealth, position, and influence, to represent the
 Contd......

EARLY TEXAS NEWS
Continued  "SYMPATHY FOR LOUIS PHILLIPPE"--
    public opinion of the city, to prepare an address of sympathy
    with him in his misfortunes, and to send it over to him by some
    delegates of acknowledged respectability and standing in the
    community.--Boston Post."
-----------------------------------------------------------------
THE NORTHERN STANDARD-SATURDAY, JUNE 10, 1848
    Vol. 6, No. 7--CLARKSVILLE, RED RIVER COUNTY
-----------------------------------
"PUBLIC MEETING-- At a meeting of the citizens of Dallas County,
    Texas, held at the court house in Dallas on Wed. the 24th day
    of May 1848 for the purpose of sending delegates to the Con-
    vention for the navigation of the Trinity River, to be held
    at the Town of Huntsville, Walker Co., Texas, on the 4th day
    of July next. Gen. E. H. TARRANT was called to the chair and
    A. HARWOOD chosen Secretary. The object of the meeting having
    been stated by the chair, the meeting proceeded to business.
    On motion, the following gentlemen were appointed a committee
    to draft a Preamble and Resolutions expressive of the sense
    of this meeting:
Doct. P. DAKAN                      Calvin G. COLE
Col. Jno. N. BRYAN                  Rev. Jas. SMITH
Jno. C. McCOY                       Benj. MERRILL
Jeff TILLEY                         Wm. J. WALKER
Rowlin HUITT                        A. G. WALKER
Col. Wm. MYERS                      Hon. B. H. MARTIN
Col. S. G. NEWTON                   Col. CROCKETT
Doct. S. B. PRYER                   Col. JENNINGS.
[abstracted by Helen due to length]-Judge MARTIN was chosen
    chairman of this committee. On motion the following gentlemen
    were appointed Delegates to attend the convention at Hunts-
    ville, to wit:
Col. CROCKETT                       Judge ELKINS
Col. S. G. NEWTON                   Alex HARWOOD
Col. Jno. N. BRYAN                  Jno. C. McCOY
Rev. Jas. SMITH                     Doct. P. DAKAN
W. J. WALKER                        Doct. S. B. PRYER
W. H. HORD                          Jeff. TILLEY
On motion the meeting adjourned sine die, E. H. TARRANT,
    Chairman (This is Gen. E. H. TARRANT) Alex. HARWOOD, Secretary."
-----------------------------------
"RAILWAY MEETING--At a large and respectable public meeting, held
    at the Tremont House, on the evening, of Friday 5th April, on
    motion of J. C. SHAW, Esq. his honor, the Mayor, was called
    to the chair, and Mr. W. RICHARDSON appointed Secretary."
"The meeting was then addressed by Ebenezer ALLEN, Esq., in
    formable and pertinent manner, advocating the importance & show-
    ing the numerous benefits of the undertaking."
"A. J. YATES, Esq., moved the adoption of the resolutions,
    and made a few remarks on the importance and advantages of the
    enterprize, and the motion was seconded by Lorenzo SHERWOOD,Esq.
    whose plain, practical and conclusive arguments in their favor,
    were well calculated to produce conviction of the minds of
    the audience." "The resolutions having been unanimously adopted
    the following gentlemen were appointed a Committee under the
    4th Resolution, to wit: Messrs. SYDNOR, STUART, RHEA & JAMES,
    YATES." Continued......

Continued: "RAILWAY MEETINGS"-----
"We, would first call your attention to the present condition
of that portion of the State through which the proposed Road
(Railroad) will pass the northern of Red River counties of
this section of the State, including the counties of Grayson,
Fannin, Lamar, Red River, Bowie, Cass, Titus, Hopkins, Hunt,
Collin, Denton and Dallas, are now estimated to raise about
40,000 bales of cotton, which finds its way to market mostly
by Shreveport, at an expense, including hauling and freight,
of about five dollars per bale, and is exposed to all the losses, damage and ____tainties of the Red River navigation."
[abstracted by Helen]
------------------------------------

"Maj. WEBSTER's REMAINS--On Monday morning, the 1st inst., the
remains of Maj. Edward WEBSTER, of the Massachusetts Volunteers,
who died in Mexico, arrived at Boston, in the bark CHIEF, from
Vera Crux--The remains were in charge of Lieut. WING, of the
Massachusetts Volunteers. The war horse of the deceased was
also on board.--The remains of the son arrived, just as the
father was performing the last sad offices to his beloved
daughter, Mrs. Julia APPLETON, who, like her brother, died
in the bloom of youth."
------------------------------------
        [Next three articles announcing PEACE WITH MEXICO]
------------------------------------

"I will  preach, at the Presbyterian Church on the 3rd Sabbath
in June; at which time, the subscribers to the Baptist Meeting
Houses are requested to attend; for the purpose of selecting
a Committee to superintend the Building of the same.
A. E. CLEMMONS."
------------------------------------

"DIED--At Victoria, on the 13th January, 1848, Dr. Walter FOS-
GATE, a native of the State of New York. The deceased, will
be recollected by the soldiers of (18) '36, as a surgeon in
the Texas army, stationed at the hospital at Victoria, and
subsequently appointed Staff Surgeon. He was a man possessed
of as much natural kindness of temperament, and honest simpli-
city of heart, as ever falls to the lot of a human being.
Having experienced his friendly attentions more than once,
and many an hour enjoyed ourself in coversions with one whose
cast of character was decidedly intellectual, and cultivated,
we wish to record at his death, our sense of his general
worth, and great goodness of character.
DeM  (Charles DeMORSE, the editor)"
------------------------------------

"Departed this life, at his residence in Bowie county, on the
20th May, Littleton W. HOUSE. Mr. HOUSE was native of middle
Tennessee, born in Rutherford County, in the year 1810. He
has left an affectionate wife, and numerous friends to mourn
his loss." The Murfreesboro, Tenn. papers, please copy."
------------------------------------

"MASONIC NOTICE,--The Brethern of the Masonic Fraternity, are
respectaully invited to attend the celebration on the 24th inst.
in the Town of Clarksville, in memory of St. JOHN the Baptist.
Done by order of Friendship Lodge, No. 16  W. H. VING, Secretary."
------------------------------------

"SUCCESSION OF JAS. H. JOHNSTON, Dec'd.--The undersigned, was
   duly appointed Administrator of the estate of James: H. JOHN-
   STON, Deceased, late of Red River county, by the Honorable
   Judge of Probate for said county, at the May term of the court
   A. D. 1848.  This is therefore to notify all persons indebted
   to said estate, to make immediate payment, and all persons
   having claims against said estate, to present them to the
   undersigned, properly authenticates, with that time prescribed
   by law for payment.  Wm. S. TODD, Adm'r.
   Clarksville, June 6th 1848."

---------------------------------

"THE STATE OF TEXAS, COUNTY OF NAVARRO, District Court, Fall term,
   1848--To the Sheriff of said county, Greeting:  In the name
   and by the authority of the State of Texas, you are hereby
   commanded to summon the unknown heirs of Edward DAVIS, deceased,
   by publication for twelve successive weeks, in the Northern
   Standard, a newspaper printed at Clarksville, Red River, County,
   Texas, to appear at the next term, of the District court, to be
   holden in and for the county of Navarro, at Corsicana, the
   county seat of said county, on the fourth Monday in Sept. A.D.
   1848, to answer the Petition of Wm. F. HENDERSON, of Navarro
   county, Robert M. TYERS, John R. HENRY, and John KARNER, residents of Limestone county, all of said State of Texas, Plaintiffs; which said petition alleges that is important to Plaintiffs for the heirs of Edward DAVIS, aforesaid, to be made
   parites plaintiffs, to this suit, and that they are to petitioners unknown.  Petition further states, that siad plaintiffs, together, with one William M. JACKSON, and one Edward
   DAVIS, made a joint contract in writing, under their hands
   and seals, on the 13th day of July 1839, and that pursuant
   to said contract, which is annexed to and made part of petition,
   said parties located certain points and Bluffs on Trinity
   River, in the then county of Robertson, now Navarro county,
   but the parties died not then make a survey of said lands so
   located and selected; and afterwards said William M. JACKSON,
   deceased, and neither he, during his lifetime, nor his heirs
   or representatives, thereof July notified, complied with and
   performed the conditions of the said contract, incumbent on
   him the said JACKSON.  Petition further states that after the
   decease of said JACKSON, the surviving parties to said contract,
   in order to carry the same into effect, fur [not legible] some
   warrants to the amount of one third of a league of land each,
   or fourteen hundred and seventy-six acres each, which were
   duly surveyed and were recorded in the office of the county
   surveyor of said Robertson county, and the copies of the field
   notes of each survey, are also annexed to and made part of said
   petition; that after said surveys were made, said Edward DAVIS
   deceased, and that the names of his heirs, successors or representatives, are to petitioners unknown, and further that
   petitioner believes they are non-residents of Texas; that said
   William M. JACKSON, his heirs or representatives, have forfeited
   all rights to land under said contract, and that according to
   the tenor of the same, the heirs of the said DAVIS and your
   petitioners, have a common and undivided interest and are joint
   and common owners of each tract of land surveyed as aforesaid,
   without regard to the same in which each separate tract was
   surveyed; and said lands now remain undivided, the condition of
   Contd......

Continued "THE STATE OF TEXAS, COUNTY OF NAVARRO".....

the Frontier having prevented petitioners and said Davis, during his lifetime from making a division of said lands, as contemplated by the terms of their contract, wherefore petitioners pray for a writ of Partition, that the respective shares of petitioners and the heirs of said Edward DAVIS, be set aside by bounderies and proper deeds made to each party for the same, and for publication in the newspaper, citing said unknown heirs etc., and for general relief etc. Herein fail not and make due return of this writ, with your action on the same.

   Witness J.M. RIGGS, Clerk of the District Court for the county and my seal of office, at office this ___day of May A.D. 1848 and of the Independence of the United States the 72nd year.          James M. RIGGS, D. Clk. N.C. by A. HENDERSON, Deputy
TO THE UNKNOWN HEIRS OF EDWARD DAVIS--You, and each of you, are hereby commanded, in accordance with the foregoing authority, to appear at the next term of the District Court for the county of Navarro and State aforesaid, to be holden at Corsicana the county seat of said county on the fourth Monday in September 1848, to answer the above stated petition, wherein Sheriff W. F. HENDERSON, Robert M. TYERS, John R. HENRY, and John KARNER are Plaintiffs and the unknown heirs of Edward DAVIS are Defendants. James A. JOHNSON, Sheriff of Navarro.
-----------------------------------

"A CONFERENCE COLLEGE. At the late session of the East Texas Annual Conferance of the M.E. Church South, the following preanable and resolutions were adopted" [HMS Note: Due to length will not copy all of article, only references to names] "Letters addressed to S.A. WILLIAMS or J. W. FIELD, San Augustine; or to H. B. KELSEY, Marshall, will meet with prompt and respectful attention." "As we have no religious paper in the Conference, we respectfully ask the Northern Standard, Western Star, Western Argus, Jeffson Democrat, Texas Union, Nacogdoches Times, Rusk Pioneer, and Texas Christian Advocate at Houston to publish this notice for three months, as a matter of public interest."
H. B. KELSEY; B. A. WILLIAMS; J. W. FIELD, Comm.
May 20th 1848
-----------------------------------

"STATE OF TEXAS, BOWIE COUNTY___BEAT NO. 3--We the undersigned, having been appointed appraisers, to view and examine an estray horse shown us by James R. BOYCE, taken up by him as an estray, do find the same to be a dark bay, with black legs mane and tail, left hind foot white, some saddle marks about five or six years old, nearly fifteen hands high, and do value the same to be worth sixty dollars."
Given under my hand, this 27th May A. D. 1848
J. M. KIMBLE; E. S. TANSOR, Sworn to and subscribed before be this 27th May 1848  D. M. CHISHOLME, Beat No.3 (J.P.)
A true copy from the Record, June 2nd A.D. 1848
J. C. McGONIGAL, Clk. C.C.B.C. By his deputy S. H. McFARLAND
-----------------------------------

"CORRESPONDANCE OF THE DOLLAR NEWSPAPER-Philad.--New York,
   May 1, 1848" The story of the unknown suicide, found in
   an open lot on 14th street, has been developed, and is
   melancholy enough. His name was Alexander HAMILTON NORWOOD--
   his age 41. His father and family are people of wealth,
   fashion and influence, and reside in one of the many spendid
   mansions on Fourteenth street, near Union Square, in the
   highest ton of the upper ten thousand. The poor deceased,
   when a boy, for some cause unexplained, left the paternal
   roof and took to the sea, which he clung to till 1831, soon
   after which his father purchased for him a small farm in
   the country, on which he resided several years, but which
   he finally lost by becoming involved in lawsuits and other
   difficulties. Since then he has led rather a vagrant life,
   and the last several weeks he has been an inmate of the
   Sailor's Snug Harber. There is something mysterious, strange
   and unnatural shrouding over the whole affair. It would
   seem that he kept upon good terms with his father, for they
   were together much on Friday, when he complained of in-
   juries to his feelings by the treatment, he had received
   at the Harbor, and soon after leaving him he shot himself,
   as before stated. The report was heard in his father's
   house and around the neighborhood, but no one took any concern in the cause of the report, and his corpse lay in the
   vacant lot in which it fell till the following morning, when
   it was found by strangers."
---------------------------------

"SOUTH CAROLINA--Dr. MAJOR, a travelling lecturer on the Philo-
   osopy of Animal Magnetisum, lately visited Barnwell, S.C.,
   where suspicion was soon excited that he was an agent of the
   abolitionists. A meeting of the citizens was held on the
   subject, the perambulating lecturer was heard in his defence,
   he failed to satisfy the citizens as to the correctness of
   his conduct, notice to quit the parish was given him, a committee was appointed to hasten his departure, and he forthwith made tracks. If caught again, he may not be treated
   with as much forbearance as was shown him by the citizens
   of Barnwell."
---------------------------------

"THE CHERAW GAZETTE states that a distressing occurence happened
   in the upper part of that district, near Mount Croghan, a few
   days ago. It appears that the woods had got on fire near
   the plantation of Mr. SUMMERFORD, who with his wife and others
   went out for the purpose of protecting his fencing. While
   the party were in the woods, a tree that had taken fire fell
   upon and instantly killed Mrs. SUMMERFORD. Sometime that
   night Mr. SUMMERFORD was prevailed upon by the neighbors, who
   came in to set up with the corpse, to retire to rest. Not
   making his appearance in the morning, his room was entered,
   where he was found dead in his bed."
---------------------------------

"TO THE ELECTORS OF RED RIVER COUNTY"-[abstracted by Helen]
   W. B. STOUT placed his name before the public as a candidate
   for the office of Chief Justice of Red River County."
---------------------------------

"DREADFUL CASE OF HYDROPHOBIA--William KNIGHT, residing Francis
   Square, west of the Ridge Road, in Francisville, was attacked
   last week with hydrophobia, resulting from having been bitten by his own dog, about two months since.  He was attacked
   with illness about three days since, but the nature of the
   disease was not suspected until he was siezed with convulsive
   ravings on water being poured from one basin to another in
   his presence.  Last evening, during a dreadful fit, he attempted to rush from the house, and he was with difficulty
   restrained by six men, who happened to be in there at the
   time.  They succeeded in trying him down to his bed with a
   clothes line, when his ravings became most awful, and could
   be heard for a square around.  He died at 9 o'clock that
   night.  Those who were at his bed-side and witnessed his
   death, describe it as being a dreadufl sight.  The unfortunate man for some time previous to his dissolution attempted to bite everything within  his reach, and having obtained
   a stick, he sank his teet into the hard wood with the force
   of a vice.  During the time, he uttered the most piteous
   howlings, the sounds somewhat resembling those made by
   dogs when tortured by this terrible disease.  The best medical skill was exerted, but as it has ever been with this
   fearful malady, no relief could be afforded.

   The unfortunate man returned home about three months since
   from Austria, where he had been employed as a superintendent
   in the building of locomotives, in the extensive manufactory
   of Mr. NORRIS in that country.  Dr. HARTSHORN and five or
   six others physiscian were called in to consult upon his
   case, but their skill proved unavailing." Dollar Newspaper.
--------------------------------------------------------------

THE NORTHERN STANDARD-SATURDAY, June 17, 1848
   Vol. 6, No. 8, Clarksville, Red River County

---------------------------------

The next few columns are all political, HMS.

"CANNIBALISUM IN IRELAND--At the late-Galway Assizes, a man
   named John CONNELLY pleaded guilty to a charge of sheep-
   stealing.  The self-covicted criminal was sentenced to three
   months' imprisonment and hard labour.  Mr. DOPPING, the resident magistrate, stated in open Court that he knew of his own
   knowledge, that the prisoner and his family were starving when
   the offence was committed--that one of his children had died;
   and he had been credibly informed that the mother ate part of
   its leg and feet after its death.  He had the body exhumed
   and its appearance coroborated the information fully."
-----------------------------------------

"We are requested to State that the announcement of A. J. TITUS,
   for the County Clerkship, was prematurely made.  He will not
   be a Candidate."
-----------------------------------------

"UNFORTUNATE OCCURRENCE--On Wednesday evening, Wm. K. McKENZIE,
   the son of the Rev. J. W. P. McKENZIE, started from home in
   company with Joseph DICKSON, to attend a wedding.  Passing
   the place of Mr. FOR_____, but a short distance from the
   Rev. Mr. McKENZIE'S, and riding at a brisk gate, they ran

EARLY TEXAS NEWS

Continued--"UNFORTUNATE OCCURRENCE".....

    upon a cow lying down, and were both thrown from their
    horses. The cow rose, and the horse of young McKENZIE fell
    over with him. He was taken up insensible and never spoke
    after, breathing his last at about eleven o'clock, P.M.
    The deceased was a correct, worthy youth, of about seven-
    teen years of age."
--------------------------------

Due to length of this policical letter, all has not been copied.HMS

"LETTER FROM C. M. CLAY--From the Louisville Courier--To the
    Editors of the Louisville Journal--Madicon County, Kentucky
    May 18th 1848. Signed Your obedient servant, C. M. CLAY"
--------------------------------

The left side of the next article has been cut off by microfilm
    taker. H.M.S.

"MARRIED--Wednesday evening last, by the Rev. A. Da_____
    Burrel P. SMITH, Esq. to Miss Sarah HENDERSON, daughter of
    Col. L. D. HENDERSON, of this county. "
    ___Holly Springs papers, please copy.
--------------------------------
[Red River Co., Tex. Marriages Records shows above marriage to
    have license/bond issued 12 June 1848.]
--------------------------------

ADVERTISEMENT: "Books and paper for sale at the Drug Store
    of LOOK & ROWE, Frank H. CLARK" Clarksville June 17th 1848.
--------------------------------

"STATE OF TEXAS, COUNTY OF LAMAR--In Probate Court, March
    Term, A.D. 1848-Reuben W. REYNOLDS, and Henry TRIMBLE, ad-
    ministrators of the Estate of Andrew B. SMITH, deceased,
    filed their petition for final settlement; of said estate
    at the July Term of the Honorable Probate court 1848. The
    heirs, creditors and all persons interested are hereby not-
    ified to be and personally appear, on the last Monday of
    July 1848, at the court house in the Town of Paris, then and
    there to show cause if any they ran, why they shall not have
    their accounts allowed, and this succession closed. Given
    under my hand and the seal of said court, at Paris this 13th
    June A. D. 1848. John R. CRADDOCK, Cl'k C.C. & Ex. off.
    C. P. C. Paris, June 13, 1848."
--------------------------------

"PUBLIC MEETING--A meeting of the citizens of Galveston,
    convened on Friday evening, 19th inst., at the Alphonse
    House, agreeably to a previous call.
    On motion, His Honor Mayor BATES, was called to the chair
    and J. W. JOCKUSH appointed Secretary."
"The chair explained the object of the meeting to be to
    apoint delegates to represent this County at the Convention
    to be held in Huntsville on the 4th of July next with a view
    to take suitable steps for improving the navigation of the
    Trinity river; whereupon on motion made the Chair appoint-
    ed the following committee to draft resolutions expressive
    of the sentiments of the meeting, to wit: H. STUART, M. M.
POTTER, J. C. KUHN, Col. WARREN, A. BALL, W. M. SARGEANT,
J. S. SYDNOR, M. B. MENARD, H. McLEOD and W. RICHARDSON."
[Due to length, all of this article has not been copied,HMS]

"We had hoped to hear of the arrival of the steam boat
Thos. F. McKINNEY at some of the upper landings, but see by
the NEWS, that she has been unable to stem the current at
some of the rapids, for want of power."

---------------------------------

"MARRIED--On Wednesday evening last, at the residence of
Jas. J. WARD, Esq, in Red River County, by John A. BAGBY,Esq.,
Mr. Henry SMITH to Mrs. Mary ____. WARD.
    We acknowledge the receipt of some of the wedding cake and
tender the usual congratutaions."

---------------------------------

Red River County, Tx. Marriage Records shows:
    21 June 1848--Henry SMITH to Mary D. WARD.

---------------------------------

"DIED--At his residence in Brenham, Washington County, on Tuesday, the 16th inst. Thos. JOHNSON, Esq., late Solicitor in
that district, leaving an interesting family, and a large
circle of friends to mourn his loss.
    The deceased was well known as formerly one of the District
Judges of the State, and subsequently the Editor of the
National Vindicator. He enjoyed the reputation of being a
very honest man. As District Attorney he was a vigorous
and powerful prossecutor.
Paris, Lamar County, on the 20th inst. Capt. Geo. W. JEWELL."

---------------------------------

ADVERTISEMENT: Masonic Dinner at Star Hotel    H. GOODING
    Clarksville, June 24 th 1848.

---------------------------------

ADVERTISEMENT: MOSES GREENWOOD & CO, Commission & Forwarding
    Merchants, 5 Foucher St., New Orleans.
    M. GREENWOOD; J. R. REALD; T. E. ADAMS.

---------------------------------

ADVERTISEMENT: WATCHES AND JEWELRY--The undersigned respect-
    fully informs the citizens of Clarksville, and the surround-
    ing country, that he has lately opened at his store upon
    the public square.    Thos STEVENSON,    June 24th 1848.

---------------------------------

ADVERTISEMENT: BLACKSMITHING--At the old Stand near the
    square.    BAGBY & CO.

---------------------------------

ADVERTISEMENT: PAINTING--S. H. CLARK, at DURFEE's Cabinet
    Ware Room       Clarksville, June 24th 1848.

---------------------------------

ADVERTISEMENT: HOUSE SIGN & CARRIAGE PAINTING, Shop at
    SHANALEAN's Cabinet Shop    L. W. YEAGER, Clarksville,
    June 24th 1848.

---------------------------------

ADVERTISEMENT: Cabinet Warehouse--Furniture--Jas.B. SHANAHAN
    Clarksville, June 24th 1848.

---------------------------------

ADVERTISEMENT: John P. DALE, Tailor, has resumed business
    at his old shop, South West corner of the Public Square,
    and will do work in his line in the latest style.
    Clarksville, June 24th 1848.

---------------------------------

ADVERTISEMENT: "Saddlery, Thos. R. Wilson"
  Clarksville, June 24th 1848.
---------------------------------

ADVERTISEMENT: "Wm. POWERS, Hatter, Red River District at his
  shop in Clarksville."   Clarksville, June 24th 1848.
---------------------------------

"ESTATE OF ROBERT WHITAKER--The undersigned having been qualified at the May term 1848, of the Honorable Probate Court
  of Red River County, as Executor with the will annexed of
  the estate of Robert WHITAKER deceased, late of said county
  hereby notifies all persons indebted to said estate to make
  immediate payment, and all persons having claims upon it, be
  present them to him, duly authenticated, within the time prescribed by law, or they will be barred." JAS. GILLIAM
  Red River County,  June 24, 1848
---------------------------------

STATE OF TEXAS, COUNTY OF LAMAR, PRECINCT No. 10,   In Justice
  Court, Brad. C. FOWLER, Presiding J.P. 9th June, A.D. 1848.
  John R. CRADDOCK, Plff. vs. James M. MORPHIS, Deff.:   To the
  Sheriff of Lamar County and State of Texas Greeting:   Whereas
  it appears from the return of the attachment, that James M.
  MORPHIS defendant in the above named cause, is not to be
  found in the county aforesaid, and whereas John R. CRADDOCK
  Plaintiff aforesaid has made oath in due form of law, that
  James M. MORPHIS defendant aforesaid as a transient person,
  so that the ordinary process of the law, cannot be served
  upon him.
  These are therefore to command you to summon said defendant James M. MORPHIS by publication, to appear before me,
  at my office in the town of Paris, on the third Saturday in
  July next, the same being the 15th--then and there, to answer
  John R. CRADDOCK plaintiff aforesaid in action of settlement,
  sued out for the sum of twenty-six dollars, and seventy-six
  cents, and in this behalf defend.
  Given under my hand, and official signature, at Paris, the
  9th day of June, A.D. 1848.    Brad. C. FOWLER, J.P.
  TO JAMES M. MORPHIS:
  You are hereby commanded to appear according to the above notice, to answer the complaint of John R. CRADDOCK,Plaintiff
  in the above named action.
  June 19th A.D. 1848.    CYRUS K. HOLMAN,Sheriff Lamar County
---------------------------------

"STATE OF TEXAS, COUNTY OF LAMAR, IN PROBATE COURT May Term 1848"
  Jas. S. GILLET administrator, and Frances CRABTREE administratrix of the Estate of Solomon CRABTREE deceased, filed their
  petition praying the sale of a negro boy, Joe, belonging to
  the Estate of said decedent.  This is therefore to notify the
  unknown heirs, creditors etc., to be and personally appear at
  the next term of the Honorable Probate court to be held at the
  court house in the Town of Paris on the last Monday of July 1848,
  then and there to show cause if any they can why the prayer of
  the petitions shall not be granted.
  Given under my hand and the seal of Court at Paris this
  22nd June 1848.   John R. CRADDOCK,Ctk. C.C. & Ex. Off. Ctk.P.C.
---------------------------------

"BACON--Sides for sale at ten cents per pound at retail, at the
Bakery, by OLIVER INGLES." Clarksville, June 24th, 1848.

---------------------------------

"THE POLAR EXPEDITION--Sir John RICHARDSON has reached Buffalo,
where he is to be joined by Dr. RAY and about twenty men from
Montreal, who together will set out for Hudson's Bay, via
Detroit and the sault St. Marie. In the prosecution of the
voyage of exploration, in search of Sir John FRANKLIN's ex-
ploring expedition. Sir John FRANKLIN set out on this last
voyage of discovery, in the year 1844."

---------------------------------

"DEATH OF AN EDITOR--Richard H. TOLER, the able and accomplished
Editor of the Richmond Whig and Enquirer, died on the 5th inst.
aged 49 years. He was one of the ablest and most talented
conductors of the press, in the Union."

---------------------------------------------------------------
THE NORTHERN STANDARD--July 1, 1848--CLARKSVILLE,RED RIVER COUNTY
Vol. 6, No. 10

---------------------------------

"MEETING AT BUFFALO--At a meeting, held by a numerous and respectable portion of the citizens of Henderson County at Buffalo, on
Tuesday, May 16th, for the purpose of devising means for opening
and improving the navigation of Trinity River, the following
preceedings were had:
    On motion of Dr. GRAHAM, Hon. BENNET, H. MARTIN was unanimously
called to the chair, and George L. STORER appointed Secretary
of the meeting. [The following was abstracted by Helen due to
length of the above article:]"Messrs. T.J. JENNINGS, J.H.REAGAN
and Mr. BLAKE, of Leon County, all addressed the meeting"
"A committee of twenty be appointed, to draft resolutions: E.
MALLARD, Dr. GRAHAM, Judge GREY, Thos. BOX, S.Q. GIBBS,B.GOOCH,
Hon. John DAMRON, Maj. J.D. SCOTT, J. WALKER, D. BAUGH,
L. GODDARD, Thos. REAVES, Joseph BARTLETT, George WHALY,
J. A. ROBINSON, John H. REAGAN,Esq., James DAVENPORT, A.M. MOORE,
and L.B. SANDERS." "Resolved: That we appoint Col.S.O.GIBBS,
Dr. H. M. ALLEN, Hon. John H. REAGAN, Judge GREY, J. E. CHISM,
E. MALLARD, Dr. S. G. PARSONS, B. GOOCH (and by motion Hon.
Bennet H. MARTIN was added) as delegates to represent Henderson
County in the convention which is to be held at Huntsville,
Walker County on the fourth day of July next." "On motion the
meeting adjourned, sine die." "B.H. MARTIN, Chairman, G.L.STORER,
Secretary."

---------------------------------

"The portion of the Comanche tribe under the chief Santa ANNA,
came into town last Wednesday. The old Chief professed much
friendship. He alledged as the reason for coming into the
settlements, that the buffalo had left their ranges farther
north and had come down in this direction, and that it was necessary for them to follow the herds in order to their subsistence.
The old Chief and party visited the Governor, with whom a talk
was had, They were required to remove immediately beyond the
designated line, and they took the hint and sloped yesterday
morning, Capt. CONNER's company is following them to watch
their movements." Austin Democrat

EARLY TEXAS NEWS

"From the St. Louis Reveill, May 18, INDIAN WAR IN OREGON--
Seventy days later from Walla Walla.  Massacre of the Presbyterian Mission--Jos. L. MEEK, Esq.,the celebrated Oregon
guide, arrived here yesterday, en route for Washington City,
with despatches for the United States-Bovernment.  He informs
us that himself and a party of seven men, headded by Lt.
BOWMAN, left Walla Walla, on the 5th of March, and travelled
over nineteen hundred miles with the same animals in sixty
days--a part of the way, in crossing the mountains, the snow
was four feet deep.  He is a special messenger from the Government of Oregon to the President of the United States asking
for immediate assistance from this Government, to defend the
citizens of that territory from the depredations of the Indians.
Four of the most powerful tribes have alread commenced a horrid
and bloody war.

Mr. MEEK represents the state of affairs in Oregon as most
alarming and distressing.  Four battles had already been fought,
in all of which except one--and attack upon an advance guard
which fell back upon the main body--the whites maintained
their ground.--The last and most desperate battle previous to
his departure, was fought in February, on Big Plains, near
Walla Walla.  Five hundred whites, commanded by Col.GILLIAM,
maintained their position manfully against two thousand or
more Indians warriors, of four tribes, for seven hours--till
night--when the Indian gave back a little, and both parties
camped on the field.  During the night the Indians retreated.
No whites were killed but a great number wounded.

A horrid massacre was perpetrated on the 20th of November
last, by the Cayuso Indians at the Presbyterian Mission, at
Wailalpu, in Wall Walla valley.  Dr. WHITMAN and nine others
were killed, and sixty or seventy persons, men, women and
children, were taken prisoners.  By the couragesous and energe-
tic efforts of Peter SKEEN OGDEN, Esq., Chief Factor of the
Hudson Bay Company, at Fort Vancouver, the surviving prisoners
were ransomed, and restored to their friends.

The following is an abstraction from a letter written to
Gov. ABERNATHY, announcing the massacre of Dr. WHITMAN;  Our
lamented friend, Dr. WHITMAN, his aimiable and accomplished
lady, with nine other persons, have fallen victims to the
fury of these remorseless savages, who appear to have been
instigated to this appalling crime by a horrible suspicion
which had taken possession of their superstitions minds, in
consequence of the number of deaths from dysentery and measles,
that Dr. WHITMAN was silently working the destruction of their
tribe by administering poisonous drugs under the semblance of
salutary medicines.

With a goodness of heart and benevolence truly his own, Dr.
WHITMAN had been labor-incessantly since the appearance of the
measles and dysentory among his Indian converts to relieve
their suffering, and such has been the reward of his generous
labors."
---------------------------------

"ATROCITIES IN YUCATAN--The Washington Union gives the following
sketch of some of the atrocities perpetrated in Yucatan.  If
true it is, indeed, horrible!  It is furnished by Don Justo SIERRA,
continued....

the Commissioner of Yucatan, now in Washington; a gentleman, says the Union, of education, and a nephew of a distinguished Mexican, who was formerly driven from his country on account of his liberal principles, took refuge in Texas, whose destiny he shared, and whose revolution he promoted.

Horrible Atricities Committed by the savages in Yucatan--During the siege of Valladolid, the savage Indians proposed that commissioners should be sent out to them to treat for peace. The parish priest of that city, a young occlesiastic of unblemished conduct and well known piety, (Dr. Manuel Sierra de O'RIELLY, a brother of Don Justo SIERRA, the present Commissioner of Yucatan, at Washington,) was nominated for that purpose, together with the chief of police, and two other respectable citizens. Dr. SIERRA had acquired, by his charity and benevolence a wide-spread popularity with the Indians of the city and its vicinity and the happiest result were anticipated from the mission.--Two days were passed in pacific conference with the savages, after which they committed the unheard of brutality of assassinating him and his colleagues in the church. Their lives were feloniously taken in reward for their (perhaps) indiscreet confidence in the integrity and honor of a race, who alas are too well known for their perfidy.
[The following was abstracted by Helen:] "Guaitna who had been fifty-three years among the Indians--during the whole of which period his life had been among the Indians--during the whole of which period his life had been devoted to their service--was forced from his bed, where he was ill with a disease and taken to the church and hung from the bell rope of the church. More 30,000 men, women and children have been assignated in the frontier settlements and villages by the savages."

---------------------------------

"LOOK OUT FOR A KIDNAPPER--There has been a man lurking about this vicinity for some time past, endeavouring to steal negros--His object no doubt is to take them to Mississippi and sell them, as he is connected with a man lately from Vicksburg. The villian is about 30 years of age, stout and healthy, dark red complextion, dark hair and eyes, about 5 feet 11 inches high, broad, square and rather stoop-shouldered.

The above notice was handed us by a respectable citizen whose negroes have been tampered with by this scoundral."
Arkansas Democrat.

---------------------------------

"PRUSSIAN RYE--TEXAS GROWTH--Judge OCHILTREE has furnished us with, several green heads of Prussian Rye from the plantation of William A. LAWRENCE at mound prairie Anderson County. These heads are very much larger, than any we ever remember to have seen, and we are told that the stalks are now six feet high. It is said that the seed was introduced into Alabama by the Hon. Dixon H. LEWIS, three years ago. Its growth, in all places where it has been tried is said to be superior to all other species of rye, and its yield without a parallel. Our planters will do well to give it a trial. Star State Patriot."

---------------------------------

"RESOURCES OF TEXAS--IRON ORE--Last week Mr. W. M. FREEMAN of
Cass County presented to us a specimen of Texas Iron, separate
from the ore by Mr. NASH, near the south-west corner of Cass
County, and not more than 30 miles from this place."
[HMS did not copy all of article] Star State Patriot.

---------------------------------

"The following is a list of the Ranging Companies, their stations,
and the Captains in command on the frontier of Texas:

    Capt. FITZHUGH's Company on the East Fork of Trinity, with
a detachment 30 miles above, near Red River.
    Capt. JOHNSON's Company, west fork of Trinity, detachment
30 miles below on Chambers' Creek.
    Capt. CONNER's Company on the Navasoto, between the Brazos and
      Trinity.
    Capt. ROSS, Ft. Waco Village, detachment on hte Leon, 30 miles
      distant.
    Capt. McCULLOCH, Hannlton's Valley, 60 miles north of Austin.
    Capt. HIGHSMITH's Company, on a fork of the Sandy, 18 miles
      frmo Fredericksburgh and near the (Enchanted Rock.)
    Capt. CRUMP on the Medina, 20 miles south of San Antonio.
    Capt. GILLET, on Areyo Saco, 60 miles south-west of San Antonio.
    Capt. VEATCH, on the Rio Grande, above the Pecsidio Crossing.
    Capt. LAMAR, at Laredo, on the Rio Grande.
    Capt. SUTTON, near San Patricio, on the Nueces, detachment of
      Corpus Christi."

---------------------------------

ADVERTISEMENT:  "For President, Lewis CASS, of Michigan.  For
    Vice President, Wm. O. BUTLER of Kentucky.  Democratic Electors.
    For the State, Jas . B. MILLER, T.G. BROOCKS.  For the Eastern
    District, Wm. C. YOUNG.  For the Western District-M.A. DOOLEY."

---------------------------------

ADVERTISEMENT:  "For Chief Justice-Hugh F. YOUNG requested his
    withdrawal from the canvass for Sheriff and is a candidate for
    Chief Justice of the County Court of Red River County."
    "For Assessor--John M. BIVINS as a candidate for Assessor and
      Collector of Red River County."
    "For Sheriff--Lewis D. BARRY for sheriff of Red River County."
    "For Sheriff--Col. Robert S. HAMILTON as a candidate for Sheriff
      of Red River County."

---------------------------------

"SUCCESSION OF N. J. STAATS--Whereas the undersigned was duly
    appointed by the Hon. Probate Court for Red River County, at
    the May term 1848, administrator of the estate of Nelson J.
    STAATS deceased, late of said county, this is therefore to
    give notice to all persons indebted to said estate to make im-
    mediate payment, and all those having claims upon it to present
    them to me duly autheaticated, within the time presecribed by
    law, or they will be forever barred.    BENJ. BOOTH, Adm'r.
    Clarksville    July 1, 1848.

---------------------------------

"NOTICE--I hereby forewarn all persons from trading for four
    notes, executed by the undersigned, to one Charles A. WARFIELD,
    two for the sum of three hundred dollars each, one due on the
    25th day of December A.D. 1849 and the other due the 25th day
    of December 1850, and one for two hundred dollars due the 25th
    day of Dec. 1851--and one for fifty dollars, due the 25th day
    continued...

of December 1848 all dated in the month of January A.D. 1848
as the consideration for which said notes was given, has failed,
and I am determined not to pay the same unless compelled by law."
SARAH HAMILTON      Paris 12th June 1848

--------------------------------

"APPOINTMENTS OF NOTARIES PUBLIC FOR THE COUNTY OF RED RIVER--
   Confirmed by the Senate at the 2d acession of the Legislature
   of the State of Texas, Burrell P. SMITH, Martia FULBRIGHT,
   George S. YOUNG, Isaiah W. WELLS.

   I, John STILES, Chief Justice of the county of Red River  do
hereby certify that I have been legally notify by W.D. MILLER
Secretary of State for the State of Texas of the above appoint-
ments and that the same were confirmed by the Senate of the
State of Texas at its session of 1847 and 48.
   Witness my official seal and signature this 26th day June
A.D. 1848." John STILES   Chief Justice of Red River County.

--------------------------------

"THE STATE OF TEXAS, COUNTY OF TITUS--Taken up by Lindsey BURK,
   and estrayed before William BURK, a justice of the peace for
   Titus County, Beat No. 2, a dark bay mare 14½ hands high, supposed to be nine or ten years old, branded on the left hip with
   the letters C.S. and on the left shoulder with letters J.V., a
   scar on her back, a white spot a little in front of it, right
   hind foot partly white, and star on her forehead, appraised to
   fifty five dollars by J.M. CARTWRIGHT, John HUMPHREYS.
Sworn to and subscribed before me this 20th day of April A.D.
1848.    William BURK, J.P.
Filed for Record, on the 9th day of May 1848.  J.COOK, Clk'k.
A true copy from the records of my office,this the 18th day
of May 1848."  J.COOK, Cl'k. C.C.T.C.T.

--------------------------------

"THE STATE OF TEXAS, COUNTY OF TITUS--Taken up by Samuel McCROREY,
   and posted before J.W. DABBS, an acting Justice of the Peace,
   in precinct No.3 of the county aforesaid on the 27th day of
   April 1848, one sorrel horse supposed to be twelve years old,
   and branded on the left shoulder with J.S. appraised to
   thirty dollars by Rufus GODWIN  Daniel McCALL.
Sworn to and subscribed before me this 27th day of April 1848.
J.W. DABBS, J.P.      Filed for Record, April 27th 1848.
J. COOK, Clk. C.C.T.C.T."

---------------------------------------------------------------

THE NORTHERN STANDARD--SATUARDAY, JULY 8, 1848-CLARKSVILLE,
RED RIVER COUNTY--Vol. 6, No. 11

--------------------------------

"From the Cirilian of the 4th ult-LATE FROM THE RIO GRANDE--The
   schr. STAR, Capt. PARKER, arrived yesterday from Brazos San-
   tiago, having left that port the day previous.
   The Matamoros Flag of Sunday expresses the belief, universal
there, that treaty has been ratified.  The same paper says-The
robber chief who planned the murder of the ROGERS family, more
than two years ago on the Colorado, was arrested some days ageo
at Reynosa, and is now confined in the Guard House at this
place, Mr. William ROGERS, of Corpus Christi, who had his throat
cut at the time, but who survived and made his escape, was sent
for, and visited the Guard House.  He unhesitatingly pointed
out the Mexican, and pointed him to the scar on his throat.

EARLY TEXAS NEWS

"NOTICE-The undersigned having located permanently in this
    place, respectfully tenders his professional services to the
    citizens of Clarksville and vicinity."  I. P. MORGAN, M.D.
    Clarksville, July 9th, 1848
------------------------------------

"ESTATE OF ISAAC BATEMAN--Whereas the undersigned was appointed
    by the Honorable Probate Court of Red River County, at the
    May term 1848, administrator upon the estate of Isaac BATEMAN,
    deceased, late of said county, this is therefore to notify all
    persons indebted to said estate to make immediate payments
    and all those having claims upon it present them to the under-
    signed duly authenticated according to law.  Jonathan BATEMAN."
    Clarksville July 4th 1848.
------------------------------------

"A LIST OF LETTERS--Remaining in the Post Office, at Clarksville,
which if not taken out by the last day of September next, will be
sent to the Post Office Department as dead letters."

| | | |
|---|---|---|
| A. | DONLEY, S. P. | LACEY, Robert J. |
| ALDRIDGE, Moses D. | DEAN, Levi | LEVINE, Nicholas |
| B. | DEAN, Jesse | LABEY, William |
| BELL, William | DANIEL, Aline | LEE, William |
| BRYAN, John A. | DARNELL, Foster S. | M. |
| BLANTON, W. C. | DALE, Thomas | MONTGOMERY,Thos.B. |
| BAKER, Hiram 2 | DURIN, Jesse | McCARLY, Robert |
| BAUGESS, Franklin | E. | McFARLAND, James |
| BURGHEN, Younger | ENNIS, N. F. | MILLER, A.G. |
| BUNYAN, Richard B. 2 | ELLIS, N.D. | McNIEL, Jesse |
| BREKEAD, William | EPPERSON, B.H. Hon. | MAREA, John |
| BATES, Elizabeth Mrs. | ENGLISH, Campbell | McKULTER, William |
| BAIN, John | EDMONSON, Samuel | MURRIN, Jehu |
| BLACKBURN, James | F. | MARTIN, William |
| BLACKWELL, Wiley | FUNDERBURG, Wm. B.2 | MATHIS, W.R. |
| BURDEN, Nathaniel | FLEMING, B.M.C. | MOTLATT, William |
| BREEDING, C.C. | G. | McCLEASH, J. |
| BATEMAN, Evan | GREGG, Thomas | McLAURIN,James |
| BARNARD, Calvin. | GREEN, Rolin | McCARTNEY,B.H. 2 |
| C. | GLASS, J.A. | McCARTY,H.S. 2 |
| CALHOUN, Harriett Miss 2 | GRANT, Mr. | MORRIS, James |
| CHURCHHILL, John | GILBREATH, James G. | MAIN, John |
| CHATFIELD, Richard | H. H | N. |
| CHATFIELD, Andrew | HOLBROOK & ROMAN | NORVILLE,S.G.,Esq. |
| CRIER, Elijah | HOGAN, Woodson 2 | O. |
| CLANTON, Martha Miss | HUSBANDS & BUCHANAN | O.H.WELL John |
| COCKE, Benjamin F. | HOUSTON, Robert | P. |
| CALDWELL, Samuel | HARLAND, N.R. | PHILIPS, James |
| CHISM, V. Wm. | I. | PERINS, Jesse |
| CLEMMONS, E.A. Rev. | INGRAM, M. & V. Messrs | PHILIPS,William |
| COLLINS, William | J. | POPE,James |
| CORNELIUS Mart D. | JOHNSON, Amanda Mrs. | PATRICK,Lockey Jane |
| CLAPP, William | JENKINS, Charles | PARKS, Elizabeth |
| CAMPBELL, Ann G. Mrs. | JONES, Dennis | PUTMAN,B.B. |
| CAMPBELL, Francis A. 2 | JOHNSON, Peter B. | PERKINSON, Benjamin |
| CORLEY, Samuel Rev. 3 | K. | PEARSON, James D. 2 |
| D. | KELLEY, Susanna Mrs. | PRICE, Elizabeth 2 |
| DANTTON, John | KING, Eliza Ann Miss | POST, Master 4 |
| DANAGHO, Roberts B. | L. | R. |
| DUTY, ?Henry? | LAWSON, I.D. | ROLIN,Jane |

LIST OF LETTERS REMAINING IN POST OFFICE, Continued from Pg. 87

| | | |
|---|---|---|
| RENNINGTON, Mr. | SPARKS, A. | TURGGLE,John H. |
| ROBSON, John | SIMS, Samuel | TALTON, John F. |
| REEVES, J.H. | SMITH, M. | TATE, James M. |
| REDDING, A.J. Dr. 4 | SMITH, Thomas | TUCKER, Jeffersson |
| REDDING, W. T. | SMITH, James | THOMAS, F.M. 2 |
| RUSSELL, N.M. | SINGLETON, A.J. | TERRY, John |
| RUSSE, John | SKERRY, Richard | W. |
| RIPLEY, Ambrose | STEPHENS, A.F.,Mrs. | WILKINSON,Mary Mrs.2 |
| RICE, Elias | SUTTON, Thomas | WITHINGTON,Wm.T. |
| RICE, A. J. | SMITH, Burrell P. | WARD, William |
| RICE, William L. | STEARNS, Aaron | WHITSON,Esther Mrs. |
| ROGERS, John K. | SEALS, William | WARD, James |
| S. | SMITH, John S. | WEST,Edward 2 |
| SHERRY, Bernard | SHERIFF Red River Co. | WALKER,J.W. |
| SAMPSON, James Rev 2 | T. | WIMS,Wilkins |
| STEWART, Joseph S. | TRAVELSTEAD,E.C.,Lieut. | WELBORN,Chas. C. |
| SAWNS, Israel | TRAVELSTEAD,Anthony | |

John A. BAGBY,P.M.,Clarksville
July 1st 1848.

---

THE NORTHERN STANDARD--SATUARDAY-JULY 15, 1848-CLARKSVILLE,RED RIVER CO. Vol. 6, No. 12.

---

"DAVID DAVIS vs DAN'L. WELCH--ATTACHMENT, Whereas David DAVIS having applied to the undersigned William H. WYNN a Justice of the Peace in due form of law, for an attachment against the property of Daniel WELCH, and having obtained the same, and whereas it appears to me that the said Daniel WELCH, is not a resident of this State, and that his residence is unknown, Now the said Daniel WELCH, wherever he may reside, is hereby notified of the pendency of the said Attachment, that the same has been levied in the hands of Nathaniel VISE, and said Nathaniel VISE summoned as Garnishee, and if the said Daniel WELCH, does not appear before me at my office in the county of Lamar, in the town of Paris, in the State of Texas, on the first Saturday in August next, I will proceed to give judgment, on said attachment, in the same manner as if the said defendant were present--to answer and defend the same, and I will as the law directs award execution, order of saile, or other process, as the case may require. To the Sheriff of Lamar County Greeting: You are hereby commanded to summon the said Daniel WELCH, to appear and answer according to the above complaint, by publication in the Northern Standard, a newspaper published in the town of Clarksville in Red River County and State of Texas, for four weeks before the return day of this writ. Herein fail not, and make due return how you have executed writ. Give under my hand, and seal this June 8th A.D. 1848. Wm. H. WYNN, Justice of Peace.
To DANIEL WELCH: You are hereby commanded to appear according to the above notice. CYRUS K. HOLMAN, Sheriff Lamar County, Texas July 10th, 1848."

---

"STATE OF TEXAS, BOWIE COUNTY--We the undersigned being duly summoned to appraise the value of a certain Roan mare with white
hind feet and a spot in her forehead with some saddle marks,
10 or 12 years old, 13½ or 14 hands high, shown us by Presley
MAULDING, after being duly sworn, do appraise the same to
thirty dollars.  James P. ALFORD  William LUNN
Sworn to and subscribed before me this 20th June A.D. 1848.
                              John LOOP,J.P.
Filed and recorded June 20th 1848. J.C.McGONIGAL,Cl'k.C.C.T.C.
                              By Sam'l. McFARLAND,Deputy.
A true copy from Record July 1848."
------------------------------------

"DEMOCRATIC RATIFICATION MASS MEETING--At Clarksville on Saturday
the 22nd inst., FREE BARBECUE provided, sufficient for all who
will attend, and several speeches will be delivered: Clarks-
ville, July 15th, 1848.:(List of Names) Wm. C. YOUNG, Geo. H.
BAGBY, Geo. GORDON, A.J. TITUS, Jas. LATIMER, W.R. SCURRY,
J.W.P.McKENZIE, Granville LEWIS, A.R. DICKSON, R.SCURRY, R.M.
HOPKINS, J.C.HART; Chas. DeMORSE, A.J. RUSSELL, Jas. GILLIAM,
Isaiah KING, Shelby CRAWFORD, E.M. SMITH, Edward WEST, A.H.
LATIMER, John WARE, John A. BAGBY, B. P. SMITH, P. DUTY, Wm.
CRITTENDEN, Jesse ADAMS, Nelson DOAK."
------------------------------------------------------------------

THE NORTHERN STANDARD-SATURDAY, JULY 22, 1848-CLARKSVILLE,RED RIVER CO
Vol. 2, No. 13
-------------------------------------------

"MEMORIALS TO CONGRESS--To the Honorable the Senate and House of
Representatives of the United States of America in Congress
Assembly: Gentlemen:  It is made my duty to forward to your
honorable body the memorial passed by the legislature of Oregon,
and the papers containing the documents refered to in the memorial; all of which is enclosed herewith.  I have the honor to
remain, gentlemen, your obedient servant."
                              Geo. ABERNETHY, Governor of
                              Oregon Territory.
-------------------------------------------

"IRELAND--The peace of Ireland continues undisturbed.  The public
attention seemed absorbed in the prosecutions which were going
on against Mr. W. S. O'BRIEN, Mr. MEAGHER and Mr. MITCHELL.--
THE STATE TRAILS--ARREST AND COMMITTAL OF MITCHELL TO NEWGATE,
FOR TREASON--Since Saturday last, strange and startling news
has been received from Ireland.  On the evening of that day
Mr. MITCHELL was arrested and sent to Newgate, on a charge of
treason, said to be contained in his paper, the United Irish-
man of May 6th and 13th."
-------------------------------------------

"MARRIED--In Lamar on the 11st inst. by the Rev.__.C. PATTON,
A. B. KILINE to Miss T. C. RECORD.
Also on the 11st inst., by B. C. FOWLER, Esq. ROBERT McFARLAND
to Miss Martha GARDNER."
-------------------------------------------

"THE TROUBLES IN OREGON--[abstracted by Helen]  In regards to
   other story in this book about the Indian Massacres in Oregon.  The following is the list of the murdered persons:
   Dr. WHITMAN; Mrs. WHITMAN; Mr. ROGERS; Mr. HUFFMAN; Mr. SANDERS
   (schoolmaster); Mr. MARSH: John SAGER; Francis; Sager;(youths)
   Mr. KIMBALL: Mr. GELLEN; Mr. BEWLEY; Mr. YOUNG,Jr.; Mr. SALES;
   Mr. HALL (supposed to have been killed at John DAY's river)
   HALL made his escape and reached Vancouver, but was unwise
   enough to attempt to get to the (lower country) after which
   time he was not heard of, except that the Indians reported
   that he had been killed."

   "Another letter, dated Fort Nez Perces, Dec. 30, mentions
   that the intelligence had been received there by this Mr. HALL--
   so that it appears he escaped after all.  The writer (Mr.McBEAN)
   proceeds: (I immediately determined on sending my interpreter
   and one man to Dr. WHITMAN's to find out the truth, and, if
   possible, to rescue Mr. MANSAN's two sons, and any of the sur-
   vivors.  Before the interpreter had proceeded half way, the
   two boys were met on their way hither, escorted by NICHOLAS
   and FINALY.)."

   "The Oregon Spectator of January 27th contains a particular
   account of the efforts of Peter Sken OGDEN, Esq. chief factor
   of the Hudson Bay Company, to effect the restoration of Dr.
   SPALDING and the other persons who were taken prisoners by the
   Kayuse Indians, at the time of the murder of Dr. WHITMAN.  Mr
   OGDEN arrived at Walla-Walla on the 19th December, having accomplished the journey from Ft. Vancouver in ten days.  He had
   with him sixteen men.  Immediately on his arrival at Ft. Nez
   Perces' he despatched couriers to call a meeting of the Kayuse
   chiefs."
   "About the 29th or 30th of Jan. the following captives were
   rescued:  Joseph and Hanah SMITH and their five children: Mary
   SAUNDERS and five children; Harriet KIMBALL and her five children:
   Josiah and Margaret OSBORN and three children; Rebecca HAYS and
   daughter; Jos. STANFIELD, Sally Ann CANFIELD, and five children:
   Eliza. HALL and five children: Elam and Irene YOUNG and two
   children: Miss S. BEWLEY; Miss E. MARSH, six mission children:
   Mr. and Mrs. SPALDING and three children; Mr. HART, Jr.
   JACKSON, Mr. CANFIELD, Mr. CRAIG, and Miss JOHNSON-Total 61."
-----------------------------------------------------------------
THE NORTHERN STANDARD-SATURDAY--JULY 29, 1848-CLARKSVILLE,RED RIVER CO.
Vol. 6, No. 14
-------------------------------

"SINGULAR MISTAKE-The body of Major E. Kirby SMITH, who fell in
   one of the late battles, was to be sent home to the United
   States.  The coffin was waited for by a military funeral committee, and the desolate hearted wife of the deceased, at Syra-
   cuse.  But when the coffin arrived, and was opened for one last
   glance at the dead, it was found to be the wrong body."
-------------------------------

[abstracted by Helen] "FROM THE MISSISSIPPIAN OF June 30th--A
   WHIG'S PROTEST AGAINST THE NOMINATION OF GEN. TAYLOR BY THE
   WIG NATIONAL CONVENTION"  This letter was written by Mayfield
   JOHNSON, of Hinda County, Miss.
-------------------------------

"STATE OF TEXAS--Bowie County--We the undersigned being duly
    summoned to appraise the value of a certain Roan mare with
    white hind feet and a spot in her forehead with some saddle
    marks, 10 or 12 yrs. old, 13½ or 14 hands high, shown us by
    Presley MAULDING, after being duly sworn, do appraise the same
    to thirty dollars.    James P. ALFORD    William LUNN
    Sworn to and subscribed before me this 20th June A.D. 1848
    John LOOP, J. P.       Filed and recorded June 20th 1848-J.
    C. McGONIGAL, Clk. C.C.C.C. by Sam'l. McFARLAND, Deputy.
    A true copy from record July 1848."
---------------------------------

[abstracted by Helen due to length]  "EXODUS OF MR. GREELY--The
    Phildadelphia Bulletin give humorous account of the hasty de-
    parture of the editor of the Tribune from Philadelphia, after
    the nomination of Gen. TAYLOR.(Mr. Horace GREELY)."
----------------------------------------------------------------

THE NORTHERN STANDARD-SATURDAY--AUGUST 5, 1848-CLARKSVILLE, TEXAS
RED RIVER COUNTY--Vol. 6, No. 15.
---------------------------------

"MARRIED-On Thursday evening last, by the Rev. Saml. CORLEY,
    Mr. J.H.B. DINWIDDIE to Miss Sarah Jane GILLIAM, daughter of
    James GILLIAM, Esq., all of this vicinity.
    We acknowledge the cake, and tender our good wishes to the
    young people."
---------------------------------

"OBITUARY-Died at Holly Springs, Miss. on the 4th of July,
    Miss Sarah E. DARNALL, aged 28 years.

    The deceased lady, was for some years a resident of Clarksvil-
le, and had lately gone to Mississippi, in the hope that change
of climate, and travelling would loosed the iron grasp of a
mortal disease, which for years had laid the weight of its
heavy hand upon her.  But vain the expectation.  The destroyer
but dallied with his victim, allowing the sunshine of hope
occasionally to light up the despondency of disease.

    Miss DARNALL will long be remembered in this community, by
many friends whom free social intercourse had endeared her to,
and who sympathize sincerely in the sorrow which her death
brings upon the family circle here.

    The deceased however, was not one of those to whom death
comes as a grim destroyer, demanding a terrified victim; but
in the fullness of a faith in the Redeemer which was sincere
and long cherished, passed away to the world of spirits,
cheerful, hopeful, undoubting.  To her sinking frame and glazing
eye, with a mind unweakened to the last, the world of the future
was a round of pleasure, confidently anticipated, when in the
beneficence of her Saviour's love, she should live again, a
life free of care, and aching pains, blessed beyond the imagin-
ings of this world.  The last rites of the Church were administered to her before her departure and she passed on to the
other life, prepared."
---------------------------------

"$25 REWARD-Ranaway from the subscriber, some time in May last,
    my negro man named KIT, 35 years of age, 5 feet 8 or 9 inches
    high, slim, round shouldered, crooked feet, and small scar on
    Continued....            92.

Continued--$25 REWARD......
his nose, looks like a piece had been bit off, slow spoken, and
tolerably fine, rather cracked in his voice.

I will pay the above reward for his apprehension, and delivery
to me, at my residence in Bowie county near the Spanish Bluffs,
or $15 if confined in any jail, so that I get him again.
Hiram A. RUNNELS"                  July 19th, 1848.
------------------------------------

[abstracted by Helen due to length of article]
"IRELAND-SENTENCE OF MITCHEL--At the sitting of the court on Saturday, May 27 the prisoner was sentenced to fourteen years
transportation.  After Baaron LEFROY had delivered judgment,
Mr. MITCHEL, who heard his sentence quite unmoved, asked leave
to address the court."

"A crowd of barristers and gentlemen crowded round the dock,
to shake hands with Mr. MITCHEL.  A deafening cheer then re-
sounded through the court.  The police interfered to preserve
order, and prevent the dock from striving to lay a hand on Mr.
MITCHAEL, as he was being taken from his place by the jailors.
A scuffle ensued--the judges fled from the bench, to which
they returned in about two minutes, during which the heat of
the excitement lasted.  Messrs. O'GORMAN, MEAGHER, and DOHENY
were handded up by the police.  An officer of the line, who
was near the constables, offered his arm to Mr. MEAGHER, who
declined it, saying he would not take the arm of any man
wearing the British uniform."  "At about 4 o'clock on the
same day Mr. MITCHEL was removed in heavy irons, and placed
on board her Majesty's steamship Sheerwater, on his way to
Spike Island, Cork, where he arrived on Saturday, the 28th ult."
"An extraordinary edition of the Cork paper published on last
Sunday evening gives the following:  The vessel that brought
John MITCHEL to Spike arrived in the harbor at an early hour
to-day and before it dropped its anchor, the marty ____was landed
on the island, and handed over to the custody of the Governor."
    [see page 89]
--------------------------------------------------------------------
THE NORTHERN STANDARD-SATURDAY-AUGUST 12, 1848, CLARKSVILLE,
RED RIVER COUNTY--Vol. 6, No. 16.
------------------------------------

"MARTINIQUE--The brig Columbus, Capt. WEBSTER, arrived at New
York on the 18th from St. Pierre, Martinique, bringing news
to the 2d inst.  The reports which reached this city by the
ship Europe about two weeks ago, of wholesale murders of the
whites in St. Pierre by the black population, are fully cor-
roborated.  The Columbus had on board J.B. DUCHAMP, E. DUCHAMP,
L. DUCHAMP, F. CRASSOUS, Thos. REGNARD, and T. DESCRETTO,
formerly all wealthy planters, with their families and servants, in all 35 persons, who narrowly escaped with their
lives in the night, leaving all their property behind, and
took refuge on board on the C., being kindly received by the
captain, The Journal of Commerce says:  Fears were entertained
that the blacks would attack the brig; but Capt. W. determined
to resist at all hazards, to save the lives of those who had
thus sought protection, for which they fell grateful to him."
"The inhabitants were fleeing wherever they could get refuge;
a number had gone to New Orleans."
------------------------------------

From N.O. Pivoyune--July 6th [HMS believes this to be the news-
    paper called New Orleans Pivoyune.]
"ARRIVAL OF JOHN MITCHEL AT BERMUDA" [abstracted by Helen]
    "We learn from an officer of the British steamer Great Western,
    which arrived off Ship Island on the 2d, inst., the following
    interesting particulars in relation to John MITCHEL, the
    Irish patriot."
---------------------------------
"ZANESVILLE, Ohio, June 19, 1848--To the Editor of the Aurora:
    Sir: In the Zanesville Courier of this date I noticed an
    article headed "The Broken Sword." Letter was written by
    William WILLIS."
---------------------------------
From the Vermont Patriot--"INTERESTING TO WOOL-GROWERS, Lowell,(Mass)
    Feb. 10, 1848. Mr. Dear Sir:" Letter signed Sam. LAWRENCE,
    Henry S. RANDALL, Esq., Cortland N. York."
---------------------------------
"MEETING OF THE DEMOCRACY OF HUNTSVILLE--The meeting is des-
    cribed by the Banner, as one of the most enthusiastic charac-
    ter, and was addressed by Gen. DAVIS of Liberty, the Hon.
    H. J. JEWETT of Leon, F.S. STOCKDALE, Esq. of Grimes county,
    and Messrs. W. A. LEIGH and A.P. WILEY of Huntsville."
---------------------------------------------------------------
THE NORTHERN STANDARD-SATURDAY-AUGUST 19, 1848-CLARKSVILLE, RED
RIVER COUNTY  Vol. 6, No. 17
---------------------------------
"CORRESPONDENCE OF THE UNION-St. James, July 2d, 1848
    My Dear Sir: Letter written by Robert Carter NICHOLAS."
    "Dr. E.D. RENTFRO and other composing the (Central Correspond-
    ing Committee) of the Whig Convention, Huntsville."
    "Gentlemen--Letter written by James WEBB."
    [all this article abstracted by Helen]
---------------------------------
"The murder of the Princess WINDISHGRATZ, the wife of the Austrain
    commander..She was killed by a Jager, prompted by private
    malice against the Prince. This man had taken a room in the
    house adjoining to that of the Prince, and remained, with a
    loaded rifle, watching his opportunity. Seeing some one moving
    behind a curtain in the Princess's apartments, and believing it
    to be the Prince, he fired and the unfortunate Princess fell
    weltering in her blood.

    This unhappy lady was the daughter of Field Marchal Prince
    SHWARZENBERG, and her mother is the lady who perished in the
    flames, while endeavoring to save her child, at the confla-
    gration of the Festive Hall, erected as a ballroom to celebrate
    the marriages of NAPOLEON with Maria Louisa of Austria an
    occurence which at the time caused immense sensation.

    This tragedy occurred on the 12th June.--Some soldiers of
    the garrison rushed into the house from which the shot had been
    fired by which the Princess fell, and killed several persons.
    In the meantime, the Czechs collected in large numbers around
    the residence of the Prince, and sang insulting songs, accom-
    pained by hooting and threats. The Prince, with the firmness
    Continued....

94.

Continued..Murder of Princess WINDISHGRATZ...
  and dignity of an old Roman, left the body of his murdered wife,
  and facing the crowd, thus addressed them:  Gentlemen--If it
  is your desire to insult me, because I am of noble birth, go
  to my palace and do there as you may think fit.  I will even
  give you a guard, that you may not be disturbed in your
  amusement.  But if you act thus because I am commander of
  Prague, and purpose making a demonstration in front of this
  building, I tell you candidly that I shall prevent such a step
  with every means at my command.  My wife now lies a lifeless
  corpse above stairs, yet I address you in words of kindness.
  Gentlemen, do not drive me to severe measures."  A fight followed between the Czechs, the Prince's grenadiers.  In the midst
  of all of the battle that day the Prince suffered another misfortune, His son received a mortal wound during the distur-
  bances, from which he afterwards died." (All of this took
  place on 12th of June.)
------------------------------------

"The volunteers on the Texas frontier are to be discharges, and
  their places supplied by regulars"
"of the emigrants who arrived in Canada during the year 1847,
  it is estimated that at least six-sevenths were Irish."
----------------------------------------------------------------

THE NORTHERN STANDARD-SATURDAY-AUGUST 26, 1848-CLARKSVILLE,
RED RIVER COUNTY  Vol. 6, No. 18.
------------------------------------

"FROM THE LOUISVILLE DEMOCRAT--JOHN J. CRITTENDEN AGAINST MR.CLAY--
  A STAB IN THE DARK--THE TRUTH WILL OUT--A letter from Mr.
  ANDERSON--a young lawyer of Cincinnati--to Mr. SNELSON, formerly
  of Jessamine County, Ky., is now in Washington."[abstracted HMS.]
------------------------------------

"We learn from H. RANDOLPH, Esq., who has just arrived in this
  city, that the Commissioners appointed to select a site for
  the Penitentiary, have finally made choice of Huntsville,
  Walker County, for that purpose.  We are inclined to the opinion that their decision will meet with general approbation.
  They came to this determination about a week ago--Galveston
  News. [HMS Note:  take note "arrived in this city, means Galveston.]
------------------------------------

"STOP THE MURDERER--$500 REWARD--I will pay the sum of five hund-
  red dollars for the apprehension and delivery to the Sheriff of
  Henderson County, Texas, of the body of Wm. F.C. BUTLER.
    Said BUTLER, on the 31st day of July, 1848, murdered, in the
  town of Buffalo, without cause or provication (as the evidence
  shows) my brother, John P. MOORE.  DESCRIPTION OF THE MURDERED--
  Said BUTLER is almost five feet ten inches high, with blue
  eyes and rather light or auburn hair, about 33 or 34 years of
  age, disabled in the right hand by the cut of a knife, which
  has caused some of his fingers to stand straight.  He is of
  thin visage, n--- Ronna, and rather sharp.  He sings and talks
  Indian, well.  Weighs about 15 or 16 pounds".
A. M. MOORE        Buffalo, August 8th 1848.
------------------------------------

EARLY TEXAS NEWS

"ATTENTION BATTALION--The Commissoned officers of the First
    Regiment, Second Division, First Brigade, Texas Miltia, are
    hereby ordered to convene at the town of Clarksville on the
    first Saturday, the first day of September next, for the pur-
    pose of holding a Regimental Court Martial, agreeable to pre-
    vious notice, given on the mustar ground on the 4th day of
    July last.  By order of Hugh F. YOUNG, Col. Commanding
    Edw'd. HUNTER, Assistant."   Clarksville, August 11th 1848.
    ------------------------------------

"LIBEL ON GEN. CASS-REFUTED"  A letter from Gen. Jefferson DAVIS,
    senator from Mississippi to Mr. Wm. C.H. WADDELL of New York,
    dated 29 June 1848.
    -----------------------------------------------------------------
THE NORTHERN STANDARD-SATURDAY-SEPTEMBER 2, 1848-CLARKSVILLE,
RED RIVER COUNTY  Vol. 6, No. 19
    ------------------------------------

"TEXAS IRON--Mr. NASH who is constructing a foundry in Cass
    County, has sent us a small specimen of the metal, obtained
    by melting in his brick kilo, ore gathered from the surface.

    We have shown the specimen to Mr. John W. WEST of our Town,
    who is a practical Blacksmith, and after making a nail of it,
    pronounces it, as good as he ever saw.--

    The nail made of it, was bent like a fishhook, around and
    back again, some twenty times, without breaking.  Some other
    persons of judgment in this particular, to whom the piece was
    submitted, pronounce it a superior article."
    ------------------------------------

"OBITUARY--Died at the residence of Mrs. Martha RUNNELS on the
    9th, inst., Mrs. Zerilda RUNNELS, consort of Mr. Edward RUNNELS
    of Bowie county.  The deceased was a daughter of the late
    Col. HEATHERLY of Lamar, a native of Madison County, Ky.

    She died at the early age of 19 years, ere she had known
    the cares or sorrows of life and with a bright prospect before
    her of an immortality of bliss.  She had left a little infant
    and an affectionate husband, besides numerous friends and re-
    latives to deplore her untimely death.  To them the unexpected
    stroke is severe indeed.  Not quite one year ago she stood
    at the altar a youthful and blooming bride, hope and joy beamed
    from her eye, and reasonably might she have looked forward to a
    long life of prosperity and happiness.  But alas! How uncer-
    tain, vain, and fleeting are all human hopes and calculations.
    Those bright eyes are dimned in death, that healthful rosy
    cheek is pale, and in the cold and narrow grave lies that
    youthful active form.

    The writer of this tribute knew her well and fully appre-
    ciated her gentless and amiability of character.
                            A Sympathising Friend."
    ------------------------------------

"MARRIED-At Dallas on Tuesday August 15th by William HEARD, Esq.
    Mr. U. MATTHIESSEN of Paris, Texas, to Miss Josephine, a daugh-
    ter of J. B. McDERMOTT, of Dallas County, Texas."
    ------------------------------------

"$50 REWARD--Runaway from the subscriber, at his farm, in the
North west corner of Lamar county, on the 13th of August a
negro Boy, name GREEN about 20 years of age, about 5 ft.
high, weighs about 150 lbs. or 160 lbs. and of black color.
He has a scar above one of his eyes, very plain, made by
running against a cane in driving stock. He is rather
spare made and slim frame, speaks quick, and has a large
eye showing a good deal of white. He went off without a
coat or shoes, had on a coarse home made cotton shirt, without ?whiteheads?, and yellow cotton peintaloomes. He had a
straw hat, with a broad yellow ribbon tied on it.

    Whoever will return said negro to me, or lodge him in
jail, so that I can get him, shall receive the above reward.
SQUIRE MAYES      Lamar County    Aug. 31st 1848."
-----------------------------------

"ESTATE OF DOROTHY HARTY, Desc'd--Whereas the undersigned was
 appointed administrator of the estate of Dorothy HARTY, deceased,
 late of Red River County, at the July term of the Probate cou
 court of said county, this is to notify all persons indebted
 to said estate to make immediate payment, and all those having
 claims upon it, to present them to the undersigned, within
 the time prescribed by law, or they will be barred.
JONATHAN HARTY, Adm'r.  Red River County, Sept. 2, 1848 "
-----------------------------------

"STATE OF TEXAS--Powatan L. SMITH--$67 vs. Attachment--Josiah
 THOMPSON--County of Hopkins, Greeting:  To the Sheriff or
 any constable of said county ..You are hereby commanded to
 summon by publication in the Northern Standard as the law
 directs, Josiah THOMPSON, to be and personally appear at ___
 court to be holden at my office in a Precenct No. 1, at my
 residence, the Last Saturday in September next, to show
 cause if any, why a judgement shall not be rendered against
 him.        Given under my hand this the 25th day of Aug. A.D.1848.
        MILTON WARDLOW, Justice of Peace
To: Joshiah THOMPSON--You are herby cited to appear in accordance
 with the above summons.  Wm. MASON, C.H.C.  August. 27th,1848.."
-----------------------------------

"STATE OF TEXAS--Sheriff of Titus County--Greeting:  A summons
 for Williard J. PIRTLE to appear in the District Court of the
 county of Titus to be held second Monday in September A.D. 1848
 to answer the petition of John W. WITHER, now filed in my office.
 William J. PIRTLE is a non-resident of the State, that he is
 indebted to petitioner in the sum of one hundred and thirty-two
 dollars and sixty-seven cents, for Goods, Wares and Merchandise.
 Witness Bernard HILL, clerk of our District Court of the county
 of Titus, and his seal of office, at Mt. Pleasant, this the
 8th day of August A.D. 1848.
 I certify the above to be tru copy of the original writ."
J. D. LILLY, Sheriff of Titus County.
[HMS Note:  William instead of Williard was printed at one spot]
-----------------------------------

THE NORTHERN STANDARD-SEPTEMBER 9, 1848-CLARKSVILLE, RED RIVER CO
Vol. 6, No.20
----------------------------------

"NOTICE-Taken up and brought before Alex. M. CROOKS an acting
 Justice of the peace within and for the County of Red River
 and State of Texas, on the fifth day of September, 1848, a
 negro Man, slave, who calls himself WASHINGTON and states
 that he belongs to a man whose name is David DICKSON or DICKERSON
 living near Fulton, State of Arkansas.
 R. S. HAMILTON, Sheriff Red River County"
----------------------------------

"THE STATE OF TEXAS--Summons for William SCURLOCK to appear in
 my office in Millsville on the first Saturday in October 1848,
 to answer five petition of Jos. J. SMITH now filed in my office.

   Petioner makes affadavit and alleges that the said, William
 SCURLOCK is not a resident of the State.
 Given under my hand in my office, this 4th day of September 1848.
 MARCUS W. CAUDLE, J.P.      Whitfield MOORE,Constable of Prec 4"
----------------------------------

"WASHINGTON CORRESPONDANCE--A letter written by Davis S. KAUFMAN.
 Headlined as Washington City, July 21, 1848.  Letter to editor."
----------------------------------

"TO KISS OR NOT TO KISS--The N.Y. Sunday Despatch says:"The
 theatrical and critical world is divided with regard to the
 propriety of a dead Romeo kissing a living Juliet.  It has
 arisen from the fact of Mr. ANDERSON, when dead as Romeo, having
 returned with a vigorous smack, the salute of Fanny WALLACK
 when she kissed his corpse.  It was done so heartily that the
 audience tittered throughout, and the gentlemen in the upper
 tiers were almost boisterous in their expression of fun."
 Of course, the temptation was so strong that ANDERSON couldn't
 resist it."
-----------------------------------------------------------------

THE NORTHERN STANDARD--SATURDAY--SEPTEMBER 16, 1848-CLARKSVILLE
RED RIVER COUNTY  Vol. 2, No. 21
----------------------------------

"SKETCH OF THE LIFE OF GEN. LEWIS CASS--Lewis CASS was born at
 Exeter, in New Hampshire, on the 9th day of October 1782.
 His father Maj. Jonathan CASS, was a soldier of the Revelution,
 who enlisted as a private the day after the battle of Lexington.
 He served in the army until the close of the war, and was in al
 all the important battles in the Eastern and Middle States,
 where he was distinguished for his valor and good conduct.,
 and stained the rank of captain.  He was afterwards a major
 in WAYNE's army and died at an advanced age, after a life of
 usefulness and honor, at his residence, near Dresden, Muskingum
 county, Ohio.  His son, Lewis CASS, the subject of this brio-
 graphy, emigrated, at the age of 17 to the then Northwestern
 Territory, and settled first at Marietta, WashingtonCounty.
 He was thus called by the convention of Ohio, one of the (early
 pioneers) of that immense, western region, which has already
 risen to such a magnitude in our own days, and is destined to
 attain one so much greater herafter."
 [Due to length of article it was abstracted by Helen]
----------------------------------

"Thirty-two negro slaves to be sold at Public Sale in Red River
County.  13 men, about five of whom are good mechanics, eight
grown women, also good house servants, the balance boys and
girls, from one to fourteen years old, levied upon as the
property of Samuel S. TURNER, to satisfy said execution in
favor of Wm. M. LAMBETH vs. siad TURNER, this the 12th day
of September 1848.  Robert S. HAMILTON, Sheriff.  By E. WEST,
Deputy Sheriff      Clarksville Texas Sept. 12, 1848.
--------------------------------
"ESTATE OF ELI H. CAMPBELL, Dec'd.--Whereas the undersigned was
duly appointed by the Honorable county court of Bowie County,
at the August term 1848, administrator of the estate of Eli H.
CAMPBELL deceased, late of said county, this is therefore to
notify all persons indebted to said estate to make payment as
soon as their notes fall due, or I shall prosecute them legally,
and all persons having claims against the estate, to present
them to me, duly authenticated, according to law, or they will
be barred."  SAMUEL HUGHES, Administrator.
Bowie County  Sept 6, 1848
--------------------------------
"THE STATE OF TEXAS--To the Sheriff of Red River County--Greeting:
You are hereby commanded to summon, by publication according to
law in the Northern Standard, Nancy BANKSTON (who is declared
upon oath to be a non-resident of this State) to be and appear
before the Honorable the District Court of your said county,
on the first day of the next term thereof, to be holden at
the court House in Clarksville, on the fifth Monday in October
next, to answer the petition of Hamilton BANKSTON, now filed
in our said court of which the following is a brief statement
of the substance: viz. "Hamilton BANKSTON represents unto the
Hon. John T. MILLS, Judge, that sometime in the year of our
Lord 1841, he was married to one Nancy LICK-- that after said
marriage be done and performed all the duties incumbent upon
him as such husband--that afterwards to wit:  on the day of
A.D. 1842, the said Nancy regardless of her said marriage vows
to him, and without any just cause or provocation--abandoned
his bed and board and has and still doth refuse to return, and
said Hamilton further vows to him is guilty of adultery, and
is and has been for a long time being in adultery with one
_____HOUSTON, in the State of Arkansas--and said Hamilton
prays that he be decreed a Divorce, "a vinculo matrimonu"
from said Nancy.
Witness Wade H. VINING, Clerk of said court, and the Impress
of the seal thereof, at office in Clarksville, this 9th day of
Sept. A.D. 1848, and of the Sovernignty and Independence of
the United States the 73d year.    W. H. VINING, Clk.
Test:  By John W. CHENOWETH, Depty. Clk.
I hereby certify that the above is true copy of the original
writ now in my hands.    Robt. S. HAMILTON, Sheriff R.R.C.
September 9, 1848."
--------------------------------
THE NORTHERN STANDARD--SATURDAY--SEPTEMBER 23, 1848--CLARKSVILLE
RED RIVER COUNTY   Vol. 6, No. 22
--------------------------------

Continued--THE NORTHERN STANDARD-September 23, 1848-----

"APPONT MENT BY THE PRESIDENT BY AND WITH THE ADVICE AND CONSENT
OF THE SENATE, Francis H. MERRIMAN, attorney of the United States
   for the district of Texas, in the place of George W. BROWN, dec'd."
----------------------------------

"Our old Townsman Ebenezer ALLEN, Esq., accompanied by A.J.
   YATES, Esq. arrived in Town, on Tuesday last."
----------------------------------

"CERTIFICATE of James LATIMER, Esq."  [abstracted by Helen]
   I have been called upon by Major DeMORS, to certify the circumstances under which he came to Clarksville to publish the
   Standard.  Major DeMORSE came here at the instance of all the
   members from Red River District, upon a proposition to furnish
   a printing establishment and materials through the action of
   some of the citizens, if he would conduct it.  We found him
   in Austin, were satisfied of his capacity to conduct such a
   Journal creditably, and made the arrangement with him purely
   as a business matter.
   We knew the people of the county were anxious to have a press
   established and had once made an effort to procure one, and we
   were satisfied that they would readily advance the means.  All
   the circumstances attending his coming were entirely honorable
   to himself.     A. H. LATIMER     Clarksville, Sept. 21, 1848."
----------------------------------

"CERTIFICATE OF THOS. CASSIDY--I certify that on the Sunday previous to the late election for county officers, George F. LAW-
   TON, J.J. MUSGROVE, Dr. I.P. MORGAN, I.M. BLACKWELL and myself,
   being in the grocery of Mr. Gilbert RAGIN, Mr. MUSGROVE asked
   LAWTON said that he had been riding until he was tired correct-
   ing some reports made and circulated by Hugh F. YOUNG and
   Ballard C. BAGBY, (viz:) that he (LAWTON) had voted a single
   vote for B. H. EPPERSON in the late election for the Legislature, which he paid was not so, that he had voted a full ticket,
   but had not voted for DeMORSE, MUSGROVE remarked that if he
   had what was the difference:  who is De MORSE: LAWTON."
   [abstracted by Helen]--DeMORSE was Whig, and remained so until
   some articles were published in his paper against Russel LAT-
   IMER, whom (LATIMER) he refused the use of his columns to give
   publicity to his answer to the articles, whereupon old man
   LATIMER wernt to DeMORSE and told that if he did not change his
   course in his paper that he would do away with his press and
   establish another.  Mr. LAWTON then spoke of the inconsistency
   of not allowing the use of his paper to the LATIMER family.
   (the old man LATIMER is Jas. LATIMER)     THOS. CASSIDY"
   Clarksville    Sept. 8, 1848.
----------------------------------

"DIED--In Paris, Lamar County, Texas on the 2nd inst.; Antonia
   Coles FOWLER, the only daughter of B. C. and Mary A. FOWLER,
   aged 1 year 11 months and 22 days."
----------------------------------

"ESTATE OF JESSE CHERRY--The undersigned, having been appointed
   administrator of the estate of Jesse CHERRY, deceased, late of
   Titus County, by the Honorable County Court of said county, at
   the Aug. term 1848, hereby gives notice, to all persons indebted
   Continued...
                              100.

Continued--"ESTATE OF JESSE CHERRY"
  to said estate, to make immediate payemtns, and all those
  having claims upon it, to present them within the time prescribed by law, or they will be barred.   HARRIS H. LILLY "
  Titus County    Sept. 14, 1848.
---------------------------------

"STATE OF TEXAS County of Red River, Prec. No. 6--Appraisal
  of a horse on 16 Aug. 1848--Isaac WARD and John McCRORY,appraisers
  Sworn to before Peter RINGO, J.P.
  Filed 19 Aug. 1848--Geo. F. LAWTON, Clerk."
  [above abstracted by Helen]
-----------------------------------------------------------------------

THE NORTHERN STANDARD--SATURDAY--SEPTEMBER 30, 1848--
CLARKSVILLE RED RIVER COUNTY    Vol. 6, No. 23
---------------------------------

"DEATH OF CAPT. MARRYATT--This distinguished novelist is dead.  We
  think it very probable that the unexpected termination of his
  life, was caused by the receipt of a telegraphic despatch,
  announcing abroptly the liberties taken with his name and
  reputation by the Whig Elector for this District, at his
  murderous onslaught at Boston, upon the name and fame of the
  Capt. and of that unfortunate sovereign of his country.
  (the bloody tyrant Charles the Fifth).  The Captain's nervous
  system from long debility, was in a tender condition, indeed
  it was said he had been breaking blood vessels for some time
  past.  We have no wish to trifle with serious matters, but
  have no doubt that the report of Mr. EPPERSON's unintentional
  murder of his character, finished the business--it was enough
  to have caused the rupture of an artery."
---------------------------------

From the Charleston Mercury, Aug. 22(1848)
"DEMOCRATIC MEETING--Pursuant to Public notice a large and
  highly respectable meeting of the democrats of Charleston
  district was held at the Theatre on Monday evening last.

    On motion of J. W. WILKINSON, Esq., the following gentle-
  men were appointed officers of the meeting.  Hon. John HUGER,
  President.  Vice Presidents:  Hon. Wm. ?BUBOSE?, Hon. H. L.
  PINCKNEY; Hon. Paul C. GRIMBALL; Hon. Berkeley GRIMBALL,
  H. W. PERONNEAU; Thomas LEHRE; Thomas MILLIKEE; Thomas G.
PRIOLEAU, John STROHECKER, Samuel BARKER, Hugh WILSON; Andrew
  TURNBULL, John COLCOCK, Dr. J. W. SCHMIDT; Henry BAILY;
  William BIRD; Charles M. FURMAN; Dr. Elias HORTIN; Frederick
  SHATLER; R. D. LAZARUS; Robert HUME; William J. BULL; W.J. BEN-
  NETT; Dr. Samuel CORDES; O. L. DOBSON, R. IZARD MIDDLETON; Geo.
  H. INGRAHAM; R. R. BEE; Benjamin S. RHETT; Edward BRUNWELL.
  Secretaries--A. P. HAYNE; John W. Che----HOROUGH; W. A. CLEVE-
  LAND; T. C. PAINE."

---------------------------------

From Washington Correspondence..Washington City, Aug. 10, 1848

"Mr. Editor, Please publish the following letter from Major HETTIE.
  This will give you a mail twice a week from Mansfield to Clarks-
  ville.  We are still pressing the Department for stage service.
  David S. KAUFMAN."
Continued.....

EARLY TEXAS NEWS

Continued.....

"POST OFFICE DEPARTMENT, CONTRACT OFFICE, Aug. 10th, 1848--Sir:
The Postmaster General has ordered the additional weekly trip
of the mail between Mansfield and Clarksville advised by
G. L. CLAPP, Esq. The other suggestions made by his letter
have been attended to. I have the honor to be, Very respectfully your obe't ser't, S. R. HOBBIE, Assistent P. M. GENERAL
Hon. D. S. KAUFMAN, House Representives."

-----------------------------------

"MARRIED--On Thursday the 24th inst., by the Rev. Sam. ?orley,
Col. Richard PETERS to Miss Eliza Ann BEATY, daughter of the
late Robert E. BEATY, all of this county."

"On the 10th inst. in Titus County by John D. _?_?_, Mr.
James H. KEITH to Miss Jane O.__?_?_. " [HMS Note: The above
marriage notices were caught in left side of binding for
microfilming and therefore could not be read.]

-----------------------------------

ADVERTISEMENT: C. C. GALAWAY, Attr. at Law, Gilmer, Upshur
County.       Sept. 16, 1848

-----------------------------------

"Sons of Temperance..The Brothers of the Clarksville Division of
the (Sons of Temperance), meet at half past 3 o'clock P.M. on
Tuesday, Oct. 3rd at the Masonic Hall.--A procession will form
and march to the Presbyterian church, when a public installa-
tion of the officers will take place; after which an address
by the Rev. J.W.P. McKENZIE. All are invited to attend.
Sam'l. CORLEY W.P.       J.M. MONTGOMERY R.S.
Clarksville Sept. 28th 1848.

-----------------------------------

"ADMINISTRATOR'S SALE..[abstracted by Helen] To be sold on 1st
Tuesday in Nov. by Probate Court of Red River County--750 acres
or thereabouts lying in the county of Harrison, being part of
the tract located upon the headright certificate of Alexander
JOHNSON.[abstracted,HMS.]-On a credit of 12 months-the following
tracts to wit 480 acres in county of Titus, Southwest corner
of the survey made upon the headright certificate of David CLARK.
Also the North half of a half league and half labor survey,
made for CRAIG & DENTON, situated in the county of Cass, made
upon the Headright certificate of Joshua PETERS.
Also 1576 acres off of the south west half of a survey made
upon the Headright certificate of Sarah READ, situated in the
county of Hopkins.
Also 836 acres upon a survey made for CRAIG & DENTON assignesses
of James GRAHAM, lying in the county of Cass.
Also 100 acres of a survey made upon a certificate issued by
the Secretary of War to Robt. A. PRICE, situated in Lamar Co.
Also 1259 acres, south corner of a survey made for CRAIG & DENTON
upon the headright of Joshua PETERS, situated in Cass County.

The purchasers of the last mentioned tracts, will be required
to give bond with approved security for the amount of the purchase money, and a lien upon the lands.
Jno. B. CRAIG, Adm'r. of Jno. B. DENTON, Dec'd. Sept.27th 1848."

-----------------------------------

"$50 REWARD--Ranaway from the subscriber, on hte 12th inst. a
negro man named ARMSTEAD, about 28 yrs. of age, black complex-
ion, about 5 ft. 3 or 4 inches high, well made, heavy set,
very stout and will weigh about 150 lbs. He is quick, free
spoken, and the left side of his head has been shaved about
six weeks since and has a scar on it, made by the poll of
an axe. On the back part of one of his legs at the bend of
the knee there is a large scar resenbling an old burn.

He rode off on a sorrel mare with flax mane and tail, star
in her forehead about 14 hands high, long heavy body and bears
the marks of the harness on her. The boy had on, when he left
a shirt and pants of common twilled negro cloth. It is probable he will attempt to make his way to the Indian Nation.
I will give 40 dollars for the delivery of the negro to me,
10 miles from Shreveport on the Greenwood road or for his
confinement any jail so that I get him, and 10 dollars for
the mare.     A. W. TUCKER     Sept. 14th 1848."

------------------------------------

"STATE OF TEXAS, County of Bowie--County Court for October Term,
1848--To the Sheriff of said County--Greeting:  Whereas
Samuel A. BLYTHE of the county of Bowie, has filed his petition
in my office, for a division and distribution of the estate of
Samuel K. BLYTHE, deceased, in which it is alledged that Martha
GRAIM formerily Martha BLYTHE, Lackey GRAIM forly Lackey BLYTHE,
James S. BLYTHE, and Edward BLYTHE, are Legatees of said estate
and non-residents.  These are threrfore to command you by the
authority of the State of Texas to summon the Legaters above
named, by publication in the Northern Standard, a newspaper
published in Clarksville in the adjoining county, Red River,
in the State of Texas, for four successive weeks, to be and
appear before the honorable county court of said county of
Bowie, on the last Monday in Oct. next, to show cause why
said estate should not be divided and distributed, according
to prayer of petitioner.

Herein fail not, but make due return as the law directs.
Witness Sam'l. H. McFARLAND, Clerk of said court, and the impress
of the seal thereof, at office in Boston, this the 23rd day of
Sept. A.D. 1848, and of the Independence of the United States,
the 73rd year.

I hereby certify that the above is a true copy of the original
writ, now in my hands September 23, 1848.  David JARRAT, Sheriff
of Bowie County.  By his deputy, A.L. HULM."
Boston,     September 23, 1848.

------------------------------------

"LOST CERTIFICATE--Lost or mislaid, the conditional head right
certificate granted to Henry RITCHIE, by the Board of Land
Commissioners for Red River County, 3rd class dated December
5th 1839; and numbered 252 and calling for 320 acres of land.
Said certificate is the property of the estate of John MARTIN
deceased, late of Red River County.  If it is not found within
the time prescribed by law for advertising, I shall apply at
the proper office for a duplicate."
W. W. FOREMAN, Guardian of the Heirs of John MARTIN.
Clarksville,     Sept 30th 1848.

------------------------------------

"LOST CERTIFICATE--I have lost my head right certificate for
   one league of land, first class No. 80, granted to me, by the
   Board of Land Commissioners for Red River County, January 31st
   1838.  If said certificate is not found within the time prescribed by law, for advertising, I will apply at the proper
   office for a duplicate."  Geo. BRINLEE
Boston, Bowie County      Sept. 14th 1848.
--------------------------------

ADVERTISEMENT:  STAR HOTEL, MT. PLEASANT TITUS COUNTY--Washington
   GRAY      Sept. 14th 1848.
--------------------------------

"STATE OF TEXAS--County of Red River--To the Constable of Pre-
   cinct No. 4 greeting:  In the name and by the authority of the
   State aforesaid you are hereby commanded to summon, William
   SCURLOCK, by publication for three successive weeks, in the
   Northern Standard a newspaper, printed at Clarksville Red River
   County Texas, to be and appear before me at my office in Mill-
   ville on the first Saturday in October 1848, to answer the
   petition of Jos. J. SMITH now filed in my office.

   Petitioner makes affidavit, and alledges that the said
   William SCURLOCK is a non resident of the State that he is
   indebted to petioner in the sum of twenty-three dollars and
   thirty eight cents, for goods wares, merchandise sold and delivered, and money loaned etc.

   Herein fail not and have you then and there this writ, with
   your action on the same.

   Given under my hand in my office, this 4th day of Sept. A.D.
   1848.      Marcus W. CAUDLE, J.P.
To WILLIAM SCURLOCK
You are hereby summoned to appear according to the above notice.
Whitfield MOORE, Constable of Prec. No. 4 R.R.C.T."
--------------------------------

"STATE OF TEXAS--County of Red River, Prec. No. 6-Shown us by
   Francis BLUNDELL, one bay filley supposed to be two years old
   last spring about 14 hands high no marks brands perceivable,
   appraised at $20.50 this the 16th day of Aug. A.D. 1848.
   John McCROBY, Isaac WARD-Appraisers.
   Sworn to before me this 16th of Aug. 1848, Peter RINGO,J.P.
   Filed Aug. 19th A.D. 1848. Geo. F. LAWTON,Clerk.
   A true copy from the records. Geo.F. LAWTON,Clerk."
--------------------------------

ADVERTISEMENT:  MOSES GREENWOOD & CO., Commission & Forwarding
   Merchants. M. GREENWOOD; J. M. BEALD; T. ?R?. ADAMS-
   New Orleans.
--------------------------------

ADVERTISEMENT: ALFRED & CO., wholesale grocers, receiving, Com-
   mission and for Wardens Merchants, Fire proof warehouse, Levee
   Street, Shreveport, La.  Refer to: C.C. ALEXANDER-Clarksville;
   T. J. & W. P. CORNELIUS-Clarksville; A. M. & L. C. ALEXANDER-
   Paris; RAGSDALE & WRIGHT-Paris; Joseph HARRISON-Bonham; PACE &
   BRO.-Bonham; BEATHELET, HEALD & CO.-Doaksville; Charles P.
   STEWART-Mayhew, C.N.
--------------------------------

THE NORTHERN STANDARD-SATURDAY-OCTOBER 7, 1848-CLARKSVILLE RED
RIVER  Vol. 6, No. 24
----------------------------------

IRELAND--"Numerous arrests have taken place throughout the countyr;
as many as sixty having taken place in TIPPERARY.

The Roman Catholic clergy of Tuam have got up a memorial to
the Queen on behalf of the State prisoners, praying that the
prerogative of mercy should be exercised in faver of the insurgents who recently took up arms against the Crown.

An active chase is kept up both by land and sea for Mr.
Richard O'GORMAN.  He was traced Kilrush; but what became of
him afterwards no one can tell.  It is said that he is in the
Derry mountains, at the head of 600 men; but other accounts
assert that he escaped in an American vessel.  A reward of
£390 has been offered for his apprehension.

Arrest of T. F. MEACHER; Mr. LEYNE; and P.O'DONOGHUE--On
Sunday morning, about 1 o'clock, these three leaders, while
walking along the road between Clonculty and Holycross, were
met by a large party of police, who, suspecting them, demanded
their names.  They immediately complied, and were arrested by
Inspector MADDEN, in the Queen's name.  The police fell in, one
at either side of each prisoner, and they marched them to the
barracks at Rathcaupan, about a mile off, where they were
brought before the resident magistrate.

That official asked, in the course of the inquiry, whether
Mr. MEAGHER intended to surrender himself; to which he emphat-
ically replied that he did not, and that he scorned the idea
of asking for his life; and that the only condition on which
he would have ever been induced to surrender himself was, that
all parties implicated to the movement should have permission
to leave the country.  Mr. MEAGHER then proceeded to write some
long statement which has not been made public."
----------------------------------

"AN EXTENSIVE PEACH ORCHARD--Mr. James CASSADY, of Cecil Co.,Mary-
land has a peach orchard of 30,000 trees of 28 varieties.  They
will yield this season about 60,000 baskets."
----------------------------------

"ADMINISTRATOR'S NOTICE--Whereas the undersigned was appointed administrator of the estate of Richard MILLER deceased, and letters
issued to him on the 31st day of Jan. 1848, from the Probate
Court of Hopkins county; all who have claims against said estate
will present them according to law, and all who are indebted
to said estate will make payment.    John B. CRAIG, Adm'r."
Oct. 7th 1848.
----------------------------------

"ESTATE OF JOHN BASSETT, dec'd--The undersigned having been duly
appointed by the Honorable County Court of Bowie county, at
the Sept. Term 1848; administratrix of the estate of John BAS-
SETT deceased late of said county, hereby notifies all persons
indebted to said estate to make immediate payment, and those
having claims against it to present them duly authenticated,
within the time prescribed by law.  Martha BASSETT, Adm'r.
Sept. 26, 1848.
----------------------------------

"LOST CERTIFICATE--The certificate for one league and labor of
land first class, granted by the Board of Land Commissioners
for Red River county, to Howard REAMS has been lost.

   If said certificate is not found within the time prescribed
by law for advertising, I will apply at the proper office for
a duplicate."          Howard REAMS.
Bowie County   Sept. 30th 1848.
-----------------------------------

"LOST CERTIFICATE--I have lost my head right certificate for one
league of land, first class No. 80, granted to me, by the
Board of Land Commissioners for Red River County, January 31st
1838.  If said certificate is not found within the time prescribed by law, for advertising, I will apply at the proper
office for a duplicate."   Geo. BRINLEE
Boston  Bowie County   Sept. 14th 1848.
-------------------------------------------------------------------

THE NORTHERN STANDARD-SATURDAY-OCTOBER 14, 1848-CLARKSVILLE
RED RIVER COUNTY  Vol. 6, No. 25
-----------------------------------

"ANOTHER BASE, SLANDER NAMED TO THE COUNTER-Mr. B. B. KERCHIVAL
is one of the _?_ _?_ _?_ exceptionable citizens of Michigan.
_?_ _?_ born in Kentucky; has resided __?_ ___?_ in Michigan
has been a member of _?__ _?__ _?_ _?_ __? Detroit Whig Journal.
-----------------------------------

ADVERTISEMENT;  A. K. ELLETT, M.D.  Clarksville
-----------------------------------

ADVERTISEMENT:  Drs. GORDON & WALKER, of Clarksville and vicinity
Feb. 1, 1848.
-------------------------------------------------------------------

THE NORTHERN STANDARD-SATURDAY-OCTOBER 21, 1848-CLARKSVILLE
RED RIVER COUNTY     Vol. 6, No. 26
-----------------------------------

"DANIEL DRAYTON, the negro stealer, was sentenced by the Criminal
Court of Washington, to 20 years imprisonment in the penaltentary."
-----------------------------------

"DELLAR NEWSPAPER--This paper, published in Philadelphia, by
A. H. SIMMONS & CO."
-----------------------------------

"PUBLIC MEETING IN LAMAR COUNTY-[abstracted by Helen] was held
at court house of Lamar County on the 18th of Oct. 1848.  Meeting organized by Col. Travis G. WRIGHT to the chair and appoint-
ing H. D. WOODSWORTH, secretary. Hon. Wm. H. BOURLAND explained
objects of the meeting-- a protest against a called Session of
the Legislature of the State of Texas. Hon. G. A. EVERTS addressed the meeting.  Wm. R. SCURRY, Esq., addressed the meeting.  Hon. Wm. H. BOURLAND introduced some Resolutions.
The Governor's letter to the Committee of Colorado County was
then read by W. H. MILWEE, Esqr. and the opinions there impressed, warmly approved of by the meeting. T. G. WRIGHT,Chairman."
-----------------------------------

EARLY TEXAS NEWS

"RAILWAY MEETING AT PARIS-[abstracted by Helen] meeting of the
citizens of Lamar with a view to facilitate the construction
of contemplated Rail Road from Galveston to Red River.  Called
to the chair: John R. CRADDOCK, Esq. and Hon. H. R. LATIMER.
U. MATTHIESSEN appointed Secretary.
Resolutions submitted by Ebenizer ALLEN and A. J. YATES, Esqs.
and F. B. GILLIAM, M.D.        H. R. LATIMER, Chairman.
U. MATTHIESSEN, Secretary"      Paris 3rd October 1848
--------------------------------

"NOTICE TO THE COLUNTEERS WHO SERVED IN THE WAR WITH MEXICO--Sam.
F. MOSELEY will be at Clarksville, during the first week of
the ensuing court, beginning on Monday the 30th ult., prepared
to take proofs and receive powers of attorney to draw the
extra pay due the volunteers who served in the war with Mexico."
Paris, October 18th 1848.
--------------------------------

"TITUS COUNTY ESTRAY NOTICES-A claybank horse, seven years old,
white valued at $40. before me this 5th day of August.
W. J. HAMILTON, J.P.T.C. Texas.  Jas. DAVIS, and John W.
PRICE-Appraisers.
A true copy from the record of my office this the 30th day of
September 1848.    J. COOK, Clk. Co.Court Titus County."
--------------------------------

"We the undersigned being duly sworn for the purpose, do certify
that we have viewed two steers"  "The two supposed to be worth
$40 taken up by Abram ASTUN, August the 28th 1848."
     Green T. HUNT, Jerden HAYS, Appraisers
Sworn to and subscribed before me this 28th day of Aug. 1848
     L. BURK, J.P.
A true copy from the original now on file in my office, this
30 th of September 1848.  J. COOK, Clk. Co.Crt.Titus County.
--------------------------------

"NOTICE --Is hereby given, that the undersigned was appointed
by the Hon. Probate Court of Lamar County, at the May  term
thereof, administrator of the estate of Joseph REDDING, deceased
late of said county.  All persons therefore, having claims
against said estate, will present them duly authenticated
within the time prescribed by law or they will be barred,
and those indebted to said estate are requested to make
immediate payment to the undersigned. DANIEL T. ALEXANDER, Adm'r."
October 18th 1848.
--------------------------------

"NOTICE FOR FINAL SETTLEMENT-State of Texas County of Red River
County Court--Whereas, Albert H. LATIMER, administrator of the
estate of James W. DICKSON deceased has filed his petition in
said court for a final settlement of said estate, and a distribution thereof.

   Notice is therefore given to all persons interested therein,
to appear at the next Nov. term of said court to be held at
the court house in the town of Clarksville, on the last Monday
in Nov. next, and show cause if any they have, why said settlement partition and distribution should not be made.
   By order of Hugh F. YOUNG, Chief Justice of Red River County.
   Given under my official signature and seal of said court, at
office in Clarksville, this 18th day of Oc.A.D. 1848."
                                  Geo.F. LAWTON,Clk.C.C.RR C

EARLY TEXAS NEWS

"NOTICE-Strayed from the subscriber near McKinney, in Collin
county, one sorrel mare, four years old."[description given]
"Any person delivering said animal to us in Buffalo, Dallas,
McKinney, Bonham, Paris or Clarksville, will be liberally re-
warded.        C. C. ALEXANDER & Bros.
Clarksville, October 12th 1848.

------------------------------------

"LIST OF LETTERS--Remaining in the Post Office at Pine Bluffs
Red River County, Texas, for the Quarter ending September 30,1848.
MIMS, Gideon,          MEBANE,P.Rebecca Mrs.   VANDERGRIFT,Margaret
MANIS, G. James        SMITH, H. Charles             Miss
MEBANE, J.Margaret Miss DILLINGHAM, L.J.       REDDING, A.J.
               Isiah W. WELLS, Post Master
        October 6th 1848.

------------------------------------

"LETTERS-Remaining in the Post Office at Clarksville, Texas on
the 30th day of September, 1848-which if not taken out by the
31st Dec. next, will be sent to the Post Office Dept. as dead letters'

| | | |
|---|---|---|
| A. | GRAHAM,John | McCARTY,John H |
| ADAMS,Mr.or James | GEORGE,Almiria | McCALL,Marshal |
| ADAMS, Jesse | GUNTER,Chas.or Daniel | McREYNOLDS,James H. |
| ANDERSON,John | MATTHEWS | McREYNOLDS,Wilson |
| B. | GELLESPIE,Isaac S. | MATHIS,R.W. |
| BLACKBURN,James | GREGG,W.M. | MONTGOMERY,T.B.  2 |
| BARNES,Mrs. Jane R. | GLOVER,Joseph | MOBLY,Miders |
| BROTHERS,Jasper | GAMBLE,Thomas | MORROW,B.C.L. |
| BUTLER,Thos.  2 | H. | MAGUS,Berry |
| BURMMITT,Geo. | HOOD,Mrs. Mary | P. |
| BURRY,Jasper A. | HAMILTON,Miss Sarah | POTTER,Wm.R. |
| BENGE,Lewis | HAMLETON,James | PATTON,V.B. |
| BARKER,W.W. | HALE,James W. | PIRTLE,Wm. |
| BLOODSWORTH,John | HUDIBURG,Rev.C.S. | PEARSON,James D |
| BROWN,James C.  2 | HARRIS,Nathaniel | PERRY,N.B.,Dr. |
| BOYCE,Miss ?Janice? | HILLBURN,F.M. | POST Martin Epperson' |
| BURK,James R. | HARRIS,Temple  3 | Ferry Red River Co |
| BRISTO,David | HOGAN,W.B.  2 | PITMAN,Samuel |
| C. | HILBURN,Chas.C.  2 | R. |
| COLLINS,Mrs. Didarnia | J. | ROACH,Wade H. |
| COCK,Calvin J.  2 | JACKSON,F.M. | RICHARDSON,Mr. |
| COOK,R.M. | JENKINS,Charles D. | S. |
| CHESSIER,James | JACKSON,John | SHREEVE,Pleasant |
| CHILDERS,Levi G. | JONES,Wm. E. | STALLINGS,Abraham |
| CLAMPIT,Elisha | JAMES,Christian 2 | SCHOPSHIRE,J.H. |
| CAMERON,John | K, | SMITH,W.M.  2 |
| CRONE,Mrs.Carline | KELBY,Q.D. | SOUTH, William |
| CHARLES,Shelby Capt. | KYLE,R.G.  2 | STEPHEN,A.F.Mrs. |
| CRAIG,J.C. or E.T. | KELLY,Douglus | STORY,Samuel |
| Clerk Land off.Red.River Co. | KENNU,Corinia | SCURRY,W.R. Attr.& C. |
| D. | L. | STANLY,G.W. |
| DALE,Thomas | LEWMAN,Gilbert | SEAL,Darling |
| F. | LONG,James | SCHRACK,L.M. |
| FRIDDLE,George | LYDA,S.S.  2 | T. |
| FULGHAM,Thomas | M. | TISDALE,Ann Eliz.Mrs. |
| G. | MARTIN,A.C. | TRIMBLE,Wm. |
| GAIGE,Edward N. | MARLOW,H.W. | TINNEN,Wm. H. |
| GORDON,George Dr. | MOON,John A. | U. |
| GRAHAM,John D. | MILL,John | UMPHREY,Joseph P. |

Continued...

EARLY TEXAS NEWS

Continued--Letters remaining in Pine Bluffs Post Office....

| V. | WARD,Frederick | WILLIAMS,Eliz.J. |
| District Clerk | WHITESIDES,Wm.N. 2 | WILLIAM,M.Williams |
| VERNON,Margaret Miss | WHITE, ?L.? ?L.? | WAGLEY,John |
| W. | WHITE,John G. | WARNES,James 2 |
| WONNATT,Natty G. | WARD,Dr. | Z. |
| WARD,Jeremiah 2 | WHITHINGTON,Wm.T. | ?ZEDICUM,Fred. |

John A. BAGBY, Post Master
September 30th 1848.

----------------------------------------------------------------

THE NORTHERN STANDARD-SATURDAY-OCTOBER 28, 1848-CLARKSVILLE
RED RIVER COUNTY     Vol. 6, No. 27.

----------------------------------

"We are indebted to Hon. Thos. J. HENLEY of Indiana, for public
   documents."

----------------------------------

"FATHER AND SON--Moses CORWIN (brother of Tom, the wagon boy) is
   the Whig candidate for Congress in the Champaign District, Ohio,
   and is opposed by his son, John A. CORWIN."

----------------------------------

"CAPT. ESTILL's Company of Panola (Miss.,) Volunteers, returned
   from Mexico a few weeks ago, all democrats, good and true, resolved to vote for CASS and BUTLER.  When they left home they
   were all Wigs, save Ten.  So says a gentleman directly from that
   state.        Alas--Poor whiggery"

----------------------------------

"ALL FOR TAYLOR--A correspondent of the Wytheville Republican,
   himself a democrat, says that when Capt. PRESTON's company of
   volunteers were discharged, it numbered sixty-two men, of whom
   50 were CASS and BUTLER men.  So it goes.  The whigs are claiming
   all the volunteers, and they may count themselves well off if
   they get one-fourth of them--Fincastle Democrat."

----------------------------------

"WHY HE CHANGED--The Louisville Democrat says:  Capt. M'DOUGALL,
   of Indianpolis, informed us yesterday, that nine whig captains
   of his regiment have repudiated whiggery, and are going for
   CASS and BUTLER:  and out of 26 lieutenants, one only was for
   TAYLOR, and he was wavering.  He says he has found, upon the
   slain of the Mexican army, whig documents against the war, and
   in favor of the Mexican cause; that they were scattered pro-
   fusely through the city of Mexico, to prevent a retification
   of the treaty of peace."

----------------------------------

"THE STATE OF TEXAS--To any lawful officer of Titus County--Gre-
   eting:  You are hereby commanded to summon Wesley WRIGHT, (who
   si declared on oath to be non resident of this State) by making
   publication according to law, to be and appear before Elam RID-
   DLE, an acting Justice of the Peace, in Prec. No. 3, 2nd class,
   in and for said county of Titus, on the last Saturday in November, A.D. 1848, at the office of said Justice in the town of
   Mt. Pleasant, then and there to answer the complaint of
   Turner H. EDMONSON, founded on an account for $35.

   Herein fail not, but make due return of this writ, with your
action endorsed thereon as the law directs.

Continued...                    109.

Continued....
   Witness the hand of said Justice, this the 18th day October
   A.D. 1848.                    Elam RIDDLE,Justice of the Peace
   I certify that the above is a true copy of the original now
   in my hands.        Wm. C. HARPER, Constable, T.C.T. "
   October 28, 1848.
------------------------------------

"NOTICE--The undersigned was duly appointed Administrator of the
   estate of Henry S. LEE, deceased, at the March term of the
   honorable Probate Court of Lamar County, 1848.  This is to
   notify all persons indebted to said estate to make immediate
   payment.  And all those having claims upon it, to present them
   to the undersigned, within the time prescribed by law, or they
   will be barred.        John LEE, Administrator "
   Paris, 23rd October 1848.
------------------------------------------------------------------

   This concludes what abstracts Helen Swenson was able to do
before moving from the Austin area.  This is not all of the
newspapers on microfilm for this period of time.

   As this goes to print, it is known that Helen Swenson and
family will be moving back to the Austin area by summer of 1984.

BAGBY, ----- 81
BAGBY, Ballard G. 100
BAGBY, Geo. H. 90
BAGBY, John A. 66
BAGBY, John A. 81
BAGBY, John A. 89
BAGBY, John A. 90
BAGBY, John A. 109
BAILEY, E. 22
BAILEY, E. 22
BAILEY, Henry 101
BAILEY, J. B. 11
BAIN, John 88
BAKER, ----- 23
BAKER, ----- 27
BAKER, ----- 36
BAKER, Hiram 88
BAKER, W. W. 108
BAKERS, ----- 26
BALL, Warren A. 80
BANCAL, ----- 34
BANKS, Thomas 38
BANKSTON, Nancy 99
BARKER, Samuel 101
BARNARD, Calvin 88
BARNES, Jane R. 108
BARNET, Thos. 24
BARNETT, Thomas 29
BARNEY, Jabez 7
BARNEY, Jabez 9
BARRERER, Augustin 21
BARRETT, D. C. 36
BARRETT, D. C. 38
BARRETT, D. C. 38
BARRON, H. W. 53
BARRON, Henry Winston 53
BARRON, Newell 53
BARRY, Lewis D. 49
BARRY, Lewis D. 57
BARRY, Lewis D. 86
BARTLETT, Joseph 50
BARTLETT, Joseph 83
BARTON, William 5
BASSETT, John 105
BASSETT, Martha 105
BASTELLO, Francisco Xavier 21
BATEMAN, Evan 88
BATEMAN, Isaac 88
BATEMAN, Jonathan 88
BATES, ----- 80
BATES, Mrs. Elizabeth 88

BATTERSON, Isaac 25
BATTLE, M. M. 1
BATTLE, M. M. 4
BAUGESS, Franklin 88
BAUGH, D. 83
BAXTER, ----- 73
BAYLEY, E. 45
BEAN, Peter E. 48
BEATHELET, ----- 104
BEATY, Eliza Ann 102
BEATY, Robert E. 102
BEAUJOLIAS, ----- 63
BEAUMONT, ----- 33
BECKMANS, ----- 18
BEE, R. R. 101
BELCHER, Gov. 18
BELL, J. H. 22
BELL, J. H. 42
BELL, J. H. 43
BELL, J. H. 46
BELL, William 88
BENGE, Lewis 108
BENNET, Hon. 83
BENNETT, W. J. 101
BERRIMENDEZ, Juan Martin de 14
BEVILL, John 29
BEWLEY, ----- 91
BEWLEY, S. 91
BINGHAM, Francis 7
BINGHAM, Francis 14
BIRD, Micajah 8
BIRD, William 101
BIVINS, John M. 49
BIVINS, John M. 57
BIVINS, John M. 86
BLACKBURN, James 88
BLACKBURN, James 108
BLACKWELL, I. M. 100
BLACKWELL, Wiley 88
BLAKE, ----- 83
BLANTON, W. C. 88
BLATCHFORD, Rev. Dr. 18
BLOODSWORTH, John 108
BLOUNT, J. H. 29
BLUNDELL, Francis 104
BLUTHE, Samuel K. 103
BLYTHE, James S. 103
BLYTHE, Martha 103
BOGART, John G. 18
BOGART, Wm. 38
BOGGS, Jas. 72

BOGGS, Jas. 73
BOHEMIA, ----- 63
BOON, Thomas 19
BORDEN, ----- 36
BORDEN, G. 31
BORDEN, Gail 34
BORDEN, Thomas H. 10
BORDEN, Thomas H. 33
BORDEN, Jr. G. 31
BORDEN, Jr. G. 39
BORDEN, JR. Gail 25
BORDENS, ----- 23
BORDENS, ----- 26
BORDENS, ----- 27
BORLAND, ----- 65
BORLAND, ----- 69
BOSTIC, Levi H. 10
BOSTWICK, Caleb R. 43
BOURBONS, ----- 64
BOURLAND, James 55
BOURLAND, Wm. H. 106
BOURRIENNE, ----- 32
BOX, Thos. 83
BOYCE, Janice 108
BOYD, Lynn 57
BOYD, M. S. 72
BRACKNEY, ----- 51
BRACKNEY, ----- 58
BRADBURN, Col. 13
BRAINBRIDGE, Com. 18
BREEDING, C. C. 88
BREEDLOVE, ----- 41
BREEDLOVE, James W. 9
BREKEAD, William 88
BRENAN, Thomas H. 11
BREST, ----- 32
BREWER, Stephen 72
BRIDGES, William H. 8
BRIGHAH, ----- 15
BRIGHAM, ----- 1
BRIGHAM, ----- 18
BRIGHAM, ----- 43
BRIGHAM, A. 1
BRIGHAM, A. 10
BRIGHAM, A. 44
BRIGHAM, Asa 18
BRIGHAM, Asa 22
BRIGHAM, Benjamin R. 44
BRIGHAM, S. B. 30
BRINLEE, ----- 104
BRINLEE, ----- 106

BRISTO, David 108
BROOCKS, T. G. 86
BROOKS, Christopher 55
BROOKS, Christopher 55
BROTHERS, Jasper 108
BROWN, Gen. 18
BROWN, George W. 100
BROWN, Henderson 52
BROWN, Henry S. 19
BROWN, Henry S. 44
BROWN, James C. 108
BROWN, John 40
BROWN, Sylvester 17
BROWNELL, ----- 57
BRUNWELL, Edward 101
BRYAN, Jno. N. 74
BRYAN, John A. 88
BRYAN, Joseph 31
BRYAN, Joseph 31
BRYAN, Joseph 34
BRYAN, Joseph 34
BRYAN, Wm. 38
BUBOSE, ----- 101
BUCHANAN, ----- 88
BUCK, Billy 32
BUCKNER, Aylett C. 10
BULL, William J. 101
BUNDICK, Comisario S. 10
BUNYAN, Richard B. 88
BURDEN, Nathaniel 88
BURGHEN, Younger 88
BURK, James 108
BURK, L. 107
BURK, Lindsey 87
BURK, William 52
BURK, William 87
BURKE, ----- 3
BURLESON, Edward 38
BURMMITT, Geo. 108
BURNET, David G. 43
BURNET, David G. 44
BURNET, David G. 45
BURNHAM, Jesse 24
BURNS, ----- 42
BURRY, Jasper A. 108
BURTON, Isaac W. 47
BUSTELLO, Domingo 21
BUTLER, ----- 109
BUTLER, Thos. 108
BUTLER, Wm. F. C. 95
BUTLER, Wm. O. 86

BYRNE, S. H. 51
BYRNE, S. H. 59
BYROM, J. S. D. 21
BYROM, J. S. D. 42
BYROM, J.S. D. 17
BYRON, J. S. D. 29
BYRON, John S.D. 15

CADIZ, ----- 32
CAGE, Benjamin Franklin 15
CALDER, Sir Robert 32
CALDWELL, James H. 38
CALDWELL, James P. 49
CALDWELL, Samuel 88
CALHOUN, Harriett 88
CALVIT, Joseph 42
CAMBERLENG, Hon. C. C. 18
CAMERON, John 72
CAMERON, John 108
CAMPBELL, Ann G. 88
CAMPBELL, Eli H. 99
CAMPBELL, Francis A. 88
CANFIELD, Sally Ann 91
CARDENAS, Jose Maria 21
CARDENAS, Jose Marie de 14
CARPENTER, J. 66
CARR, J. B. 33
CARRAJAL, Jose Maria de Jesus 21
CARTWRIGHT, J. M. 87
CARVAHAL, Manuel 21
CARVAJAL, Jose M. J. 24
CARVAJAL, Jose Maria 30
CASMECASSE, M. 35
CASS, ----- 56
CASS, ----- 109
CASS, Lewis 86
CASS, Lewis 98
CASSADY, James 105
CASSIDY, Thos. 100
CASSIDY, Thos. 100
CASTIGLIONE, Francois Xavier 9
CASTILLO, J. M. 14
CASTONADO, ----- 32
CATLETT, Fairfax 30
CAUDLE, Marcus W. 98
CAUDLE, Marcus W. 104
CAZENEAU, Wm. L. 31
CHAMBERS, John G. 51
CHAMBERS, T. J. 20
CHAMBERS, T. J. 21
CHARLES, Shelby 108
CHASE, Wm. 6

CHATFIELD, ----- 52
CHATFIELD, Andrew 88
CHATFIELD, Richard 88
CHAUNCEY, Com. 18
CHAVES, Ignacio 21
CHENOWETH, John W. 60
CHENOWETH, John W. 99
CHERRY, Jesse 100
CHERRY, Jesse 101
CHESSIER, James 108
CHILDERS, Levi G. 108
CHISHOLME, D. M. 77
CHISM, J. E. 83
CHISM, Wm. V. 88
CHRISTY, Wm. 38
CHURCHILL, John 88
CLAMPIT, Elisha 108
CLANTON, Martha 88
CLAPP, G. L. 102
CLAPP, William 88
CLARK, A. B. 6
CLARK, Frank H. 80
CLARK, Ger--dus 18
CLARK, S. H. 81
CLAVETT, Joseph 21
CLAY C. M. 80
CLAY, ----- 50
CLAY, Cassius M. 69
CLAY, Nestor 10
CLEMENS, E. A. 88
CLEMENTS, Joseph 10
CLEMINTINA, Maria 63
CLEMMONS, A. E. 75
CLEVELAND, J. A. H. 46
CLEVELAND, W. A. 101
CLIFFORD, ----- 66
CLINTON, Gov. 18
CLINTONS, ----- 18
CLOOUD, J. W. 15
CLOUD, J. W. 14
COCHRANE, James 27
COCHRANE, James 39
COCK, Calvin J. 108
COCKE, Benjamin F. 88
COFFIN, Admiral Isaac 18
COFFMAN, Lovell 72
COGSWELL, ----- 68
COLCOCK, John 101
COLE, Calvin G. 74
COLEMAN, R. M. 26
COLEMAN, R. M. 38

COLES, J. P. 46
COLES, John P. 10
COLLINGWOOD, ----- 32
COLLINS, ----- 51
COLLINS, ----- 58
COLLINS, Didarnia 108
COLLINS, J. W. 3
COLLINS, Ruben D. 52
COLLINS, William 88
COLLINSWORTH, ----- 29
COLLINSWORTH, ----- 30
COLLINSWORTH, G. M. 21
COLLINSWORTH, G. M. 42
COLWELL, ----- 68
CONKEY, ----- 68
CONNER, ----- 83
CONNER, ----- 86
CONNER, John 58
CONWAY, ----- 58
COOK, ----- 62
COOK, J. 87
COOK, J. 107
COOK, J. P. J. 52
COOK, R. M. 108
COOK, Jr. John 62
COOKS, Alex. M. 98
COOLRIDGE, ----- 54
COOPER, William 45
CORBIN, Wm. P. 30
CORLEY, Samuel 88
CORNELIUS, Mart D. 88
CORNELIUS, T. J. 52
CORNELIUS, T. J. 104
CORNELIUS, W. F. 52
CORNELIUS, W. P. 104
CORWIN, John A. 109
COS, ---- 25
COS, ----- 24
COS, ----- 26
COSTELLO, P. 53
COTTEA, G. B. 11
COTTEN, G. B. 6
COTTEN, Godwin Brown 16
COUNSEL, Dr. J. S. 12
COWAN, Thos. L. 72
COX, C. G. 17
COX, Dr. C. G. 10
COX, Dr.C. G. 14
CRABTREE, Solomon 82
CRADDOCK, J. R. 72
CRADDOCK, John R. 52

CRADDOCK, John R. 59
CRADDOCK, John R. 60
CRADDOCK, John R. 80
CRADDOCK, John R. 82
CRADDOCK, John R. 107
CRAIG, ----- 91
CRAIG, ----- 102
CRAIG, E. T. 108
CRAIG, J. C. 108
CRAIG, Jno. B. 102
CRAIG, John B. 105
CRATFIELD, ----- 58
CRAWFORD, Shelby 90
CRIEDLAND, Benjamin 23
CRIER, Elijah 88
CRITTENDEN, John J. 57
CRITTENDEN, W. P. 72
CRITTENDEN, Wm. 90
CROCKETT, ----- 74
CRONE, Carlin 108
CROOKS, Ramsey 69
CROWOVER, B. 72
CRUMP, ----- 86
CRUMP, R. P. 60
CUDDIHY, Pat. 53
CUMIDS(?), James 10
CUMMINS, William 3
CUNNINGHAM, ----- 47
CUNNINGHAM, A. P. 47
CUNNINGHAM, David A. 47
CUSHMAN, Susan 68

DABBS, J. W. 87
DAKAN, P. 74
DALE, John P. 81
DALE, Thomas 88
DALE, Thomas 108
DALLAS, G. M. 60
DALMONASTER, ----- 61
DAMRON, John 83
DANAGHO, Roberts B. 88
DANIEL, Aline 88
DANTTON, John 88
DARNALL, ----- 92
DARNELL, Foster S. 88
DARTMOUTH, ----- 46
DAUMALE, Henry 64
DAVIS, ----- 66
DAVIS, ----- 94
DAVIS, David 89
DAVIS, Edward 76
DAVIS, Edward 76

DAVIS, G. W. 25
DAVIS, G. W. 25
DAVIS, Jas. 107
DAVIS, Joseph 39
DAY, John 91
DE LA GARZA, Jose Antonio 21
DEAN, Jesse 88
DEAN, Levi 88
DEAN, Willis 59
DEAN, Willis 60
DEGGES, ----- 71
DELAPLUINE, ----- 23
DELONG, ----- 68
DEMORS, ----- 100
DEMORSE, ----- 100
DEMORSE, Charles 75
DEMORSE, Chas. 90
DENTON, ----- 102
DENTON, Jno. B. 102
DESCRETTO, T. 93
DEVENPORT, James 83
DEWITT, Col. Green 9
DEWITT, Green 10
DEWITT, R. V. 40
DICKERSON, David 98
DICKINSON, Benj. B. 3
DICKSON, A. R. 90
DICKSON, David 98
DICKSON, James W. 107
DICKSON, Joseph 79
DICKSON, Mrs. Wm. P. 57
DILLAIRD, Nicholas 9
DILLINGHAM, J. L. 72
DILLINGHAM, John A. 72
DILLINGHAM, L. J. 108
DILLON, ----- 53
DIMMET, P. 34
DINSMORE,Jr. Silas 17
DINWIDDLE, J. H. B. 92
DOAK, Nelson 72
DOAK, Nelson 90
DOE, Fanny 32
DOHENY, ----- 53
DOHENY, ----- 93
DONLEY, S. P. 88
DOOLEY, M. A. 86
DOPPING, ----- 79
DORLEANS, ----- 63
DOSS, B. H. 59
DOSS, R. H. 52
DOWNING, John 19

DOYLE, William S. 52
DUBOIS, ----- 40
DUCHAMP, E. 93
DUCHAMP, J. B. 93
DUCHAMP, L. 93
DUKE, John H. 57
DUKE, Philip 7
DUKE, Thomas M. 10
DUNN, John R. 33
DUNN, John R. 33
DURIN, Jesse 88
DURRAND, ----- 70
DUTTY, P. 90
DUTY, Henry 88
DWYER, Jeremiah 5
DYER, C. C. 24
DYER, Clement C. 29

ECKFORD, Henry 18
ECKLE, ----- 22
EDMONSON, Turner H. 109
EDMUNSON, Samuel 88
EDMUNSON, Wm. 72
EDWARDS, Mr. 2
EGALITE, Phillippe 63
ELLETT, A. K. 58
ELLETT, A. K. 106
ELLIS, B. F. 66
ELLIS, N. D. 88
ELOCHIUGEN, ----- 61
ELY, Rev. Dr. 18
EMANUEL, A. 48
ENGLISH, Campbell 88
ENIS, N. F. 88
EPPERSON, ----- 56
EPPERSON, ----- 101
EPPERSON, B. H. 50
EPPERSON, B. H. 100
EPPERSON, B. H. Hon. 88
EPPERSON, E. H. 56
ESTILL, ----- 109
EUART, ----- 15
EVERETT, ----- 29
EVERETT, S. H. 29
EVERITT, S. H. 48
EVERTS, G. A. 106

FALCON, Don Miguel 37
FALCON, Jose Miguel 40
FENTON, Charles 54
FERDINAND, ----- 63
FERDINAND, ----- 64
FERGUSON, ----- 5

FERROL, ----- 32
FIELD, J. W. 77
FINALY, ----- 91
FISHER, S. Rhoads 5
FISHER, S. Rhoads 14
FISHER, S. Rhoads 30
FISHER, S. Roads 45
FISHER, Wm. 26
FITZHUGH, ----- 86
FLEMING, B. M. C. 88
FLETCHER, George 50
FLETCHER, Joshua 4
FLORES, Edwardo Rivas Jose 21
FLORES, Gasper 21
FLORES, Jose Francisco 21
FLORES, Pedro 21
FLORES, Ramon Trevino Manuel 21
FLORES, Salvador 21
FOLEY, B. M. 1
FORBES, F. 72
FORBES, T. C. 72
FOREMAN, W. W. 103
FOSGATE, Walter 75
FOSTER, Issac 9
FOSTER, John 42
FOSTER, Randolph 9
FOWLER, ----- 19
FOWLER, ----- 100
FOWLER, B. C. 90
FOWLER, Benjamin 19
FOWLER, Brad C. 52
FOWLER, Brad C. 59
FOWLER, Brad C. 82
FOWLER, Brad C. 82
FOWLER, Brad G. 52
FRANKLINS, John 83
FREEMAN, W. M. 86
FRIDDLE, George 108
FRIER, D. B. 33
FUENTE, Rafael De La 40
FULBRIGHT, D. 72
FULBRIGHT, Martia 87
FULGHAM, Thomas 108
FUNDERBURG, Wm. B. 88
FUQUA, Ephraim 10
FUREBACH, ----- 42
FURMAN, Charles M. 101

GAGER, ----- 41
GAIGE, Edward N. 108
GALAWAY, C. C. 102
GALITZEN, ----- 28

GAMBLE, B. C. L. 108
GAMBLE, Thomas 108
GANDER, Tom 32
GARCIA, Don Francisco 31
GARCIA, Jose Antonio de la 14
GARDNER, Marhta 90
GARRETT, Jacob 29
GARZA, ----- 29
GARZA, Jose Manuel de la 21
GARZA, Refugio De la 21
GATES, ----- 14
GAZETTE, Caddo 54
GELLEN, ----- 91
GELLESPIE, Isaac S. 108
GENERAL, P. M. 102
GEORGE, Almiria 108
GIBBS, S. O. 83
GIBBS, S. Q. 83
GILBREATH, James G. 88
GILLET, ----- 86
GILLET, Jas. S. 82
GILLIAM, ----- 57
GILLIAM, F. B. 107
GILLIAM, James 92
GILLIAM, Jas. 82
GILLIAM, Sarah Jane 92
GILLLIAM, Jas. 90
GILMER, James B. 52
GLASS, J. A. 88
GLOVER, Joseph 108
GODDARD, L. 83
GONZALES, ----- 26
GOOCH, B. 83
GOOCH, B. 83
GOODING, H. 81
GOODING, Henry 54
GOODWIN, Rufus 87
GOOSE, Dolly 32
GORDON, ----- 58
GORDON, ----- 106
GORDON, Geo. 90
GORDON, George 108
GORMAN, Jr. R. O. 72
GOSSETT, J. L. 73
GOULD, ----- 47
GRAHAM, ----- 83
GRAHAM, John 22
GRAHAM, John 43
GRAHAM, John 108
GRAHAM, R. 60
GRAHAM, R. H. 58

GRAHM, John D. 108
GRANT, ----- 88
GRANT, Diego 24
GRAVES, Richard 8
GRAY, ----- 40
GRAY, ----- 56
GRAY, B. W. 56
GRAY, B. W. 60
GRAY, Franklin C. 15
GRAY, Thomas 10
GRAY, Thomas 10
GRAY, Thomas 12
GREELY, Horace 92
GREEN, ----- 97
GREEN, Garrison 33
GREEN, James W. 50
GREEN, James W. 59
GREEN, Jas. W. 50
GREEN, Jas. W. 59
GREEN, Rolin 88
GREENVILLE, P. M. 60
GREENWOOD, Moses 81
GREENWOOD, Moses 104
GREGG, Thomas 88
GREGG, W. M. 108
GREGORY, Mr. 16
GRESHAMS, ----- 58
GREY, ----- 83
GREY, ----- 83
GRIMBALL, Berkerley 101
GRIMBALL, Paul C. 101
GRITTEN, ----- 36
GRITTON, Edward 36
GUERRORO, General 6
GUEST, Martia 72
GUNTER, Chas. 108
GUNTER, Daniel 108
GURLEY, ----- 65

HALE, James W. 108
HALE, S. M. 44
HALL, ----- 91
HALL, Eliza 91
HALL, John W. 44
HALL, John W. 45
HALL, W.D. C. 14
HALLARD, N. G. 73
HALLEY, ----- 30
HAMILTON, Frances R. 15
HAMILTON, Josiah F. 15
HAMILTON, R. S. 98
HAMILTON, Robert S. 49

HAMILTON, Robert S. 57
HAMILTON, Robert S. 86
HAMILTON, Robert S. 99
HAMILTON, Sarah 87
HAMILTON, Sarah 108
HAMILTON, W. J. 107
HANKS, Wyant 29
HARDIN, A. B. 29
HARDIN, A. B. 34
HARDY, ----- 36
HARLAND, N. R. 54
HARLAND, N. R. 58
HARLAND, N. R. 88
HARMON, John T. 55
HARPER, Wm. C. 110
HARRIS, ----- 40
HARRIS, Abner 42
HARRIS, David 10
HARRIS, David 45
HARRIS, Gowin 21
HARRIS, James 30
HARRIS, John R. 45
HARRIS, Joseph 52
HARRIS, Nathaniel 108
HARRIS, Thomas 52
HARRIS, W. P. 29
HARRIS, William P. 10
HARRIS, Wm. P. 24
HARRIS, Wm. P. 45
HARRISON, Gen. 18
HARRISON, Joseph 104
HARRISON, Wm. M. 55
HART, ----- 91
HART, A. 48
HART, J. C. 51
HART, J. C. 90
HARTSHORN, ----- 79
HARTY, Dorothy 97
HARTY, Jonathan 97
HARWOOD, A. 74
HARWOOD, Alex 74
HASKINS, F. J. 20
HASTINGS, John 62
HAUSER, Casper 42
HAYNE, A. P. 101
HAYNE, Col. 18
HAYS, Jerden 107
HAYS, Rebecca 91
HEALD, ----- 104
HEARD, William 96
HEATHERLEY, Henry B. 52

HEATHERLEY, Henry B. 58
HEATHERLY, ----- 96
HENDERSON, A. 77
HENDERSON, L. D. 80
HENDERSON, Sarah 80
HENDERSON, W. F. 77
HENDERSON, Wm. F. 50
HENDERSON, Wm. F. 58
HENDERSON, Wm. F. 76
HENLEY, Thos. J. 109
HENNINGTON, Robert 40
HENRY, John R. 76
HENRY, John R. 77
HENRY, Maurice 16
HERALD, Valasco 49
HERRERA, Ignacio 21
HERRIN, A. 64
HIGHSMITH, ----- 86
HIGHSMITH, S. 58
HILBURN, Chas. C. 108
HILL, Bernard 97
HILLBURN, F. M. 108
HILLINSWORTH, ----- 73
HIRAMS, S. C. 10
HOBBIE, S. R. 102
HODGE, Alexander 20
HODGE, Wm. L. 38
HOFFMAN George 18
HOGAN, W. B. 108
HOGAN, Woodson 88
HOLBROOK, ----- 88
HOLDEN, ----- 43
HOLLEY, Mrs. Mary Austin 20
HOLLOMAN, H. H. 66
HOLLOMANS, ----- 66
HOLMAN, Cyrus K. 82
HOLMAN, Cyrus K. 89
HOLMES, Thomas 29
HOOD, J. L. 29
HOOD, J. T. 34
HOOD, Mary 108
HOPKINS, E. 64
HOPKINS, Eldridge 60
HOPKINS, R. M. 90
HORD, W. H. 74
HORTIN, Elias 101
HOUSE, Littleton W. 75
HOUSTON, ----- 29
HOUSTON, ----- 73
HOUSTON, ----- 99
HOUSTON, A. 34

HOUSTON, A. 34
HOUSTON, Robert 88
HOUSTON, S. 29
HOUSTON, Sam 48
HOUSTON, Sam. 67
HOUSTON, Samuel 29
HOUSTON, Samuel 31
HOWELL, T. A. 43
HOWELL, Thomas A. 43
HOWELL, William 43
HOWTH, ----- 16
HOWTH, ----- 16
HOWTH, W. E. 21
HOWTH, W. E. 42
HOXEY, ----- 34
HUDIBURG, C. S. 108
HUDSON, R. Q. 72
HUFF, Geo. 44
HUFF, George 20
HUFFMAN, ----- 91
HUGER, John 101
HUGH, John M. 40
HUGHES, ----- 70
HUGHES, Geo. W. 70
HUGHES, Samuel 99
HUITT, Rowlin 74
HULM, A. L. 103
HULME, A. L. 51
HUME, A. L. 59
HUME, Robert 101
HUMPHREY, John 87
HUMPHREYS, Wm. 72
HUNT, Green T. 107
HUNTER, ----- 4
HUNTER, ----- 8
HUNTER, A. J. 72
HUNTER, Edw. 96
HUSBANDS, ----- 88
HUSTON, A. 29
HUTTON, James 48
HUYSAR, Bruno 21

INGLES, Oliver 83
INGRAHAM, Geo. H. 101
INGRAHAM, Ira 34
INGRAM, Ira 9
INGRAM, Ira 43
INGRAM, M. 88
INGRAM, V. 88
IRALA, Jose Mariano 24
IRWI, Thomas R. 41
JACK, Spencer H. 27

JACK, William H. 10
JACK, William H. 12
JACKSON, ----- 91
JACKSON, Alden A. M. 52
JACKSON, F. M. 108
JACKSON, Gen. 18
JACKSON, John 108
JACKSON, William M. 76
JAMEISON, Isaac B. 15
JAMEISON, Margaret 15
JAMERSON, Green B. 21
JAMERSON, Green B. 42
JAMES, ----- 74
JAMES, Christian 108
JAMES, John 34
JAMESON, G. B. 45
JASPER, ----- 47
JAY, John 18
JENKINS, ----- 52
JENKINS, Charles 88
JENKINS, Charles D. 108
JENKINS, Josiah 52
JENNINGS, ----- 74
JENNINGS, T. J. 83
JEWELL, Geo. W. 81
JEWETT, H. J. 94
JOCKUSH, J. W. 80
JOHNS, John R. 39
JOHNSON, ----- 56
JOHNSON, ----- 65
JOHNSON, A. E. C. 29
JOHNSON, Amanda 88
JOHNSON, F. W. 10
JOHNSON, F. W. 12
JOHNSON, Francis W. 5
JOHNSON, Francis W. 6
JOHNSON, Francis W. 10
JOHNSON, Francis W. 10
JOHNSON, Francis W. 24
JOHNSON, Hugh B. 29
JOHNSON, Hugh B. 34
JOHNSON, James 50
JOHNSON, James 58
JOHNSON, James A. 77
JOHNSON, Jas. H. 76
JOHNSON, John B. 39
JOHNSON, L. H. W. 30
JOHNSON, Mayfield 91
JOHNSON, Peter B. 88
JOHNSON, R. M. 57
JOHNSON, Thos. 81

JOHNSON, W. H. 56
JOHNSTON, James H. 54
JOHNSTON, James H. 76
JOINVILLE, Francis de 64
JONES, Anson 22
JONES, Anson 43
JONES, Charles 55
JONES, Charles 56
JONES, Dennis 88
JONES, H. W. 55
JONES, Isaac 55
JONES, Isaac 56
JONES, John W. 4
JONES, Lodiada 55
JONES, Oliver 3
JONES, Oliver 8
JONES, Oliver 21
JONES, Randall 24
JONES, William 56
JONES, Wm. E. 108
JUDKINS, ----- 66

KARNER, John 76
KARNER, John 77
KAUFMAN, ----- 47
KAUFMAN, D. S. 33
KAUFMAN, D. S. 67
KAUFMAN, D. S. 68
KAUFMAN, D. S. 102
KAUFMAN, David S. 47
KAUFMAN, David S. 98
KAUFMAN, David S. 101
KEELER, ----- 71
KEITH, James H. 102
KELBY, Q. D. 108
KELLEY, Susanah 88
KELLOGG, A. G. 31
KELLY, Douglus 108
KENLEY, ----- 70
KENNU, Corinia 108
KERCHIVAL, B. B. 106
KERR, James 14
KESLEY, H. B. 77
KILINE, A. B. 90
KIMBALL, ----- 91
KIMBALL, Harriet 91
KIMBLE, J. M. 77
KING, A. W. 72
KING, Eliza Ann 88
KING, Isaiah 90
KINNEY, Tom M. 66
KIT, ----- 92

KLONNE, H. 8
KNICKERBOCKERS, ----- 18
KNIGHT, M. M. 60
KOHLAATT, ----- 54
KUHN, J. C. 80
KUYKENDALL, Abner 10
KUYKENDALL, Mr. 2
KYLE, R. G. 108

LABEY, William 88
LACEY, Robert J. 88
LAMAR, ----- 86
LAMB, Caleb 42
LAMBETH, Wm. M. 99
LAMLETON, James 108
LANG, Edward 9
LAON, Simon de 21
LARKIN, Baker 7
LATIMER, ----- 100
LATIMER, A. H. 90
LATIMER, A. H. 100
LATIMER, Albert H. 107
LATIMER, H. R. 52
LATIMER, H. R. 107
LATIMER, Jas. 90
LAWRENCE, William A. 85
LAWSON, I. D. 88
LAWTON, ----- 100
LAWTON, Geo. F. 101
LAWTON, Geo. F. 104
LAWTON, George F. 56
LAWTON, George F. 100
LAZURAUS, R. D. 101
LEAGER, L. W. 81
LEAGUE, ----- 19
LEAGUE, H. H. 4
LEAKEY, ----- 2
LEE, Henry S. 110
LEE, John 110
LEE, V. P. 66
LEE, William 88
LEE, William H. 12
LEFROY, Baaron 93
LEHRE, Thomas 101
LEIGH, W. A. 94
LEON, Fernanso de 14
LEONS, Martin de 24
LEOPOID, ----- 63
LESASSIER, Luke 10
LESASSIER, Luke 13
LESASSIER, Luke 22
LESASSIER, Luke 43

LESENSSIER, Luke 10
LESTER, J. S. 38
LEVEMWORTH, ----- 20
LEVINE, Nicholas 88
LEWIS, ----- 56
LEWIS, C. 51
LEWIS, C. G. 33
LEWIS, Dixon H. 85
LEWIS, Franklin 21
LEWIS, Franklin 42
LEWIS, G. 50
LEWIS, G. 56
LEWIS, Granville 90
LEWIS, I. R. 29
LEWIS, Ira R. 31
LEWMAN, Gilbert 108
LEYNE, ----- 105
LICK, Nancy 99
LILLY, Harris H. 101
LILLY, J. D. 97
LITTLE, H. 51
LIVINGSTONES, ----- 18
LOGAN, J. O. 72
LONG, J. 55
LONG, Jacob 55
LONG, James 108
LONG, Mrs. Jane H. 11
LONG, Mrs. Jane H. 16
LOOP, John 51
LOOP, John 59
LOOP, John 92
LOOP, John P. 90
LUCKEY, ----- 71
LUNN, William 90
LUNN, William 92
LYDA, S. S. 108
LYON, Eunice 42

M'KINSTRY, ----- 11
MACDOUGAL, ----- 69
MACOMB, David B. 32
MADDEN, ----- 105
MAGUS, Berry 108
MAIN, John 88
MAJOR, ----- 78
MALLARD, E. 83
MALLARD, E. 83
MALLER, Edwin 22
MANIS, James G. 108
MANLOVE, B. 38
MANSAN, ----- 91
MANSFIELD, ----- 14

MANSON, L. C. 20
MARCY, Spoil 40
MAREA, John 88
MARIA, HENRIETTA 7
MARIANO, ----- 36
MARSH, ----- 1
MARSH, ----- 91
MARSH, E. 91
MARSH, S. 3
MARTIN, ----- 56
MARTIN, ----- 57
MARTIN, A. C. 108
MARTIN, A. C. 108
MARTIN, Albert 26
MARTIN, B. H. 56
MARTIN, B. H. 71
MARTIN, B. H. 74
MARTIN, H. 83
MARTIN, James 73
MARTIN, John 103
MARTIN, Mat W. 52
MARTIN, Mrs. 9
MARTIN, William 88
MARTIN, Wyly 24
MARTIN, Wyly 29
MARTINEZ, Manuel 21
MASON, ----- 20
MASON, ----- 52
MASON, G. B. 73
MASON, Henry B. 52
MASON, Wm. 97
MATHEWS, ----- 54
MATHEWS, ----- 108
MATHIS, R. W. 108
MATHIS, W. R. 88
MATTHIESEN, U. 107
MATTHIESSEN, U. 96
MAULDING, Presley 92
MAYS, Squires 97
MAZRO, John Coffin 18
MCBEAN, ----- 91
MCCALL, Daniel 87
MCCALL, Marshal 108
MCCARLY, Robert 88
MCCARTHY, H. S. 88
MCCARTHY, John H. 108
MCCARTNEY, B. H. 88
MCCLEASH, J. 88
MCCOMB, D. B. 24
MCCOY, James D. 9
MCCOY, Jno. C. 74

MCCROREY, Samuel 87
MCCULLOCH, ----- 86
MCDERMOTT, J. B. 96
MCDONALD, ----- 70
MCDONALD, Henry G. 55
MCEWEN, ----- 73
MCFARLAND, James 88
MCFARLAND, Robert 90
MCFARLAND, S. H. 59
MCFARLAND, S. H. 77
MCFARLAND, S. M. 51
MCFARLAND, Sam. H. 103
MCFARLAND, Samuel 90
MCFARLAND, Samuel 92
MCGINNIS, ----- 58
MCGONICAL, J. C. 90
MCGONICAL, J. C. 92
MCGONIGAL, J. C. 51
MCGONIGAL, J. C. 59
MCGONIGAL, J. C. 77
MCGOWEN, Jas. 72
MCGOWEN, S. K. 57
MCGOWES, S. K. 60
MCKENZIE, ----- 80
MCKENZIE, J. W. P. 90
MCKENZIE, J. W. P. 102
MCKENZIE, J. W. P. 79
MCKENZIE, Wm. K. 79
MCKINNEY, Thos. F. 81
MCKINSTRY, G. B. 12
MCKULTER, William 88
MCLAURIN, James 88
MCLELLAN, ----- 30
MCLEOD, H. 80
MCMULLIN, Juan 21
MCNEEL, J. G. 22
MCNEEL, J. G. 43
MCNEEL, Miss Emily 19
MCNEIL, Pleasant D. 3
MCNIEL, Jesse 88
MCQUEEN, ----- 4
MCREYNOLDS, Wilson 108
MDOUGALL, ----- 109
MEACHER, T. F. 105
MEAGBER, ----- 72
MEAGHER, ----- 53
MEAGHER, ----- 53
MEAGHER, ----- 90
MEAGHER, ----- 93
MEAGHER, ----- 105
MEBANE, Margaret J. 108

MEBANE, Rebecca P. 108
MEEK, Jos. L. 84
MELLER, ----- 58
MELTON, E. 50
MELTON, E. 58
MENARD, M. B. 80
MENARD, P. J. 29
MENARD, Peter J. 34
MENIFEE, Wm. 24
MERCER, ----- 54
MERRILL, Benj. 74
MERRIMAN, Francis H. 100
MEXIA, Col. 11
MGLAUGHLIN, Laughlin 7
MIER, Jose Maria 24
MIER, Jose Maria 30
MILAM, Benj. R. 29
MILBURN, David H. 19
MILES, F. 55
MILL, John 108
MILLARD, Henry 29
MILLER, ----- 73
MILLER, A. G. 88
MILLER, Dr. 1
MILLER, Dr. 4
MILLER, Dr.James B. 10
MILLER, J. B. 46
MILLER, James B. 22
MILLER, James B. 26
MILLER, James B. 43
MILLER, Jas. B. 14
MILLER, Jas. B. 44
MILLER, Jas. B. 86
MILLER, Richard 105
MILLER, Stephen 30
MILLER, Thomas R. 10
MILLICAN, William 3
MILLIKEE, Thomas 101
MILLS, A. G. 17
MILLS, A. G. 20
MILLS, A. G. 21
MILLS, John T. 99
MILLS, R. 17
MILLS, R. 20
MILWEE, W. H. 106
MIMS, ----- 41
MIMS, Gid. 72
MIMS, Gideon 108
MISS, Davis R. 21
MITCHAEL, ----- 93
MITCHEL, ----- 93

MITCHEL, John 94
MITCHELL, ----- 90
MITCHELL, Asa 6
MITCHELL, Eli 14
MITCHELL, Hon.Saml. L. 18
MITCHELL, John W. 44
MKINSTRY, George B. 4
MNEEL, Pleasant D. 10
MOLBY, Miders 108
MONEY, Jno. H. 25
MONEY, John H. 34
MONTES, Andres De La Viesca Y 30
MONTGOMERY, J. M. 56
MONTGOMERY, J. M. 102
MONTGOMERY, T. B. 108
MONTGOMERY, Thos. B. 88
MONTPENSIER, ----- 63
MONTPENSIER, Anthony 64
MOON, John A. 108
MOORE, ----- 32
MOORE, A. M. 83
MOORE, A. M. 95
MOORE, J. H. 25
MOORE, J. H. 26
MOORE, J. P. 73
MOORE, J. W. 46
MOORE, James 8
MOORE, John H. 32
MOORE, John P. 95
MOORE, John S. 12
MOORE, John W. 24
MOORE, Whitfield 98
MORGAN, G. W. 66
MORGAN, Hon. John J. 18
MORGAN, I. P. 100
MORPHIS, James M. 56
MORPHIS, James M. 82
MORRIS, ----- 23
MORRIS, ----- 23
MORRIS, James 88
MORRIS, Robert 23
MORTON, Rufus 52
MORTON, William 10
MOSELEY, R. J. 1
MOSELEY, R. J. 8
MOSELEY, Sam. F. 107
MOSLEY, Dr.S. S. 10
MOTGAN, M.D. I. P. 88
MOTLATT, William 88
MULDOON, Father 2
MUNSON, Henry 17

MUNSON, Nancy B. 17
MURPHY, Sylvester 12
MURRAY, ----- 70
MURRIN, Jehu 88
MUSGROVE, ----- 100
MUSGROVE, ----- 100
MUSGROVE, J. J. 100
MUSPRATT, Sheridan 68
MUSQUIZ, Felipe 14
MUSQUIZ, Ramon 9
MUSQUIZ, Ramon 40
MYERS, Wm. 74

NADAL, ----- 66
NAPOLEON, ----- 64
NAPOLEON, ----- 94
NARWOOD, Hamilton 78
NASH, ----- 86
NAVARRO, Jose Antonio 21
NAVARRO, Luciano 14
NAVARRO, Luciano 21
NAVARRO, Mr. Antonio 10
NELSON, ----- 32
NELSON, ----- 71
NEMOURS, ----- 63
NESMITH, ----- 57
NEVIN, James P. 38
NEWTON, S. G. 74
NEXON, ----- 15
NICHOLAS, ----- 91
NORTON, James 4
NORTON, Mr. JAMES 1
NORVILLE, S. G. 88
NOTT, Rev. Dr. 18

OBRIEN, ----- 72
OBRIEN, W. S. 90
OCHILTREE, ----- 85
ODENNELL, Charles 52
ODONOGHUE, P. 105
ODOWD, James K. 53
OGDEN, Peter Skeen 84
OGDEN, Sken 91
OGERMAN, Richard 53
OGORMAN, ----- 93
OGORMAN, Richard 105
OLIVARRI, Placido 21
OLIVER, ----- 52
OLIVER, ----- 58
ORIELLY, Manuel Sierra de 85
ORR, George 9
OSBORN, Josiah 91
OSBORN, Margaret 91

OVERTON, John 22

PACE, ----- 104
PADILLA, Don Anotonio 36
PADILLA, J. Antonio 37
PALMER, Levi 68
PANE, T. C. 101
PARK, Wm. A. 72
PARKER, ----- 87
PARKER, Daniel 29
PARKER, Daniel 29
PARKER, Daniel 34
PARKER, J. W. 29
PARKER, L. W. 34
PARKER, S. M. 33
PARKS, Elizabeth 88
PARLOR, Grace 42
PARROTT, T. F. L. 45
PARROTT, T. F. L. 19
PARROTT, T. F. L. 22
PARROTT, T.F. L. 16
PARSONS, S. G. 83
PASCHAL, Geo. W. 56
PASCHAL, J. A. 56
PATRICK, Geo. M. 24
PATRICK, Geo. M. 43
PATRICK, J. B. 10
PATRICK, Jane Lockey 88
PATTON, V. B. 108
PEARSON, James D. 88
PEARSON, James D. 108
PEBBLES, ----- 24
PEBLES, Robert 46
PEDRAZA, Gen. MANUEL GOMEZ 14
PEEBLES, Dr. 1
PEEBLES, Dr. 4
PEEBLES, Dr. Robert 10
PEEBLES, Robert 12
PEEBLES, Robert 26
PEERS, ----- 64
PERES, Igaacio 21
PERINS, Jesse 88
PERKINSON, Benjamen 88
PERONNEAU, H. W. 101
PERRY, ----- 4
PERRY, ----- 8
PERRY, A. G. 29
PERRY, A. G. 34
PERRY, A. G. 34
PERRY, James F. 21
PERRY, N. B. 108
PETERS, Joshua 102

PETERS, Richard 102
PETTIS, Wm. 14
PETTIS, Wm. 25
PETTUS, W. M. 34
PETTUS, Wm. 31
PETTUS, Wm. 34
PHELAN, Sylvester 53
PHELPS, Dr. J. E. 13
PHELPS, James A. 17
PHELPS, James E. 44
PHILIPS, Zeno 3
PHILLIP, William 88
PHILLIPEE, Louis 73
PHILLIPPE, Louis 63
PHILLIPPE, Louis 64
PHILLIPPE, Louis 66
PHILLIPPE, Louis 74
PHILLIPPEE, Robert 64
PHILLIPS, Ives 62
PHILLIPS, James 88
PIEDRAS, ----- 12
PIEDRAS, Jose de Las 12
PIERSON, J. G. W. 29
PIERSON, J. G. W. 34
PILLANS, P. J. 57
PINCKNEY, H. L. 101
PIRKEY, S. H. 56
PIRTLE, Willard J. 97
PIRTLE, William J. 97
PIRTLE, Wm. 108
PITMAN, Samuel 108
PLOUGOULN, ----- 36
PLOUGOUN, ----- 35
POINDEXTER, Gov. 18
POLK, James K. 60
PONTALBA, ----- 62
PONTALBA, M. de 61
PONTALBA, Madame de 61
POPE, James 88
PORTER, Beverly A. 17
PORTER, R. H. 54
PORTER, R. H. 66
POST, ----- 108
POST, Master 88
POTTER, M. M. 80
POTTER, Wm. R. 108
POWELL, Lazuras 57
POWERS, Wm. 82
PRESTON, ----- 109
PRICE, Elizabeth 88
PRICE, John W. 107

PRICE, Saml. C. 51
PRIOLEAU, Thomas G. 101
PRIOLLAND, ----- 35
PRYER, S. B. 74
PUTMAN, B. B. 88
P[EARME, Dr. 5


RAGIN, Gilbert 100
RAGSDALE, ----- 52
RAGSDALE, ----- 104
RAMEY, Lawrence 10
RANDALL, Henry S. 94
RANDOLPH, H. 95
RANDON, John 14
RAY, ----- 83
REAGAN, J. H. 83
REAGAN, John H. 83
REAGAN, John H. 83
REALD, J. R. 81
REAMS, Howard 106
REAVES, Thos. 83
RECORD, T. C. 90
REDDING, A. J. 89
REDDING, A. J. 108
REDDING, Joseph 107
REDDING, W. T. 89
REESON, Jos. 15
REEVES, J. H. 89
REGNARD, Thos. 93
REILY, James 47
REMSON, Henry 18
RENINGTON, ----- 89
RENTFRO, E. D. 94
REVER, W. K. 60
REVERE, W. K. 59
REVERE, William K. 59
REYNOLDS, A. G. 17
REYNOLDS, James H. 108
REYNOLDS, Reuben W. 80
RHEA, ----- 74
RHETT, Benjamen S. 101
RIBBLE, A. 50
RICE, ----- 66
RICE, A. J. 89
RICE, Elias 89
RICE, William L. 89
RICHARDSON, ----- 108
RICHARDSON, George F. 3
RICHARDSON, John 83
RICHARDSON, W. 80
RICHESON, ----- 1
RICHESON, ----- 15

RICHESON, ----- 18
RICHESON, ----- 43
RICHESON, E. 44
RIDDLE, Elam 109
RIDDLE, Elam 110
RIDGELEY, ----- 49
RIGGS, J. M. 50
RIGGS, J. M. 58
RIGGS, J. M. 77
RINGO, Peter 101
RIPLEY, Ambrose 89
RITCHIE, Henry 103
RITCHIE, Joseph L. 73
RIVA, Juan Manuel 21
ROACH, Wade H. 108
ROBENSON, William 44
ROBERTS, Abram 3
ROBERTSON, Edward 3
ROBERTSON, Edward 6
ROBERTSON, Edward 11
ROBERTSON, Edward 11
ROBERTSON, Edward 15
ROBERTSON, I. E. 31
ROBERTSON, James 29
ROBINS, N. 29
ROBINSON, J. A. 83
ROBINSON, William 5
ROBINSON, Wm. H. 18
ROBSON, John 89
ROCHELLE, ----- 32
RODRIGUEZ, Ambrosia 21
ROGER, ----- 87
ROGERS, ----- 91
ROGERS, Comm. 18
ROGERS, James H. 73
ROGERS, John K. 89
ROGERS, R. R. 57
ROLIN, Jane 88
ROMAN, ----- 88
ROSS, ----- 86
ROUCHEFORT, ----- 32
ROWE, Joseph 48
ROWLETT, D. 47
ROYAL, R. R. 25
ROYAL, R. R. 29
ROYALL, R. R. 29
ROYALL, R. R. 31
ROYALL, R. R. 34
ROYALL, R. R. 43
ROYSDON, De La F. 1
ROYSTER, James M. 11

RUIZ, Francisco 21
RUNNELS, Edward 96
RUNNELS, H. A. 51
RUNNELS, Hiram A. 93
RUNNELS, Martha 96
RUNNELS, Zerilda 96
RUSK, T. J. 56
RUSK, Thomas J. 47
RUSK, Thos. J. 56
RUSSE, John 89
RUSSELL, ----- 12
RUSSELL, A. J. 72
RUSSELL, A. J. 90
RUSSELL, Alexander 41
RUSSELL, N. M. 89
RUSSELL, Reddin 55
RUSSELL, Wm. J. 12
RUSSELL, Wm. J. 15
RUTGERS, ----- 18
RUTGERS, Col. 18
RUTHERFORD, Benj. H. 37

SAGER, Francis 91
SAGER, John 91
SALENAS, Peblo 21
SALES, ----- 91
SALINAS, Pedro 34
SALMAS, Jose Maria 21
SAMPSON, James 89
SANCHEZ, Nepomuccno 21
SANDERS, ----- 91
SANDERS, Charles R. 51
SANDERS, Charles R. 59
SANDERS, Jas. T. 51
SANDERS, L. B. 83
SANDERS, Lucy 51
SANDERS, Lucy 59
SANDOVAL, ----- 29
SANTA ANA, Antonio Lopez de 31
SANTA, ----- 69
SANTOS, Juan Antonio de los 14
SARGEANT, W. M. 80
SARIEGO, ----- 29
SATAN, Israel 42
SATRE, Charles D. 45
SAUL, Thomas S. 10
SAUNDERS, Mary 91
SAWNS, Israel 89
SAWYER, S. 20
SAWYER, Samuel 44
SAYER, ----- 15
SCANLAN, J. 3

SCANLAN, Michael 3
SCHMIDT, J. W. 101
SCHOPSHIRE, J. H. 108
SCHRACK, L. M. 108
SCHULTE, J. A. 8
SCHULTE, John 8
SCHWERIN, ----- 64
SCOTT, J. D. 83
SCURLOCK, William 98
SCURLOCK, William 98
SCURLOCK, William 104
SCURRY, C. 108
SCURRY, R. 90
SCURRY, W. R. 90
SCURRY, W. R. 108
SCURRY, Wm. R. 106
SEAL, Darling 108
SEALS, William 89
SEGUIN, Erasmo 21
SEQUIN, Juan Nepomuncena 20
SEQUIN, Juan Nepomunceno 21
SEVIER, ----- 66
SEVIER, Mr. 12
SHALTER, Frederick 101
SHANAHAN, Jas. B. 81
SHANALEANS, ----- 81
SHARP, ----- 41
SHARP, John 21
SHARP, John 21
SHAW, J. C. 74
SHERRIF, Co. Red River 89
SHERRY, Bernard 89
SHREEVE, Pleasant 108
SHWARZENBERG, ----- 94
SIBLEY, John 33
SIBLEY, John 33
SIERRA, Don Justo 84
SIERRA, Don Justo 85
SIMMONS, A. H. 106
SIMPSON, William 26
SIMPSON, William 39
SIMS, Bartlett 38
SIMS, Jas. W. 55
SIMS, Samuel 89
SINGLER, Wm. N. 29
SINGLETON, A. J. 89
SKERRY, Richard 89
SLAUGHTER, Thomas 6
SLEIGHT, John L. 9
SLICER, ----- 65
SMALL, James 48

SMITH, ----- 30
SMITH, ----- 41
SMITH, Andrew B. 80
SMITH, B. P. 90
SMITH, Burrell P. 87
SMITH, Burrell P. 89
SMITH, Charles H. 108
SMITH, E. Kirby 91
SMITH, E. M. 90
SMITH, Hanah 91
SMITH, Henry 3
SMITH, Henry 14
SMITH, Henry 19
SMITH, Henry 20
SMITH, Henry 29
SMITH, Henry 44
SMITH, Henry 81
SMITH, James 48
SMITH, James 89
SMITH, Jas. 74
SMITH, John S. 89
SMITH, John W. 21
SMITH, Jos. J. 98
SMITH, Jos. J. 104
SMITH, Joseph 91
SMITH, M. 89
SMITH, M. W. 21
SMITH, M. W. 21
SMITH, M. W. 22
SMITH, M. W. 22
SMITH, M. W. 24
SMITH, M. W. 44
SMITH, Meriwether W. 41
SMITH, Meriwether W. 45
SMITH, Mr. M. W. 16
SMITH, P. 56
SMITH, Thoas. I. 58
SMITH, Thomas 89
SMITH, Thos. I. 50
SMITH, W. M. 108
SMITHER, L. 8
SMITHERS, ----- 32
SNELSON, ----- 95
SNOW, ----- 53
SOMBRAMA, Jose Antonio 21
SOTO, Pagustin 21
SOUTH, William 108
SOUTHARD, Hon. Saml. L. 18
SPALDING, ----- 91
SPARKS, A. 89
SPARKS, Richard 47

SPAULDING, ----- 91
SPENCER, ----- 43
SPLANE, P. R. 17
SPRAGUE, Peleg 4
STAATS, N. J. 86
STALLINGS, Abraham 108
STANFIELD, Jos. 91
STANLY, G. W. 108
STAR, ----- 87
STARNS, Aaron 54
STARNS, Thomas R. 54
STEARNS, Aaron 89
STEPHEN, A. F. 108
STEPHENS, A. F. 89
STEPHENSON, James 73
STEPHENSON, Mr. Mrs. 16
STERNE, Adolphus 9
STERNE, Adolphus 48
STEVENSON, R. 16
STEVENSON, R. 41
STEVENSON, R. 41
STEVENSON, R. 46
STEVENSON, Thos. 81
STEWART, ----- 70
STEWART, A. B. 10
STEWART, C. B. 31
STEWART, Charles P. 104
STEWART, Charles W. 21
STEWART, Charles W. 42
STEWART, Joseph S. 89
STEWART, Wm. 64
STILES, John 72
STILES, John 87
STOCKDALE, F. S. 94
STONE, ----- 15
STONE, Isaac 45
STORER, George L. 83
STORY, Samuel 108
STOUT, W. B. 78
STRATTON, Piano Forte H. B. 22
STROHECKER, John 101
STUART, ----- 63
STUART, ----- 74
STUART, H. 80
STUMP, F. H. 73
STURDEVANT, ----- 16
SUBLETT, Phillip A. 31
SUMMERFORD, ----- 78
SUSTIL, Clemente 21
SUTTON, ----- 86
SUTTON, Thomas 89

SWENY, W. B. 21
SWENY, W. B. 42
SWENY, W. B. 43
SWIFT, Gen. 18
SYDNOR, J. S. 80
SYNDOR, ----- 74

TALTON, John F. 89
TANSOR, E. S. 77
TARRANT, E. H. 60
TARRANT, E. H. 74
TATE, James M. 89
TAYLOR ----- 50
TAYLOR, ----- 70
TAYLOR, ----- 92
TAYLOR, ----- 109
TAYLOR, James 47
TAYLORS, ----- 70
TEMPLE, Harris 108
TERREL, John 64
TERRY, John 89
THOMAS, F. M. 89
THOMPSON, Alex. 34
THOMPSON, Alexander 29
THOMPSON, H. M. 26
THOMPSON, Jesse 10
THOMPSON, Josiah 97
THORN, F. 39
THRUSTON, A. S. 56
THRUSTON, A. S. 56
TILGHAM, ----- 71
TILGHAMS, ----- 70
TILGHMAN, ----- 70
TILLEY, Jeff 74
TIMBLE, Wm. 108
TINNEN, Wm. H. 108
TISDALE, Eliz. Ann 108
TITUS, A. J. 72
TITUS, A. J. 79
TITUS, A. J. 90
TODD, Wm. S. 56
TODD, Wm. S. 76
TOLER, Richard H, 83
TONE, Th. J. 43
TORREY, Ebenezer 62
TOULON, ----- 32
TRASK, Col. 18
TRAVELSTEAD, Anthony 89
TRAVELSTEAD, E. C. 89
TRAVIS, W. B. 24
TRAVIS, W. B. 46
TRAVIS, W. Barret 26

TRAVIS, William B. 14
TRTACY, Hon. Albert H. 18
TUCKER, A. W. 103
TUCKER, Jefferson 89
TURGGLE, John H. 89
TURNBALL, Andrew 101
TURNER, Samuel S. 99
TYERS, Robert M. 76
TYERS, Robert M. 77

UGARTECHEA, ----- 24
UGARTECHEA, ----- 25
UMPHREY, Joseph P. 108

VAN BUREN, ----- 40
VAN RANSSALER, Gen 18
VANDERGRIFT, Margaret 108
VANDORN, Isaac 30
VASQUEZ, Jose Antonio 21
VEATCH, ----- 86
VEEDER, Lewis 2
VEEDER, Lewis L. 5
VEEDER, Lewis L. 9
VEEDER, Lewis L. 11
VEEDER, Mr. 8
VERNON, Margaret 109
VICUVE, Daniel 43
VIDAL, Alexander 21
VIESCA, Augustin 24
VIESCA, Don Augustia 37
VING, W. H. 75
VINING, Wade H. 99
VINING, Wahe H. 60
VISE, Nathaniel 89
VISOR, Peter 64

WADDELL, Wm. C. H. 96
WAGLEY, John 109
WALKER, ----- 58
WALKER, ----- 106
WALKER, A. G. 74
WALKER, J. 83
WALKER, J. W. 89
WALKER, Wm. J. 74
WALLACE, ----- 32
WALLACE, J. W. E. 45
WALLACE, J. W.E. 32
WALLER, Edwin 18
WALLER, Edwin 43
WALLER, Wdwin 17
WALLS,MD S. B. 8
WALTER, Edwin 29
WAND, Malinda 62
WARD, ----- 81

WARD, ----- 109
WARD, Frederick 109
WARD, Isaac 101
WARD, Isaac 104
WARD, James 89
WARD, James J. 50
WARD, James J. 59
WARD, Jas. J. 81
WARD, Jeremiah 109
WARD, Mary D. 81
WARD, William 89
WARDLOW, Milton 97
WARE, John 90
WARE, Jr. J. 41
WARE, Jr. James 45
WARE, Sr. J. 41
WARFIELD, Charles A. 86
WARNES, James 109
WARREN, Gen. 18
WARREN, John C. 18
WASHINGTON, ----- 98
WATSON, ----- 3
WATSON, Thos. R. 60
WAYNE, ----- 98
WEB, Kernal 19
WEBB, James 94
WEBSTER, ----- 62
WEBSTER, ----- 75
WEBSTER, ----- 93
WELBCRN, Chas. C. 89
WELCH, Daniel 89
WELL, John O. H. 88
WELLS, Dr. F. F. 10
WELLS, Dr.S. B. 10
WELLS, F. F. 22
WELLS, F. F. 42
WELLS, F. T. 46
WELLS, Francis F. 11
WELLS, I. W. 52
WELLS, Isaiah W. 87
WELLS, Isiah W. 108
WEST, Claiborne 29
WEST, Edward 60
WEST, Edward 89
WEST, Edward 90
WEST, John W. 96
WESTAIL, ----- 12
WESTAIL, James 12
WESTALL, Andrew 19
WESTALL, James 42
WESTALL, Mr. James 1

WESTALL, Thomas 19
WETSALL, James 22
WHALY, George 83
WHARTON, J. A. 46
WHARTON, John A. 16
WHARTON, John A. 17
WHARTON, John A. 19
WHARTON, John A. 19
WHARTON, John A. 20
WHARTON, John A. 20
WHARTON, John A. 29
WHARTON, John A. 40
WHITAKER, Robert 82
WHITAKER, W. M. 34
WHITE, ----- 65
WHITE, Gifford 47
WHITE, John G. 109
WHITE, Joseph 3
WHITE, L. L. 109
WHITE, W. C. 46
WHITE, Walter C. 9
WHITE, Walter C. 21
WHITESIDE, James 10
WHITESIDE, Mr. 1
WHITESIDES, Wm. N. 109
WHITHINGTON, Wm. T. 109
WHITING, Samuel 29
WHITMAN, ----- 84
WHITMAN, ----- 91
WHITMAN, ----- 91
WHITSON, Esther 89
WHITTAKER, Wm. 29
WILEY, A. P. 94
WILKINS, P. W. 33
WILKINSON, J. W. 101
WILKINSON, Mary 89
WILLAIMS, Hon. Nathan 18
WILLCOXON, J. R. 44
WILLETT, Col. 7
WILLIAM, ----- 52
WILLIAM, Williams M. 109
WILLIAMS, ----- 9
WILLIAMS, ----- 16
WILLIAMS, ----- 16
WILLIAMS, ----- 26
WILLIAMS, ----- 27
WILLIAMS, ----- 58
WILLIAMS, Augustus 21
WILLIAMS, Augustus 42
WILLIAMS, Eliz. J. 109
WILLIAMS, Ezekiel 10

WILLIAMS, R, M. 2
WILLIAMS, Robert H. 10
WILLIAMS, S. A. 77
WILLIAMS, S. M. 5
WILLIAMS, S. M. 10
WILLIAMS, S. M. 19
WILLIAMS, S. M. 46
WILLIAMS, Samuel M. 6
WILLIAMSON, Dr. R. M. 10
WILLIAMSON, R. M. 4
WILLIAMSON, R. M. 5
WILLIAMSON, R. M. 10
WILLIAMSON, R. M. 13
WILLIAMSON, R. M. 14
WILLIAMSON, R. M. 38
WILLIAMSON, R. M. 40
WILLING, Charles 23
WILLIS, William 94
WILSON, Charles 30
WILSON, Chas. 29
WILSON, Hugh 101
WILSON, Robert 21
WILSON, Robert 42
WILSON, Robert 45
WILSON, Robert 45
WILSON, Thos. N. 52
WILSON, Thos. R. 82
WIMS, Wilkins 89
WINDISHGRATZ, ----- 94
WINDISHGRATZ, ----- 95
WINTER, James 55
WINTER, Minerva 56
WINTHROP, ----- 60
WITHER, John W. 97
WITHINGTON, Wm. T. 89
WITTING, Samuel 29
WONNATT, Natty G. 109
WOOD, Jas. B. 29
WOODS, J. B. 34
WOODSWORTH, H. D. 54
WOODSWORTH, H. D. 106
WOOLDRIDGE, Wm. 52
WRIGHT, ----- 52
WRIGHT, ----- 104
WRIGHT, Dr. 10
WRIGHT, Geo. W. 54
WRIGHT, T. G. 106
WRIGHT, Travis G. 106
WYNN, William H. 89
WYNNE, W. H. 52
WYNNE, W. H. 59

YATES, ----- 74
YATES, A. J. 74
YATES, A. J. 100
YOUNG, ----- 91
YOUNG, Elam 91
YOUNG, George S. 87
YOUNG, Hugh F. 57
YOUNG, Hugh F. 86
YOUNG, Hugh F. 96
YOUNG, Hugh F. 107
YOUNG, Irene 91
YOUNG, Wm. C. 86
YOUNG, Wm. C. 90
ZAMBRANO, Jose Maria 21
ZAMBRANO, Juan 21
ZAMBRANO, Juan Antonio 21
ZAVALA, Don Lorenzo de 25
ZAVALA, Don Lorenzo de 26
ZAVALA, Lorenzo de 24
ZAVALA, Lorenzo de 29
ZAVALA, Lorenzo de 34
ZAVALA, Lorenzo de 45
ZEDICUM, Fred 109

www.ingramcontent.com/pod-product-compliance
Lightning Source LLC
Chambersburg PA
CBHW080334270326

41927CB00014B/3225